A YEAR AT
HARTLEBURY

or

The Election

A YEAR AT HARTLEBURY

or

The Election

BENJAMIN AND SARAH DISRAELI

with appendixes by Ellen Henderson
and John P. Matthews

University of Toronto Press
TORONTO AND BUFFALO

First published under the pseudonyms of Cherry and Fair Star
by Saunders & Otley in 1834
First published in Canada and USA 1983
by University of Toronto Press, Toronto and Buffalo
Appendixes © University of Toronto Press 1983
Printed in Great Britain

Canadian Cataloguing in Publication Data

Disraeli, Benjamin, 1804–1881.
A year at Hartlebury, or, The election
ISBN 0-8020-2439-4
I. Disraeli, Sarah.   II. Title.   III. Title: The
election.
PR4084.Y4 1983   823'.7   C83-098040-7

CONTENTS

Volume One

I A village – The parsonage and the manor-house,
and their inhabitants 3

II A neighbour 5

III A very fine castle, but seen only at a distance . . 7

IV Almshouses – the village school-mistress – a
political dialogue 10

V A very early morning visitor – news! . . . 14

VI Arrival of George Gainsborough 17

VII Fresh arrivals – the Boscawen family . . . 21

VIII The pic-nic in Bohun Park 26

IX Reflections which it creates in the minds of several
of the party 34

X The Gainsboroughs give a dinner 36

XI A death-bed scene 43

XII In which is announced most unexpected
intelligence 52

XIII The unexpected intelligence proves true . . . 56

XIV The owner of the castle 57

XV Mr. George Gainsborough's bad memory . . . 60

XVI Which he endeavours to refresh 62

XVII Mr. Bohun is visited by his relations – A fine lady
and a most gentlemanlike fellow 66

XVIII Increased intimacy between the castle and the hall . 70

XIX The gentlemen return from quarter sessions . . 73

XX Mr. Bohun surprises Mr. Chace and everybody
else, including the reader 78

XXI A friendly dinner party at the castle 82

XXII Amatory, political and mysterious 88

XXIII Amatory only 93

CONTENTS

Volume Two

I Mr. Bohun commences his personal canvass   .   . 101

II Arrival of two other candidates, and the
consequences 106

III A secret interview between two very great men .   . 115

IV The perplexities of Mr. Gainsborough, senior .   . 121

V The ladies canvass – Parliament is dissolved –
nomination day 127

VI A midnight colloquy 133

VII The first day 135

VIII The fate of Fanchester in the hands of Mr.
Gainsborough – the perplexities of a great man .   . 142

IX A member returned 152

X A ball at Bohun 155

XI The heart chastened in a sick chamber   .   . 163

XII Hartlebury at peace – Mr. Bohun in London .   . 170

XIII George Gainsborough's hopes revive.   .   . 175

XIV The mystery disclosed 178

XV A painful interview 182

XVI A friendly conversation 187

XVII A consultation 192

XVIII A catastrophe 194

Appendix I Cherry and Fair Star   202

Appendix II New light on Disraeli's early politics .   . 212

PREFACE

Our honeymoon being over, we have amused ourselves during the autumn by writing a novel. All we hope is that the Public will deem our literary union as felicitous as we find our personal one.

VOLUME ONE

CHAPTER 1

A village.
The parsonage and the manor-house, and their inhabitants

Gentle reader, wander with us awhile, along the banks of this tranquil river, as it winds its course through this verdant valley, and we will show you a fair scene.

Behold a rural green, encircled by cottages, and embosomed in wood-crowned hills. Each humble dwelling stands in the midst of a garden rich in vegetable store, and gay with the many-coloured tulip, and the golden crocus, and its slanting thatch is covered with the fragrant honeysuckle. It is the month of May, the air is filled with sweet odour and wild music. Hark! the clear note of the blithe Cuckoo, and ever and anon from yonder rich stack yard which surrounds that substantial looking farmhouse many a cheerful sound breaks on the ear. The green gradually ascends the side of the narrow valley, and, on the right on a sloping lawn, gay with laburnums, lilacs, and syringa, stands a low irregularly built house with gable ends and tall chimneys. It is the Parsonage; its porch is covered with ivy, and its large projecting windows are clustered with the brilliant scarlet flowers of the Pyrus japonica. On the lawn, and separated from the garden only by a light iron fence, stands a very small church mantled with ivy. It is sheltered from the North by a rich dark plantation of firs and yews, while around are scattered the humble but neat graves of the peaceful villagers. A road winds round the upland green to the wide gates of the mansion-house, an ancient Elizabethan Hall.

Such is the village of Hartlebury, where the Molesworths have been lords of the soil for many centuries. On the whole, they have been faithful stewards, and this fair spot has suffered little in the lapse of ages from extortionate proprietors, or tasteless improvers.

The present possessor succeeded early in life to the estate, and as he is a man of very cultivated mind, his taste as well as his feeling of what is right, has induced him to a constant residence among those who are dependent on him. He is of a mild and tolerant temper, and if he possesses a few inherited prejudices they hang gracefully upon him. For many years he enjoyed that rare felicity, a congenial and sympathising companion, but the same year had deprived him of a beloved wife, and an only son. Yet he was not alone in the world; a fair young child was by his side, who, each succeeding year, became more worthy of all his love. To cultivate her affections, and to store her mind with knowledge became the pleasant occupation of his life, and in her warm devoted love he reaped a rich reward. Helen Molesworth had now reached her nineteenth year. Beautiful, affectionate and gay — she knew little of our evil passions but from books, while she lived in the practice of a thousand virtues, enjoying the sweetest of Heaven's gifts, the power of doing good to others.

The inhabitants of the Rectory were her dearest friends, and her chief companions. The two families had been ever united in the strictest bonds of friendship, each loving in the other the virtues in which they themselves excelled. Mr. Latimer, who had been for thirty years the faithful pastor of Hartlebury, was a near relative of the Molesworth family, and had been from early life the favourite friend of the Squire. While to his amiable, sensible wife and his two children Helen had been always the object of the tenderest affection. But within the last three years great changes had taken place in this small circle. Charlotte Latimer had married, and Mr. Latimer had died, and Mrs. Latimer was gone too, for though she professed to divide her time between her children, she was so often called for by her daughter, was so useful as a nurse, and so valued as an adviser, that she had little time to give to her son's uneventful establishment.

Arthur Latimer succeeded to his father's duties. It was with a holy feeling he sought the same peaceful path of Christian usefulness. He loved Hartlebury, and all connected with it, and at Hartlebury he was enthusiastically beloved. Ever the active friend of the unhappy, the eloquent messenger of grace to fallen man, he aroused the slumbering, he re-animated the desponding, his piety was without fanaticism, as his charity was universal. With all these virtues, and the additional recommendations of being handsome and accomplished, in the world he was not popular, for he was reserved, and unbending, and had some awkward notions which if generally acted upon would destroy the pleasures of society. In proportion as people were rich and educated so he thought they ought to be virtuous and religious, and he was loth to condemn that as a crime in the poor and ignorant, which was regarded but as an innocent frailty in the wealthy and the well-informed. Where much was given, much, he believed, would be required. An old fashioned doctrine.

CHAPTER II

A neighbour

Within the last six years a new mansion had risen in the parish of Hartlebury. A Mr. Gainsborough purchased a large farm, which was quickly converted into a modern Gothic tenement of most ancient appearance bearing the euphonious title of Oakfield Lodge. The fields soon became paddocks, already the paddocks emulated a park. Mr. Gainsborough was a man of humble origin who, by unwearied industry and good fortune had amassed in trade what is styled a very handsome property. He was an honest man, with an exact, precise mind. He took kindly to his new mode of life, busied himself with his plantations, and rode three times in the week to the neighbouring town. He became a great politician, read every paper with maps by his side, and all the articles on foreign policy in the Edinburgh and Quarterly Reviews. He began to have a tolerably exact idea of the Turkish Empire just when it was on the point of being dismembered, and could put his finger without a moment's hesitation, on the situation of Egypt. He was astonished, not at his past ignorance, but at his present infinite knowledge, and, believing that everybody had the same want of it, he became rather too fond of enlightening others. His wife was one of those quiet insipid women who can be equally happy anywhere. Not because they have tastes and resources for all situations, but simply because they are totally devoid of any.

Their family consisted of three daughters and an only son. The two youngest Miss Gainsboroughs had lately married. One was the wife of a clergyman in the neighbourhood, the other of a young naval officer whom his good genius had induced to take a cottage in the vicinity of Oakfield for the united purpose of fishing and sentimentalizing. The eldest sister was still unmarried, and fast approaching a certain age. She was not very intelligent or very refined, but active and good-natured.

The son, George Gainsborough, had been for some time away. He had been originally intended for the church, but he soon manifested so little regard for his own conduct that it would not do to entrust him with the direction of that of others. Many wild scrapes and family discussions terminated in his going abroad. He had travelled over Germany and Italy, had visited Constantinople, and had finally taken an active part in favour of the Greeks.

In this country where the art most sedulously fostered is the art of making a connection, numerous are the established means of arriving at the great result. A public school, a crack college, the turf if you are rich, are all good in their way — but to travel on the Continent is a highly esteemed mode.

If such were the desire of George Gainsborough, he appeared eminently successful; his letters, whenever they did arrive, bore ample testimony to his aristocratic acquaintance, and most satisfactorily proved to all the members of his family that he was a very great man indeed.

CHAPTER III

A very fine castle,
but seen only at a distance

It was a delightful May morning. The sun shone brightly, and an agreeable breeze bearing fresh and charming perfume tempered its warmth. Helen Molesworth threw up the window, and stepped out upon the lawn. She turned with exquisite delight to the charming scene around her. The old Hall stood on a lawn gently sloping to the massy iron gates which opened into the village. Its heavy overhanging gables, richly adorned with coats of arms, its long line of projecting windows, between each of which, in a deep niche, stood a statue, made a fine contrast over the face of the building of brilliant light and rich deep shadow, and all surrounded by trees in their new dress of various green: the golden wreaths of the laburnum just bursting into bloom, the purple spikes of the lilac, the ivory syringa, the sweet-scented may, the delicate acacia, and, above all, the magnificent chestnut throwing up its pyramidal flowers over the heads of all the rest. Gay as the birds above her head, who filled the air with their wild carols of pleasure, Helen flew along the terrace to her flower-garden. As she gazed upon the variegated parterres, the rare tulips and brilliant anemones, she could have exclaimed with Wordsworth,

> And 'tis my faith that every flower
> Enjoys the air it breathes.

Arthur Latimer rode up the green, and stopped at the iron gates. She ran to speak to him.

"Helen," he said, "this surely is a morning for a canter, are you not going to ride?"

"If you will ride with me, but Papa is busy with Baker, and I would rather stay at home this beautiful day, than have no more sympathising companion than old John."

"I am quite at your service to talk, to listen, or to be silent, whichever may be your mood. I will ride round and order your horse, if you will prepare."

Miss Molesworth was soon equipped.

"Helen," said Mr. Latimer as he assisted her to mount, "you must so contrive your ride that we pass Whitby's cottage, for I have just remembered that I have a message for him. After having declared myself entirely at your service, it is most ungallant to dictate to you."

"But that will give me my favourite ride, so I forgive you. We can go round at the foot of the Castle into that long green lane, which falls into the road just by his cottage."

Their course lay through rich woods which gradually ascended the side of a steep hill. Suddenly the woods terminated in an open down. Bohun Castle, with its donjon keep, and its turreted towers, was still above them, but they looked down upon the ancient woods and the beautiful river, which wound through the landscape at their feet, ever and anon revealing itself by its silvery light as it wandered through the woodland glades.

"How beautiful," exclaimed Helen, "I never look upon this view but I discover some new beauty, some hitherto undiscovered point. How sad it is to think that while we enjoy it at our pleasure, the master of all never gazes upon it!"

"Do not pity him, Helen; he cannot deserve it. Why is he not here?"

"Ah! why is he not here? I never see this magnificent place without asking that question. He must be a very extraordinary man."

"He certainly is a most ungrateful one. With all his abundance of blessings, with the power of doing so much good, Lord here almost of a principality, he makes but little increase of the talents committed to his care."

"He is very fortunate to have so good an agent as Mr. Chase."

"Yes, Chase is an intelligent man, and a most active magistrate. I do not often know what we should do without him, and what is better he is, I believe, an honest man. The people are not oppressed, and the estate flourishes, but there is something, Helen, which an agent cannot do."

"And I am sure poor Mr. Lowndes' confused head cannot

assist him. Now if they had a clergyman like you Arthur."

"I do not know that I should do better than he does," said Mr. Latimer smiling. "We can do a great deal, but we cannot do everything. We want assistance. It is the sympathy of the landlord which above all things elevates the moral feelings of his poorer neighbours. In showing them affection, and in exciting theirs, you make them feel that we have all alike immortal souls, and that the accidents of fortune are but adventitious. Believe me, dear Helen, when your feeling heart sympathises with your poor friends at Hartlebury, you do far more than a temporary good. My precepts would lose much of their efficacy without so fair a practice."

He spoke with a warmth in which he rarely indulged: Helen could not reply. They rode on in silence. After a few minutes he said:

"And here there is not only the want of all this sympathy, but something worse. It is not a mere question, whether a man prefer one country to another, but here is a mystery, a conceal-ment, which can only induce those to believe, who think at all, that there is something disgraceful, something which cannot bear the light."

Mr. Latimer's censures were but too well deserved. Aubrey Bohun the descendent of a long line of illustrious ancestry was unknown and unregarded amidst his wide possessions. His father had died an early and sudden death soon after his birth, and his mother immediately left the Castle, and never after-wards returned to it. She was a woman of violent passions, who had been forced into a distasteful marriage. She hated the name of Bohun and detested the Castle, the scene of her wedded life, and she exerted all her influence to implant in the growing character of her son, her prejudices and passions. Her extreme beauty, her elevated rank, and above all, her influence over the heir to thirty thousand a year, placed her amongst the most distinguished in the gay world. For many years the name of Lady Alice Bohun was the most eminent among the few who rule the many. It is rarely that the cup of pleasure is in vain presented to a youth. Handsome and headstrong, Aubrey Bohun seized it with avidity, and drained it to the lees, and just before he attained his majority, an aching head and a dissatis-fied heart sent him to other countries, to seek that health and happiness he had wasted in his own.

It was now nearly ten years since the bonfires had blazed at Bohun Castle to celebrate his twenty-first birthday, but he had never returned. His mother had died, and her name had faded away among the gay crowds she had adorned — for the gay have only time to think of those who amuse them.

<hr/>

CHAPTER IV

<hr/>

Almshouses — the village school-mistress — a political dialogue

In a green lane which turned from the village by the side of the rectory-garden, on a grassy plot surrounded by a gravelled walk bordered with mignonette, stood a row of neat buildings. They were almshouses, which a wealthy spinster of the house of Molesworth had gratified her benevolent feelings in erecting for the aged of the parish.

Each abode had an allotted portion of garden-ground, which the most active of the inhabitants amused themselves in tending; but in general they were indebted to some good-natured son, or some lusty grand-child, who would spare a leisure hour to its cultivation. Oftentimes might you see a gardener from the hall or the rectory bearing some young plants, or some promised seed.

These almshouses were Helen's favourite resort. Here she took many lessons, not only in the mysteries of knitting but in the knowledge of cheerfulness and the art of content; here she learnt how a firm belief in a heavenly life cheers the close of an earthly one, though it may have consisted only of a youth of labour and an old age of suffering. Not that we wish to represent the inhabitants of Hartlebury as an exception to all human infirmities; there were some discontented among the aged, and not a few idle among the young, but on the whole, they displayed all the advantages which thirty years of sympathy had procured for them.

In a pretty green mead adjoining these almshouses, Mr. Molesworth and his daughter were now busily employed in the erection of a school-house. To build a school-house in this green mead had been one of Helen's first fancies. Many a subsequent project remarkable for its ingenuity, she had been obliged to yield to her father's gentle raillery, but this plan he had always seconded, for he liked building Gothic cottages. Certain difficulties had hitherto delayed it.

From time immemorial Dame Harrald had been the ruler of the village intellect; but she could only teach in her own cottage, and after her own fashion, and while she remained in office, any change in the school or its discipline was impossible. Dame Harrald was a sharp shrewd woman, with strong sense and native wit: she had educated three generations of the villagers, and those who had once been her scholars never ceased to be her subjects. They consulted her on all occasions, for she cured all evils bodily as well as mental, and she deserved their confidence, for she gave on the whole very good advice, and never told a secret.

But at last even Dame Harrald began to grow old; she became not a little deaf, and the eagle glance of olden days was dimmed. Her scholars detected her infirmities, and the dame, discovering incipient anarchy, abdicated, retiring, like greater folks, to her cabbages.

It was an electrifying stroke to the village: Dame Harrald in the almshouses, a new school-mistress, and a new school-house. Centuries had not produced such great events.

The building was now rapidly rising, and was a daily object of interest to the squire and Helen. One morning as, accompanied by Mr. Latimer, they were busied in an important consultation with Smith the carpenter, who was at, what he styled when he was puzzled, a stand-still, Mr. Gainsborough approached.

"Now," said Helen, with a gentle sigh, "this will never be settled today."

"Ah! Miss Molesworth," said the old gentleman, as he joined them, "I thought I should find you here: how do ye do my good

Sir? Mr. Latimer too all in deep consultation, I suppose. Bless me! how you get on here!" continued the old gentleman. "Amazing! Miss Molesworth; but you are *so* clever."

"You are very complimentary Mr. Gainsborough," said Helen smiling, "but I do not deserve any credit on this occasion. Papa and Mr. Smith must, I am afraid, have all the merit of our progress."

"Indeed, eh! we all know what taste Mr. Molesworth has. I assure you, Fanny takes the greatest interest in your school, and will be very happy to help you to teach."

Mr. Gainsborough thought he had now said all that politeness required, so he turned towards Mr. Molesworth, with a most argumentative look. Helen interposed with enquiries concerning Mrs. and Miss Gainsborough.

"They were pretty well when I left this morning, but I have not seen them these four hours, and you know Miss Molesworth it is impossible to answer for you ladies for so long a time," said the old gentleman, with a chuckle at his own wit.

He returned to the attack.

"Great news today from Portugal Sir."

Mr. Molesworth sunk resigned on a carpenter's bench.

"Will he be able to maintain himself, that is the point, eh?" continued Mr. Gainsborough.

"Do the people care a rush about him? I think that is the point," responded Mr. Molesworth.

"They would, if they were not priest-ridden," replied Mr. Gainsborough.

"What do you mean by priest-ridden?" enquired Mr. Molesworth very calmly.

"My dear Sir," replied Mr. Gainsborough, who was not a definer, "everyone knows that Portugal is the most priest-ridden country in the world, except Spain."

"And do you think you can emancipate their minds," said Mr. Molesworth, who never pressed his neighbour, "by hiring men at Wapping to cut their throats?"

"I should think that the middle class must secretly approve of it," said Mr. Gainsborough musingly.

"Of having their throats cut?" enquired Mr. Molesworth.

"No, of the expedition," replied Mr. Gainsborough. "It is the middle class of all countries who are the great supporters of liberal principles. I told them so in the town-hall the other day. 'It is you,' I said, addressing them, 'you gentlemen, the great enlightened middle class, to whom we look for the salvation of the country.' I was speaking against the new toll. They cheered me amazingly."

"The middle class had better mind their business," said Mr. Molesworth.

"How many miles is it, Mr. Molesworth, from Oporto to Lisbon? I wonder if there be any fortified towns in the way. What think you of Coimbra? Could they make a stand at Coimbra, think you, eh? We live in wonderful times— wonderful times. What will it all end in? Good, my dear Sir, good — good," continued Mr. Gainsborough, musingly. "Liberal principles must be beneficial in the long run. There is no withstanding it, that is the truth: such is the march of mind in the present day, that you can hood-wink the people no longer. And though the people are not so ready as we were led to expect, still this business of Portugal must end in good."

"It will end in the rise of Port wine, I foresee," said Mr. Molesworth.

"Do you think so, eh?" eagerly enquired Mr. Gainsborough. "I am just thinking of buying a pipe."

"Then, my good friend, lose no time," said Mr. Molesworth, "for you may depend upon it, that liberal principles always end in an attack upon the purse."

Mr. Gainsborough though a liberal, had a great opinion of Mr. Molesworth's sense, and looked a little alarmed, but he soon rallied and walked away to look out Coimbra in the Gazetteer.

CHAPTER V

A very early morning visitor — news!

One morning, very early for a morning visit, even a country morning visit, a morning visitor was however announced; and Mrs. Escott entered the room.

She was an ancient maiden lady who resided in the neighbouring town of Fanchester. She was the last of a family who traced its descent from the Conquest, and who had grown older and poorer in corresponding proportions. The Escotts had originally possessed considerable property in the neighbourhood, which had gradually passed into other hands, and Mrs. Escott's father had at last sunk down into an old-fashioned house in the town, where she still resided. In every generation the Escotts had visited all the neighbouring families, and Mrs. Escott strenuously preserved this feature of her superiority over the chief inhabitants of the town, whose industry made them richer every year, and whose good sense restrained them from seeking an intimacy uncongenial to their habits and injurious to their pursuits.

Every year Mrs. Escott regularly went through her round of visits, and she willingly paid the tax of an occasional pair of post horses to her antiquated chariot, to maintain her name among the families of the county. She comforted herself for her extravagance by the feeling that they would be hurt at her neglect. She was a good-natured woman, sometimes a little irritable, and always a little curious, but as fond of communicating as of acquiring information.

This day her small grey eyes twinkled with unusual complacency, as she returned Miss Molesworth's salutations.

"Thank you, my dear, I am very well, this summer brightens me up, a few twitches every winter, but nothing now. How is your good father? I hope he fares well."

"Papa is quite well. He has ridden out this morning, but I hope he will soon be back, for I am sure he would be sorry to miss seeing you," said Helen courteously. "You must have had a delightful ride this beautiful day."

They talked much of the weather, how long it had been fine, how long it would continue so, but at length Mrs. Escott could no longer conceal her superior knowledge.

"Have you heard the Hartlebury news yet, Miss Molesworth? No, it is impossible, now I think of it, that it can have reached you," said the old lady, fully confident of her priority of information.

"No indeed, what can have happened at Hartlebury?"

"Well, my dear, you may depend on my news, it is quite true. I was at the Gainsboroughs, for I always make it a point you know to call there, they would be hurt if they were neglected, they don't feel, of course, like you or I, they would fancy themselves slighted, I always make it a point to call. Well, while I was there, the express arrived."

"What express?" enquired Helen, rather puzzled.

"I think it was from London, no, I am not sure, I believe it was from Falmouth, where he had just landed; however it is not of much consequence where it comes from, for it said by the time they got it, that George Gainsborough would be in London."

"That is indeed news," said Helen rewarded at last for her persevering politeness, "his father and mother must be very delighted."

"Yes indeed I must say, they appeared very happy. At first, it seemed that Mr. Gainsborough would go to London to meet him, and then Mrs. Gainsborough seemed to think that would make it so much longer before she saw him, so at last it was settled that Mr. Gainsborough should only write him a letter. I told them I should tell you all about it, and they sent their compliments."

Helen smiled as she pictured to herself how much Mrs. Escott must have been in the way, in all this family rejoicing, and consultation.

"Mr. George Gainsborough has been a long time away? I think ever since his father has lived here; at least, I believe, he never was here."

"No I just heard Mr. Gainsborough say he never had seen Oakfield, and a very pretty place they have made of it. I dare say the young man will be quite charmed. A very pleasant chatty man is old Mr. Gainsborough; he often calls on me, he tells me all the news, and brings all his son's letters to read to me, very handsome of him isn't it, and very clever letters they are, I make no doubt he is a monstrous clever young man."

The servant entered with refreshments, the merits of the Gainsboroughs died away, drowned in the wine and cake.

"So I hear that Mrs. Latimer is not here. I felt quite sure she would have come back by this time," said the old lady when she finished her last glass of wine. She spoke in a tone of resentment as she thought that it would be necessary to make another excursion to call on her.

"Charlotte has not been well and could not bear to lose her mother," observed Helen in an apologetic tone. "I do not think she will be here for a month yet."

"Mrs. Boscawen is very fond of her mother, and I am sure she ought to be, she has a family so fast! I do not know what she would do without her. She puts me just in mind of my old friend Nancy Goldby; Mrs. Boscawen will have just such another family. I remember calling on her once, and seeing eight under eight years old. Bless me I do not know how she managed them all. But she had always great spirits. I am sure it would have killed me. I have lost sight of them of late, but I believe all the eight children lived to be married, no — let me see, I think Rose the third, never married, no, certainly she did not, there was a something, but she did not marry."

At this point of Mrs. Escott's reminiscences Arthur Latimer entered the room.

"Ah! Mr. Latimer," she continued, "I am very glad to see you, I was just enquiring after your good mother. I shall certainly pay her a visit directly she comes back. I have been telling Miss Molesworth a great piece of news. You see, I come to Hartlebury to pay a visit, and I know more about its concerns than either of you."

"What is your piece of news?" enquired Mr. Latimer. "I am almost afraid that I already know it. Is it that Mr. George Gainsborough has arrived?"

Mrs. Escott was evidently annoyed. Helen enquired how he

came to be so early in his intelligence.

"I just met Mr. Gainsborough on his way to catch the mail to London."

"Dear me, that is very odd," and the old lady bridled up, "when I left them, I am sure it was quite settled that he should not go."

Helen began to talk of other things, anxious to cover Arthur Latimer's perversity, and Mr. Gainsborough's delinquency.

At last her visitor rose, "I believe I must ring for my carriage, my dear. I must not wait any longer for the chance of seeing my good friend Mr. Molesworth. You must give my compliments to him, and tell him how sorry I am to have missed him."

"How pretty you look here," she observed to Mr. Latimer as he handed her to her carriage. "When we lived on the opposite side of the valley, that was before your time (Mrs. Escott referred to about fifty years since), I always used to say that there was nothing so pretty as looking down upon Hartlebury so snug, and so comfortable."

CHAPTER VI

Arrival of George Gainsborough

In a week George Gainsborough was at Hartlebury; in a few days more he had paid a visit at the Hall. He drove over with his mother and sister. Mrs. Gainsborough received with quiescent gratitude Helen's congratulations. She was sure she was very happy that he had come back, she did not think she should have known him, he seemed so grown, and his hair was so different.

This personal critique was evidently not agreeable to the hero of it, he was anxious that Miss Molesworth should think that he had been always as handsome and as captivating as he now stood before her, six feet high, with a fine expansive padded chest, an abundance of golden hair, which no one dared to insinuate was inclined to carrotty, and the most delicate moustachios.

"I hope you like Hartlebury," said Helen, with the polite intention of changing the subject of conversation.

"I think it charming, I never mean to leave it again."

"Oh! George how can you say so," said his mother, "I am sure you will never stay here."

"I assure you," interposed Fanny Gainsborough, "he admired it excessively, though I told him till he had seen the Hall, he had not seen half our beauty."

"I feel that now," said George Gainsborough with a bow.

"I am glad that you like the place," replied Helen: "for myself, I think everything about it charming, but I am afraid you will find one sad want, the want of society."

"Excuse me," observed Mr. George Gainsborough. "I must differ with you there; I should think, among all the delightful things at Hartlebury, the most delightful was the society."

"No, no," said Helen, "however polite you may intend to be, I fear you will too soon discover that there is no society."

"I hate society," observed Mr. George Gainsborough.

"I am sure you used, George, to like company more than anybody," said Mrs. Gainsborough.

"Well, Mrs. Gainsborough, he can soon prove his sincerity here, you know," said Miss Molesworth, "when he has exhausted all our resources, there are plenty of woods, and solitary hills, in which he may cultivate his love of solitude. You have not yet taken any rides through our green lanes?" continued Helen, addressing George Gainsborough.

"Yesterday I had a beautiful ride with my father to Bohun Castle, a fine feudal looking place. The owner never resides there, I think I heard?"

"No, never, he lives entirely abroad."

"What sort of a man is he?"

"That no one can tell you, for no one knows, do they Miss Gainsborough?"

"But is he old or young?"

"Young, decidedly young. We all know he must be young, and we suspect he must be handsome, for as the Housekeeper invariably informs us all the Bohuns are handsome."

"Positively young, and hypothetically handsome — I think

that is knowing a great deal about a man."

"You must go to the Castle, there is a capital gallery of pictures."

"I have seen so many pictures."

"And these are principally portraits, so perhaps you would not care for them, but you wouldn't fail to admire the Park, the Park is delightful, a fine combination of the richest cultivation, and the wildest scenery. There is a most romantic green dell with the tallest trees, and the softest turf, just made for a Watteau scene."

Mr. Molesworth now entered, and the conversation became more divided: Helen talked to Mrs. Gainsborough, and listened to Fanny, while the gentlemen discoursed of the state of Greece, the character of the Sultan, of the weather, of the hay, and of the coming harvest.

On the next day the Gainsboroughs dined at the Hall. George Gainsborough's accomplishments developed, he played on the guitar, he sang extremely well, and he quoted Byron.

Mr. Molesworth thought him a puppy, Arthur Latimer thought him very presuming, Helen thought him very amusing.

Whatsoever opinion, however, they might severally have formed of him, they could scarcely avoid intimacy, for every day brought them into collision. They met him in their rides, in their walks, in the village, or on the common. He sketched with great skill, his sketch-books were all at Miss Molesworth's command. He brought them, he fetched them away again, he replaced them with others, he had for ever an excuse for a visit. He took great interest in the School-house which was now rapidly progressing, he was ever ready to advise or to admire. One day, as he was standing by the side of Helen, and admiring the view of the village, which was visible from the School, a pretty little girl came hovering around them, she kept blushing and curtseying, and looked as if she wished to speak.

"Well, Mary," said Helen, "how is your Mother, is she better?"

"Much better, thank you, Ma'am, nearly well now." Still the little girl did not go.

"What do you want Mary? I am sure you want something of

me. Speak out, do not be afraid," and Helen kindly patted her cheek.

The little girl thus encouraged, but still blushing, and still curtseying, ventured to make her petition. Helen had promised that, when her mother was better, she should do some work for her. To work for Miss Molesworth was the greatest honour in the school, and only accorded to the industrious; and the little girl now came to claim the performance of Helen's promise.

"I will speak to Mrs. Walker about you today, Mary; you are a good little girl for being so anxious to work."

Mary looked much pleased, she walked steadily away for a few yards, and then scampered off to join her companions.

"You have granted that child's petition so kindly," said Mr. Gainsborough, "that I am emboldened to prefer one. Will you grant me a favour?"

"Do you want work, too? Are you already tired of idleness?"

"No, I do not want work, I want you to take me a ride."

"Where?"

"To the green dell in Bohun Park."

"What, the Woodman's Dell, have you not yet been there?"

"No, I every day take the most minute directions where it is situated, not that I may visit, but that I may avoid it. You described it so poetically on the morning that I first had the pleasure of seeing you, that I could not endure to view it for the first time, but in your presence."

"When you see it, you will think I described it very ill."

"But will you introduce me?"

"I shall be very happy, but we must have a very fine sunny day, it must be just such a day as this, clear and bright. Mr. and Mrs. Boscawen are coming to us next week, and we will all go together."

Mr. Gainsborough was eloquent in his thanks.

"Papa," said Helen, as Mr. Molesworth joined them, "we are projecting a pic-nic, will you ensure us fine weather?"

"Remember your promise to me," said Mr. Gainsborough, as Helen shook hands with him at parting. "The sun will be propitious if you are."

"That is a most gallant young gentleman," observed Mr. Molesworth, as Helen took his arm and they proceeded up the Green. "A specimen of the Oriental style, I presume!"

CHAPTER VII

Fresh arrivals — the Boscawen family

There was an almost alarming ringing at the Hall gates. All the dogs barked. Amid the whirl of wheels, human voices might however be detected. The Boscawens had arrived!

Helen flew into the hall to welcome her friend. "Dear Charlotte, how well you look," she exclaimed, as she embraced her. It was a long ceremony before the whole family could be unpacked. First came out the baby warm and sleeping; Mrs. Boscawen was all anxiety until he was safely conveyed out of the draughts. Then came the eldest boy, a brave youth of four, who was vociferous until he was allowed to tell cousin Helen that he was quite a man, and had ridden outside all the way with papa. Followed the second son very fractious, too young to have partaken of his elder brother's privileges, and too old to have shared the slumbering felicity of the younger. At last the children were got rid of, sent to the comfortable nursery which had been prepared for them, and the noise subsided, and Helen was able to hear that they had deposited Mrs. Latimer at the Rectory quite well, that they had just had a glimpse of Arthur as he took his mother from the carriage, and that they were all delighted to be again at Hartlebury.

Mrs. Boscawen was a pretty little woman, with sparkling hazel eyes and soft brown hair, very fond of her husband, and devoted to her nursery. She had made an excellent match. Mr. Boscawen was a man of considerable independent fortune, and of still more considerable expectations. He was not remarkably handsome, nor remarkably clever, but extremely amiable, and sensible enough.

Charlotte had not been at Hartlebury since immediately after her marriage, except during a short and painful visit at the time of her father's death, and she was eager to see all her old friends, and to hear of all that concerned them. Helen, willing as she was to communicate, could never satisfy her, and Mr. Boscawen had great difficulty in persuading his wife that early hours were indispensable after a long journey, that he was very tired, and that she must be very tired too.

People, I believe, only breakfast in the country. It is a cheerful union with us, full of hope and plans, and everyone comes down, looking all the better for early slumbers and rosy dreams. Dinner, even in the country, has a graver aspect. The party is in general slightly exhausted, they sigh for repose, the innocent excitement of the morn is over, the talkers take refuge in memory, and remind each other of early scenes and scrapes, joys and sorrows, and enumerate all the good fellows who are now dead, and all the pretty faces that are now never beheld.

The breakfast table at Hartlebury was the most charming breakfast-table in the world. Everybody lingered at it with a sort of lazy delight. And this morning the ceremony lasted longer than ever, and was of course still more lively than usual. At length the ladies rose to prepare for a round of village visits, and Mr. Molesworth proposed to Mr. Boscawen a ride over the estate.

The first village visit was of course to the rectory. Helen was eager to see Mrs. Latimer, and Charlotte to see her brother and his improvements. Here they remained a long time, so much had they all to say. Even Charlotte had a little history of the last twelve hours to tell her mother. She was glad to say the children did not seem to have suffered from their journey at all; last night when they went to bed, Mr. Boscawen thought Henry seemed a little hot and feverish, but she did not give him anything he was so fast asleep, and after all it had proved to be nothing, for he was as gay and as lively as the others this morning. They were all as happy as possible, and were coming at two o'clock, after they had had their dinner, to 'see their grandmamma.

"Well then my dear girls," said Mrs. Latimer, rising when this communication was made to her, "if I am to receive these little gentry at two, I must run away from you now, for I left Nugent with all her accompt books, and all her bills open before her, and she will be quite cross if we do not complete our affairs."

"We shall meet again," said Helen, as she kissed her: "you

will come up and dine with us?" And with the consoling assurance that they were to meet again in a very few hours, Mrs. Latimer retired.

The young ladies crossed the Rectory garden, and passing through a small side gate, entered the lane just opposite to the almshouses. Hither they bent their steps. If the first visit were to the Rectory, the second must as unquestionably be to Dame Harrald.

The old woman was standing in her doorway as they approached. She hastened forward to meet them. She was delighted to see Charlotte, and not a little secret gratification at the consideration thus shown to her, mingled with her pleasure.

"Bless you," said the dame, as she followed them into her abode, "it does me good to see you. I dare say you are surprised to find me here, Ma'am."

"I am delighted to see you looking so well, and seemingly so comfortable," said Mrs. Boscawen, and she turned to admire the room and everything it contained. Never was there such a picture of cheerful neatness. The sun shone through the broad latticed window on the well rubbed oaken chairs: in one corner stood the spinning-wheel, and on a small round table, by the side of a high backed arm-chair, was the knitting. The floor had just been fresh sanded. The mantel-shelf was adorned with many curious ornaments, the greater part fairings from her scholars, and the walls were hung with some prints of scripture history, in heavy black wooden frames, which once upon a time, many years ago, had come from the Hall. There was the Prodigal Son in an ample pair of breeches, and a three cornered cocked hat well laced: and the good Samaritan depositing his charitable burthen at a capital inn, with a handsome sign of the Rose and Crown, bearing in very legible characters, the comfortable assurance of there being within good accommodation for man and beast.

"Just the same as ever," said Charlotte, "always the neatest person in the world."

"I am not so old yet, but that I can put my room to rights," said the old dame, and she drew herself up.

This was but a slight allusion; the dame was too happy to be able to remember she was in a fallen state. They talked of the village and its historiettes, and Charlotte had the pleasure of hearing her version of many of the stories Helen had already told.

"Have you seen the new school-house yet?" at length enquired the dame. Charlotte had not yet visited it; the old woman praised its conveniences with a magnanimous dignity.

"You must knit my boys some socks, they have never had any so good as the pair you sent me for a present last year by mamma," said Charlotte, as she bid good morning to her old friend.

The ladies proceeded up the lane to the village green, stopping a few minutes to admire the new building.

"We must call at the farm," said Helen, "the Collinses will be hurt if they see us so near."

The farm-house stood at the further part of the village, and thither they directed their way, but their progress was very slow, for Charlotte had a reason for speaking to every person they met, and to every child who was playing about the cottage doors.

At the next wicket gate, under the elms, in front of the farm, was a gentleman on horseback. His back was turned to them, and he was leaning on his saddle, and talking, apparently very gaily, to a very pretty girl.

"Who can that be standing against the gate, talking to that pretty girl?" enquired Charlotte.

"That is Mr. George Gainsborough, and that pretty girl is Lydia Collins," answered Helen. "I hope he is not turning my little friend's head."

"Is it possible that that can be Lydia; why she was quite a child the last time I saw her!"

Lydia's blushing face soon revealed that she saw them, and George Gainsborough turning round, bowed, and slightly smiled, and cantered away. Lydia opened the gate, and ushered them through the small garden into the house. The door opened at once into the usual sitting-room of the family. It was tiled, but had several pieces of handsome useful furniture. There was a huge mahogany bureau, where Mrs. Collins kept her money and her accompts, a tall clock which ticked most audibly, and along one side was a dresser covered with work, and above which were hanging shelves, with a few books. Some children's toys, headless horses, and waggons without wheels,

lay on the ground, but the room looked neat and orderly. Mrs.
Collins soon made her appearance — an active, motherly
woman, with whom twelve children were never an excuse for
untidiness.

Mrs. Collins was eager in her expressions of gratification at
their visit, and scolded Lydia for not shewing them into the best
room. Accordingly, she herself opened the door into an apartment, covered with a bright Brussels' carpet, all large green
leaves and red roses, on which the sun was never allowed to
shine. Lydia began to open the shutters, but Miss Molesworth
begged her not to take so much trouble.

"You know, Mrs. Collins," said she, "I always like to see you
in the midst of all your occupation, and so I am sure does Mrs.
Boscawen."

The first bustle of reception over, Mrs. Collins soon recovered her presence of mind, and had much to tell, and a great
many questions to ask. The ages, and the names, and the
health, of the three Master Boscawens were first discussed,
then the young Collinses of the same date were brought in, to
ascertain if they were taller, or shorter, or stouter; and Charlotte having satisfactorily ascertained that neither measles, nor
whooping cough, nor scarlet fever, had been in the village for
the last year, promised that her sons should pay Mrs. Collins,
and her hens and chickens, a visit.

"Lydia Collins is certainly a very pretty girl," observed Mrs.
Boscawen, as she and Helen were proceeding homewards, "and
very pleasing too, but could you believe that poor little Susan
was only one month younger than Henry?"

CHAPTER VIII

The pic-nic in Bohun Park

Amid the wildest scenery of Bohun Park you suddenly come to a small rustic gate. Pass through it a few yards, and a magical scene is before you. The ground seems to have opened at your feet; you look over the heads of the tallest trees upon a green and bowery glen, nearly surrounded by precipitous banks covered with towering trees growing one above the other. At the furthest point these banks gradually slope down, and form a natural opening.

This beautiful spot was to be today the scene of a fine pic-nic party from Hartlebury, for which the arrival of the Boscawens had been the signal. George Gainsborough, too, was to be introduced to the picturesque beauties of which he was, as he was in the habit of constantly avowing, an enthusiastic admirer.

And even now a sparkling britchka and a cluster of gay cavaliers, looking like a fairy cavalcade from the heights above, enter upon the scene. It is the party from Hartlebury Hall. The weather was so fair and fixed, that even Mrs. Latimer had ventured to join the party, and the Gainsboroughs were also there: for since their son's return, a more familiar intercourse between them and the squire and his daughter, had almost imperceptibly arisen.

"This is charming," said George Gainsborough throwing himself from his horse, "you may travel all over the world, and never see a scene like this."

Mr. George Gainsborough was rewarded for his enthusiasm with a smile from Miss Molesworth. The party proceeded to the other end of the glen. They trod with delight the mossy and elastic turf; they gazed with admiration on the tall trees, whose tops seemed to touch the heavens, and whose stems were concealed by the richest underwood of aromatic shrubs. They were all alike enchanted, and Helen declared that the beautiful spot looked more beautiful than ever. A thousand mazy paths wound among the trees, half ascending the hill, and then again gently terminating in the glen. Amid these bowery walks they roamed, or reposed on the soft turf beneath the broad shadow of a branching tree. Everybody was witty and agreeable, or, at least, seemed so; for everybody was pleased and in good humour.

"I believe this is real happiness," said Helen, as she scented the perfumed air.

"I am sure it is," said George Gainsborough, as he threw himself on the turf by her side.

"A young lady's idea of happiness, Helen," said her father— "to be pleased, and to be idle."

"To be pleasing, you mean, Sir," said George Gainsborough, "and therefore not idle."

They were soon all moving about again; they became adventurous. One of the party proposed that they should mount the hill. Mrs. Latimer and Mrs. Gainsborough would not allow the project to be abandoned on their account; they should be very well amused in seeing the tent pitched, and watching all the preparations for the repast.

"Shall we then make an expedition to the castle?" asked Helen. "Will it be too hot?"

George Gainsborough maintained that it was not hot now, and, as they mounted the hill, it would be quite cool. Helen, too, had often made the ascent before; she knew the least steep passage. So they proceeded slowly through an arched walk formed by the entwining branches of the trees. Every now and then there came a broken piece of open, uneven ground, and then, over the trees they had passed through, they caught a glimpse of a rich view; then, again, the agreeable shade of the trees received them. They arrived, at last, at the top of the hill, at the little gate we have already mentioned, and they forgot their fatigue as they looked upon the rich landscape around them, and upon the verdant scene at their feet, which they had not long left. It was now all life and bustle: a gay marquée had just risen, and many lilliputian agents were toiling for their future enjoyment.

They crossed through the wild fern, led by Arthur Latimer and Helen, into a more cultivated scene, when, turning by a noble group of forest trees, they found themselves close to the castle.

Bohun castle was a regular show place, and was quite an income to all the inn-keepers in the neighbourhood. Few travellers came within twenty miles of it that were not induced to stay on their way, and visit the castle. The housekeeper, a stately lady, full of Bohun pride, delighted in the display of the grandeur of her charge, and was sedulous in preserving its splendour, as far as lay in her power. Though so long uninhabited, the splendid pile bore no marks of devastation – scarcely of neglect. Careful dusting had preserved the gilding, and the rich damask, though faded, was not soiled or worn. The state-rooms were in the same order as when, thirty years ago, they had received the gay revellers, who had congregated round Mr. Bohun and his beautiful bride: and, though the housekeeper inwardly sighed at the present possessor's disregard of his castle, she never allowed that there was anything extraordinary in his absence. "Mr. Bohun was, at present, on the Continent," was her evasive answer to strangers. With her neighbours she was more at her ease: she knew they were as well informed as herself, and would ask no questions where they were sure they could obtain no information.

Our party knocked at a small postern gate, the housekeeper was summoned, but she begged the party to go round to the grand entrance, as she disliked anyone to enter the castle by any other mode. Accordingly, they proceeded to the west front of the building, passed over the draw-bridge, which was now a stationary one, through the massy gates which creaked on their hinges, as with difficulty they pushed them open, and crossed the spacious quadrangle to the vast Hall, where the Housekeeper awaited them.

She conducted them up the magnificent staircase into an ante-room, which opened on one side into the private apartments, which were never shown, and on the other into the state chambers. She led them through corridors and guard-rooms, great and little cabinets, large and small drawing-rooms, and spacious saloons, all gilding and painted ceilings, and state bed-chambers, where monarchs had slept. There was the chapel, too, covered with crimson velvet, the dim library, full of monastic books, and the dismantled theatre and the long picture gallery. There had formerly been a brilliant flower-garden along the terrace; that was no longer kept up, but a splendid view was to be seen from every window. Through loop-hole, or lattice, or lordly oriel, a rich, but varied, scene was ever present.

The party were wearied with admiration, and, before they recommenced their walk, they were glad to rest themselves awhile. The picture gallery, with its long divan-looking seats, was agreed on by all to be the best lounging place, for there would be amusement for those who were the soonest refreshed.

George Gainsborough, ever active and restless, was soon moving about the room. An unfinished picture, which was leaning with its face against the wall, attracted his attention. He turned it towards a good light. He uttered a short, but agitated, exclamation.

"It is the late Mr. Bohun, sir," said the housekeeper, attracted by his exclamation, and his fixed and ardent gaze. "It is the late Mr. Bohun, sir, in an Albanian dress, I believe, a character in some play he was acting. It was painting at the time the sad accident happened; when he fell from his horse, you know, sir," said the woman turning towards Mr. Molesworth.

Her explanation had drawn all eyes towards the picture, and towards George Gainsborough. He was still holding it, and looked quite pale.

He rallied, and laughed, and said it was so exactly like a person he had known, that it took him quite by surprise, as he suddenly turned it round.

The visitors began to think of returning. Mrs. Latimer and her companion would be alarmed if they stayed away much longer, they would fancy that some accident had happened, they must set off. So they retraced their steps, but somewhat languidly, and were all unanimous in rejoicing that their return was a descent.

The party was just sufficiently exhausted to make their repast very agreeable. It is mortifying to observe how very intense are all physical pleasures. A glass of champagne has more effect upon the mind than the finest apothegm of the deepest sage, and a sandwich or a plover's egg, a plate of jelly, or a spoonful of trifle, will often produce an effect which the wisest philosophers and the most brilliant poets have failed in bringing about.

For sometime, nothing was heard but the clatter of plates, and the drawing of corks, varied with slight offers of assistance, recommendations to take some particular food, or invitations to taste some peculiar beverage. At length Miss Molesworth uttered a sentence, and, strange to say, the same speculation was passing in almost everyone else's mind.

"I wonder," said Miss Molesworth, "I wonder if Mr. Bohun will ever return!"

"Where is he?" enquired Mr. George Gainsborough.

"No one knoweth," replied Miss Molesworth, "but I suppose at Rome, Naples, Constantinople, or some place or other which young men imagine to be much more agreeable than London, though I see not why they should be."

"London is the largest capital of modern times," observed Mr. Gainsborough senior. "It is very strange that the population of principal cities holds no relation to the population of the state. For instance Lisbon has nearly two hundred thousand inhabitants, and yet Portugal itself does not contain many more souls than London. I wonder how this is?"

"Quite enough souls to cut each others' throats," said Mr. Molesworth. "You will soon have the population of Lisbon scanty enough."

"You never were at Lisbon, George?" enquired his father, "so you cannot tell me whether it is defensible."

"I believe I can answer your question, sir, though I never have been at Lisbon. It is not fortified. But that signifies little with irregular troops. One can soon throw up a few batteries. Give me plenty of artillery, and I will defend any open town in Europe against irregular troops. The mere suburbs would be burnt, to be sure, but that's nothing," added Mr. George Gainsborough, with an air of complacent courage, which seemed to speak from experience. "I should perhaps think fit to burn them myself."

"I am sure, I hope you would never do anything so dreadful, George," exclaimed his Mother.

"You have seen war?" enquired Helen.

"I had four years of it in Greece," replied George Gainsborough, "and I can assure you, whatever they may say, that fighting with Turks is no trifle."

"Who is to have Candia?" enquired his father.

"A glass of champagne, Mr. Gainsborough?" said Mr. Molesworth.

"Nothing is more awful than a Turkish massacre," continued George Gainsborough, "none spared, women, children and all. It is indeed terrific."

"How anybody could kill a child!" exclaimed Mrs. Boscawen, with averted eyes, and shuddering breath. "It does seem to me quite impossible. Only think, Godfrey," addressing herself to her husband, "what should we do if anything were to happen in this country with our dear boys. I don't think an English mob would kill children, do you Mr. Gainsborough?"

"It is impossible to say what an infuriated populace would do," solemnly replied the politician.

"It appears to me," said Arthur Latimer, "that the transition from incendiarism to the most horrible murder is not very difficult."

"Gracious!" said Mrs. Gainsborough, "how terrible!"

"Murder, incendiarism!" said Miss Molesworth. "What are we talking about. Come, Arthur, let us remember that this is a pic-nic, and not a charnel-house. Now what do you think I was imagining in the picture gallery today?"

"A woman's imagination is beyond my device," said Mr. Molesworth, with affected gruffness. "I dare say something very silly."

"You are not inspired by the chivalrous scene, papa. Remember, you have wandered today in bannered halls, and courtly chambers, and must pay compliments even to your daughter."

"I believe she gets all the compliments I ever do pay," rejoined Mr. Molesworth, with an ill-suppressed smile.

"And I am sure she deserves them," said Mrs. Latimer.

"Indeed! yes!" echoed Mrs. Gainsborough.

"Silence, silence," cried Helen, "you forget that I am here."

"Oh! we can make up for it by cutting you up behind your back," said her father. "Arthur Latimer, you seem rather dull. Send me some pigeon-pie, and persuade Mrs. Gainsborough to join us both in a glass of wine. What shall it be, Mrs. Gainsborough? The lady must decide you know."

"Champagne, then, if you please."

"Ah! I thought so. Champagne, you know, is the ladies' wine."

"You were right, Mr. Molesworth," said Mr. Gainsborough, led by the association of ideas, "Port has risen."

"To be sure, depend upon it, friend Gainsborough, I am a sounder politician than you imagine."

"Come, Helen," said Arthur Latimer, "we have not yet been favoured with your fancy."

"You would not listen, so I have communicated it, in confidence, to Mr. George Gainsborough, who thinks the idea admirable."

"Capital!" attested Mr. George Gainsborough. "But Mr. Bohun must return to put it in execution."

"Oh! a ball," said Arthur Latimer. "I thought so. Brilliant fancy! A ball."

"Not a ball! Mr. Latimer," laughingly replied Helen. "No! not a ball, but something much more original."

"Come Helen," said her father, "I am getting curious, and Arthur, too, is dying to know. Put us out of our suspense."

"Well then, Papa, a tournament!"

"A fiddlestick! Helen!"

"Lord Helm had a tournament at Strangeways castle last year," replied Helen.

"And I hope there were plenty of bloody coxcombs," replied her father.

"The invention of gunpowder has entirely altered the whole system of warfare," observed Mr. Gainsborough. "How were you supplied with ammunition in Greece, George?"

"We trusted more to our yataghans than to anything else," replied the hero.

"Helen," said Mrs. Boscawen to Miss Molesworth, "do you know what little Henry said to Sir Frederick, before we left town?"

"No indeed," replied Helen, "but I shall be delighted to hear, for I suspect that Master Henry will turn out a very great wit."

"He certainly does say very odd things," assented his silent father, ceasing from his pasty. The assent was irrepressible.

"Well, do you know," continued Mrs. Boscawen, "Sir Frederick wanted to give them all something, and the two eldest were to choose. Walter fixed his heart on a watch, and I was to wind it up for him every night, for he never could manage to wind it up, he is so impatient; and then little Henry was to choose, and what do you think he said to Sir Frederick, quite in his sturdy way, you know? 'Why, as I am to be a soldier, I think I had better have a sword, and then, I shall learn how to use it.' Only think of the child! Sir Frederick was so pleased."

"Capital little fellow!" said Helen.

"Dear boy," ejaculated Mrs. Latimer.

"Only think!" exclaimed Mrs. Gainsborough.

"Charming," echoed Miss Gainsborough.

"That child certainly does say very odd things!" observed Mr. Boscawen.

The hours flew away. The party were amused. The sun was sinking. They were no longer hungry; they began to grow sentimental. Mr. George Gainsborough had brought his guitar by particular desire, and sang several airs. He had a good voice, and well cultivated. His subjects were tender as the evening breeze, and tremulous as the evening star. His style was perhaps too affectedly passionate, and too ornate. But the human voice is, after all, a wonderful instrument, and its influence is mysteriously powerful. Even the tones of George Gainsborough stilled or excited many a sympathetic heart, and drove from many a bosom the worldly thought of the morrow. The glorious sun-set faded away. With sweet sounds lingering in their ear, the party rose, and stretched their grateful limbs in the beautiful and fragrant air. The horses were ordered. The pic-nic had succeeded.

CHAPTER IX

Reflections which it creates in the minds of several of the party

The pic-nic of yesterday was an exception to all pic-nics. All returned in the same good humour as they had started. The weather had been faultless, and so had been the company. But the morrow's sober remembrance of it did not bring equal pleasure to all. Arthur Latimer was not as well satisfied, with the events of the preceding day, as were the rest of the party.

From the first of his introduction to George Gainsborough, he had felt towards him an instinctive dislike. But, he was angry with himself for conceiving a prejudice, which he would never acknowledge, and which, he flattered himself, he effectually concealed. What right had he to set himself up for a censor of Mr. Gainsborough's manner? But now, since yesterday, greater causes of offence had arisen. It was no longer his manner, but his intentions, that Mr. Latimer objected to, for he strongly suspected him of a systematic intention of making himself particularly agreeable to Helen. The imagination of such a thing was itself an insult. It was really ridiculous, it was absurd; it was surprising that Mr. Molesworth did not resent it. As to Helen herself, she was so unsuspicious, that such an idea could never cross her mind. Arthur was not uneasy about her: he was satisfied that she had detected Mr. Gainsborough's specious vulgarity; but she was evidently amused by him. He thought her father should certainly interfere. He thought he would speak to her himself; he would tell her, he would seek a proper opportunity of telling her, that she might perhaps, unconsciously, be encouraging pretensions to which she would never listen. But, had he any right to advise Helen on such a point? And, after all, he was satisfied that she saw through Gainsborough; she could not be injured. But she was injured, she was insulted by such pretensions. It was really disgusting to think what annoyances women were subject to.

Thus cogitated Arthur Latimer. Tomorrow, they were all to dine at Oakfield, and Arthur finally determined to regulate his conduct, by his observations.

Whatever might be the cause of Mr. Latimer's quickness of observation, there is no doubt he was perfectly right in his suspicions. George Gainsborough was excessively vain, and very presumptuous. He considered himself very handsome, with a peculiarly captivating manner, and he never was in company with any woman for half an hour, provided she was not absolutely old, and absolutely ugly, which no women are, without using his utmost endeavour to make his companion of the same opinion as himself. Miss Molesworth smiled, and his ambition fired. Why should she not be his? He was quite alive to all the obvious inequalities of the union, which would make everybody exclaim, and he was aware too, of a few more, which no one knew anything about. But he had passed through some slight adventures, and he had formed a very determined opinion, that a woman will do anything for love — much more astonishing things than marrying a handsome young man.

Helen Molesworth, desperately enamoured, ready to sacrifice everything for him, her father yielding to her entreaties and her tears, was a captivating picture, now often present to George Gainsborough's imagination. Fear never disturbed him; he never doubted he could excite this great affection, which was to work such agreeable results. No, he felt confident, not only in his own manifold attractions, but in the total absence of all rivals. Excepting Arthur Latimer, Helen saw but few persons at any time, and those few, but rarely, who could venture to aspire. Of Arthur Latimer he had no fear. They were cousins, and they had been brought up together; why should she all of a sudden fall in love with a person she had known all her life?

There was no chance of it, it was impossible, cousins never do fall in love. Of course she felt towards him as she would for a brother, and as for Arthur Latimer himself, George Gainsborough had the greatest contempt for him, for not having long ago secured so great a prize.

CHAPTER X

The Gainsboroughs give a dinner

I very much fear that my fashionable readers, who have been accustomed to society as fashionable as themselves, whenever they have found time to skim over a novel, will be very much disgusted with my dull country parties, where the same thing is done and said, every day, by the same people. But really at Hartlebury, there is very little neighbourhood, and such slight sources of entertainment to all those who depend particularly upon companionship, that I must even invite my friends, in spite of the pic-nic, which has but just past, to join Mr. and Mrs. Gainsborough's dinner today.

It was a very grand affair indeed, for the Gainsboroughs. Excited by their increasing intimacy at the Hall, and the honour of not only having the Molesworths, and the Latimers, but even the Boscawens for their guests, and proud in the confidence that their travelled and accomplished son was present to back them at this moment of almost trying triumph, Mr. and Mrs. Gainsborough resolved that the dinner should be, in every respect, worthy of the occasion. The Head Cook, at the principal Hotel at Fanchester was engaged expressly; a stray sturgeon, that perquisite of princes, could scarely have made a greater sensation than the arrival of the turbot, from ———borough, and there were two soups, Mrs. Gainsborough's idea of complete domestic splendour. Besides the party of yesterday, Mrs. Escott was a guest, and Mr. Chace, the manager of the Bohun property, but himself also a small proprietor, and an active Magistrate, was there, and Dr. Maxwell, the son-in-law of Mr. Gainsborough, and his lady. Dr. Maxwell was a well powdered and pompous looking gentleman, well preferred in the church, and considerably older than his wife.

"I heard of your party yesterday," said Mrs. Escott, speaking as she entered the room, "William Barton saw you all, never saw anything so pretty— tent, blue and white— hope Mrs. Latimer caught no rheumatism. I think it is always damp in the glen. And so you lionized the castle? You must have suffered a great deal in the ascent? such a hot day! I suppose you remained below, with Mrs. Latimer, Mrs. Gainsborough? Well, it is a noble place, quite the pride of the country, and very well kept up too, that no one can deny. That Mrs. Brand is a treasure— I wonder if Mr. Bohun will ever return? They say that the Steward has quarrelled with the head gardener about the fruit. The Steward says the succession houses are his perquisite. No, says the Gardener, the head gardener, Macpherson, a Scotchman, a very respectable man, and an excellent gardener, the Scotch are the best gardeners, very odd, no fruit in their own country— No, says Mr. Macpherson— Ah! Mr. Chace, how d'ye do? you know all about it, I dare say. I am sure Mr. Bohun owes you a debt, which he never can repay. You always put me in mind of what old Frank Escott, of Escott Hall, said to Mr. Burnley, who had the management of the Escott estates in his minority, the Somersetshire property, as well as Escott Hall: 'Mr. Burnley,' said he, 'I and my family owe you more than I can express, and they can ever repay.' Very handsome of him, was it not? Oh dear, Mrs. Boscawen, how d'ye do? little Walter, I hope, very well, and Henry, my favourite, and baby too, I never forget baby. Mr. Latimer, I won't trouble you, you are always too good. What do you think the Bishop said to Dr. Maxwell? Oh! Dr. Maxwell is here, to tell the story himself. Never mind, you shall hear it now. Good news, you know, cannot travel too fast, and everybody says, I talk very fast indeed. 'Of all the clergymen in my diocese,' said his lordship, 'Mr. Arthur Latimer is the one I should fix upon, as a model!' Very handsome of him, was it not?"

"I am delighted, Miss Molesworth," said Dr. Maxwell, and glancing at her father, and speaking in a tone of solemn courtesy, "to see our invaluable friend looking so extremely well. Without Mr. Molesworth, I know not what we should do! He is the very soul of our sessions."

"And I am sure he is very sensible of the invaluable assistance he receives from Dr. Maxwell."

"You are too good. Miss Molesworth is always too flattering, I certainly do whatever is in my power to support him. I aspire

to nothing higher than to be Mr. Molesworth's humble supporter. That I believe is Mr. Boscawen, is it not? I never had the
gratification of meeting him before. An extremely good looking, gentlemanlike man, and a very fine property too, I believe?
Nothing is more gratifying than to find fine property in the
possession of a very gentlemanlike man. Considerable expectations too, I believe? It is always gratifying to understand that a
very gentlemanlike man, with a fine property, has, in addition,
very considerable expectations. Would you have the kindness to
introduce me to him? Thank you, Miss Molesworth, you are
always so kind, you are always too kind, Miss Molesworth."

Nothing was more gratifying to Dr. Maxwell, at any time,
than to be introduced to a very gentlemanlike man, with a very
fine property, and the gratification was always enhanced to Dr.
Maxwell if the very gentlemanlike man, with a very fine property, had also in addition, considerable expectations. As Mr.
Boscawen was a silent man, he was a fine victim for the solemn
flattery of the clerical courtier. In the meantime, his wife,
whom he had impregnated with his mania, to make connec-
tions, had seized upon Mrs. Boscawen, and was delighting the
fond mother with all her familiar enquiries after the children she
had never seen, and the eager interest with which she listened to
all the narratives of their exploits and their bon-mots.

Dinner, after many anxious glances of the nervous Mrs.
Gainsborough at the drawing-room door, was at length
announced, a moment of awkwardness to most persons, but to
Mrs. Gainsborough and her son, on this day, one of peculiar
anxiety, for her great soul was with her two soups, and he was
plotting to sit next to Helen Molesworth.

Mrs. Gainsborough was supported by Mr. Molesworth, and
Mr. Boscawen. The worthy host had gallantly enfiladed himself with Mrs. Boscawen, and Miss Molesworth, with whom he
had that good natured kind of flirtation, in which good natured
old men are indulged. Mrs. Escott seated herself by Mr.
Molesworth, and Mrs. Latimer was placed by Mr. Boscawen,
followed by Dr. Maxwell, and opposed by Mr. Chace. Then
the two sisters, Mrs. Maxwell, and Miss Gainsborough, took
their places, and the two vacant ones were to be filled by Arthur
Latimer, and George Gainsborough.

"I cannot sit by my sister," said the wily son of the house, and

glancing at Mrs. Maxwell. Latimer, who did not perceive that
there was a sister on each side, and was too well bred to contest
the point, yielded himself to his mortifying fate, and had the
pleasure of seeing George Gainsborough seat himself immediately afterwards, between his other sister and Helen, make an
affected exclamation of wonder at his stupidity, at not perceiving the arrangement was equally faulty, and talk to Helen
during the whole dinner.

The general conversation was not very remarkable. Mrs.
Gainsborough only talked to her servants in an agitated and
audible whisper. Her anxious eye glanced in all directions,
detected everybody's wants, and anticipated everybody's
necessities. "Graham, soup to Miss Molesworth — Graham,
Mrs. Latimer's plate — here — there — no — yes — Spoon —
knives — remove the side dishes — hand the vegetables —
Where's Brown? — Nobody should go out of the room — Have
not I always told you, if anybody wants anything, ring the bell!
Never mind Dr. Maxwell; Mr. Arthur Latimer has been waiting this quarter of an hour. Very wrong, very provoking. You
are too kind, Mr. Boscawen, I always carve myself; I cannot say
I admire the modern fashion of troubling one's guests. With
great pleasure, Mr. Molesworth, Sherry, if you please –
perhaps you will take Champagne? Graham, Champagne to
Mr. Molesworth — (the servant muttered a dissent) — never
mind, Mr. George, bring the Champagne directly."

"What is this dish before me, Mrs. Gainsborough?" enquired
Mrs. Escott.

"Let me recommend it; you will find it very nice indeed. A
Greek dish, a receipt of George's, we call it Paté de Navarino."

"Only think," exclaimed Mrs Escott, "paté de Navarino!
Everybody must taste paté de Navarino. Very nice indeed,
quite excellent. Mr. George, I am eating your dish. He is
talking so to Miss Molesworth, he does not hear me. Mr.
George Gainsborough, I am eating your Greek dish, and find it
very excellent. You must give me the receipt for old Philip
Escott. I always send him a new receipt, whenever I find
anything very good. Well, I must say, Mrs Gainsborough, it
was very good indeed in Mr. George remembering your receipt
book in Greece. Very handsome of him, was it not, Mr. Molesworth?"

"I always understood that the Greeks never eat anything but olives and anchovies," said Mr. Molesworth, "and now that their groves were cut down, and their fisheries destroyed, that you stood a very good chance of going without a dinner. And yet, I believe, Mr. Chace, a patriot cannot live on air, like a chamelion, though he may resemble that animal in some other respects."

Mr. Chace, who was a staunch Tory, smiled a hearty assent, and took a glass of wine at the same time with Mr. Molesworth, from mere sympathy.

This new dish of George Gainsborough's was the peg on which the whole conversation of the dinner was suspended, and Mrs. Gainsborough, delighted at hearing a general clatter of tongues, which was her definition of a party going off well, was confirmed in her opinion of the excellence of her cookery, and secretly determined, that she would never give a dinner without a paté de Navarino.

Mr. Gainsborough devoted himself to Mrs. Boscawen, paid her a number of delicate little attentions, and listened to all her stories about the dear boys.

Arthur Latimer was particularly silent, and more reserved even than usual, as he especially disliked the Maxwells. The reverend head of that house, after in vain endeavouring to maintain a cross-conversation with Mr. Boscawen, consoled himself by pouring his praises of his wife into the ready ear of her mother, Mrs. Latimer. Mrs. Escott principally devoted herself to Mr. Molesworth, but occasionally scattered her agreeable observations to many a nervous ear.

There is no doubt, it must be confessed, it cannot any longer be concealed, that a dinner party among us country folks, must incur the damnatory, though not very elegant, verdict of modern society — it is "a great bore". A party, consisting of individuals who have not an idea in common, is bad enough, but a party consisting of individuals, *all* whose ideas are in common, is infinitely more wearisome. All the guests are quite certain that, though they may hear many things that are disagreeable, they are equally sure of not hearing anything that is new. Every possible combination of conversation has been previously experienced, every train of ideas has exploded a thousand times. The doctrine of their association is demonstrated every instant. You know exactly what progeny will be born, to every particular opinion that is broached; you are quite aware of the following anecdote that will confirm the truth, or illustrate the amusement of its preceding relative. Conversation proceeds with the regulated precision of the machine for calculating logarithms. But as the sublime system of the universe, in spite of all its divine regularity, is occasionally enlivened or deranged by the startling phantom, and eccentric courses of a comet, so an occasional visitor sometimes diversifies these provincial banquets, and marvellous is the effect which he produces. If he be amusing, he is well repaid for his rare talent, and its amiable exercise. His listeners are universal. Unlike fine people in London, who are always ashamed to appear amused, we never think of concealing that we are delighted. And, after his departure, a very apotheosis awaits him. He is quoted, applauded, imitated — his opinions become dogmas, his stories traditions, his manners unquestioned fashion. Certainly we are very amiable in the provinces, but as everybody laughs at us, I suppose we are very dull.

I think that in our less formal assemblies we may perhaps be rather more captivating. I often observe that a meeting which is unpremeditated, is often much more agreeable. A summer evening stroll, which ends in "taking tea" at a neighbour's, with the drawing-room windows open, music, the perfume of flowers, and rosy light — we are sometimes seen, I think, to advantage under such circumstances, and always look better in our shawls and bonnets than in the elaborate coiffure, and splendid costume of our banquets, where the dresses, like the fish, seem as if they had come down from town express.

But see, Mrs. Gainsborough and her female allies exchange significant glances, they rise, and George Gainsborough runs round, and opens the door, and says a sparkling nothing to each fair passer-by. The magic door is shut, and the host, taking up his two glasses, walks up the room to his wife's vacated seat, arranges the table before him, and, filling his goblet, commences conversation.

"A very satisfactory paper today, Mr. Molesworth, full of alarming intelligence."

"Very satisfactory indeed," replied Mr. Molesworth, "to be frightened out of one's life."

"I cannot decide between the two brothers," said Mr. Gainsborough, "the more I think of it, the more I am puzzled."

"It is fortunate that you are not placed in the awkward
predicament of being the arbitrator."

"It is quite clear to me," observed Mr. Chace, "that the
Portuguese have settled the question. I met a gentleman, the
other day, just come from Oporto, a regular liberal, and he
confessed to me that the people were to a man for Miguel."

"Ah! that is the Priests," said Mr. Gainsborough; "it is a
priest-ridden nation."

"I don't see what business we have to interfere," said Mr.
Boscawen to Dr. Maxwell, "I don't see that it is our affair at all."

"Very just!" exclaimed Dr. Maxwell, shaking his solemn
head, "I never talk politics in this house, but still I cannot
withhold my assent to so remarkably just an observation!"

"I wish there were more priest-ridden nations," said Mr.
Molesworth, "for my part, I would sooner be priest-ridden than
mob-ridden."

"A mob is a tremendous thing, indeed," said Mr. Chace, "I
shall never forget the mob at Bohun Colliery. You remember
that, Mr. Latimer? We gave them a charge, eh?"

"I remember your gallantry, Chace, and I hope, if it ever be
my misfortune to find myself in such a predicament again, I
may also find myself at your right hand."

"What sort of a mob is a Greek mob, George?" enquired the
father, drawing out his modest son.

"Oh! they were always a set of riotous fellows in the time of
Pericles," said Mr. Molesworth.

"Pericles!" mused Mr. Gainsborough "Pericles was before
your time, I think, George? He knew Colcotroni very intimately," continued Mr. Gainsborough, in a sotto voce, to his
friend on his right hand.

Arthur Latimer good naturedly passed the wine, to cover the
blunder; and enquired Boscawen's opinion of some improvements in the neighbourhood.

After a long discussion on the weather, poaching, and petty
sessions, together with an episode on a new bridge, and county
rates, coffee was announced, and the gentlemen entered the
drawing-room in the middle of a duet between Mrs. Maxwell
and Miss Gainsborough.

Mr. George Gainsborough soon fluttered round Miss Molesworth, who was sitting by Mrs. Latimer, and finally seated himself by her side. Mr. Molesworth always required a rubber. Mr. Chace, Mr. Gainsborough, and Mr. Boscawen, were his companions. Dr. Maxwell soon devoted himself to Mrs. Boscawen, with great unction— unhappy Arthur Latimer was obliged to be amusing to a coterie of petticoats.

The singing went on — Mr. Molesworth liked singing with his rubber. He was a good player, but very gallant, and often indulged in momentary badinage with the ladies during the deals. It was observed, that he always said something very smart to them whenever he gained the odd trick, or turned up an honour.

Mr. George Gainsborough's guitar soon appeared. He was so kind also as to exhibit some of his oriental costumes, and was at length even tempted to yield to the unanimous solicitation of the ladies, and enfold his complacent form in them. All this was very diverting. And when the party broke up, George Gainsborough had the pleasure of attending Miss Molesworth to her carriage, and being assured by her, *en-passant*, that he made it quite amusing, and that it was the most agreeable evening she had spent for a considerable time.

CHAPTER XI

A death-bed scene

A solemn thing it is to kneel by the bed of death, to feel, that in a moment of time, even while we think the thought, the creature may be summoned into the presence of his Creator. The trial is over — the judgment is at hand. It is indeed an awful scene: receive the admonitions it conveys to you— refuse not entrance to the good resolves which pour into your subdued soul.

Determine to seek God in your youth, if you have yet your youth to give him: and lay not aside, for his service, the scanty portion of an infirm old age, which you may never reach. Lay up in your hearts this high wisdom, and you will find that there is a sorrow to be preferred to joy; a sadness of the countenance which maketh the heart glad.

Some such thoughts as these were passing in the mind of Arthur Latimer, as he entered the house, in search of Helen. He passed rapidly across the hall, to the room in which she was usually to be found in the morning. As he touched the handle of the door, he was startled by the sounds of merriment from within; he quietly entered, and the inmates were all so preoccupied, that it was some moments before any of them were conscious of his appearance.

On a sofa, Mr. Boscawen was waging a war of cushions with his two sons, who were with shrieks of merriment, strenuously endeavouring to smother Papa. At the piano, Mrs. Boscawen was endeavouring with George Gainsborough's assistance, to master the mysteries of a Romaic song, while Helen was seated at a table near to them, copying music. Mr. Gainsborough's attention seemed equally divided between the ladies; for he turned every moment to Helen, to apologize for his vile scratches, which he feared were giving her a great deal of trouble. They really were but mere indications for his own use — he never expected to have them so honoured. And then he was obliged to hum the air to her, that she might fully comprehend it.

Helen suddenly looked up from her employment and saw Arthur Latimer. He looked very grave, and beckoned her to the window.

"What is the matter?" asked Helen.

"I have come with a message to you Helen, a petition."

"A petition which you bring I am sure to grant: who is it from?"

"From Kate Medley. She wishes to see you."

"Surely, she need not petition for a visit which I pay nearly every day."

"You do not pay such a visit as this, every day, Helen. This will be your last visit to Kate."

"Is she then so much worse?" eagerly enquired Helen.

"A great change has certainly taken place and Trueman does not think she can survive eight-and-forty hours. She is very desirous to see you again, but I should not have come to fetch you, had I not full confidence in your good sense. But after all, perhaps you had better not go!" added Mr. Latimer, looking round.

"What has changed your opinion of my good sense within the last five minutes Arthur?" asked Helen, a little reproachfully. "Why do you think now I had better not go, when you have taken the trouble to come to fetch me?"

"You seem so much engaged; your thoughts are on such different objects, that perhaps," — Here Mr. Latimer hesitated.

"Indeed Arthur you do me great injustice," said Helen, with much feeling. "I can think of nothing now but poor Kate; I should be miserable if I did not go to her directly."

There was no resisting — no possibility of doubting Helen's sincere feelings; and that he had ever, even for a moment, doubted her willingness, was a fresh charge to be laid to the account of George Gainsborough, whose inopportune presence had somewhat disturbed Mr. Latimer's philosophy.

Helen called for her shawl, and having said all that was proper to her visitor, whom she confided to the care of Mrs. Boscawen, she hastened into the village. Mr. Latimer left her at the cottage door. The lower room was unoccupied, and Helen passed up the stairs, and gently approaching the bed of the invalid, she softly withdrew the curtain.

"Kate," she said, in a low voice, fearful of startling the poor girl. "Kate I have come to see you."

The tones of her voice roused the sufferer; but she could only acknowledge the kindness by her looks: she could not speak, and Helen perceived she was labouring under a violent and almost convulsive difficulty of breathing, which had lately much affected her. She dropped the curtain, fearful to increase the excitement of the invalid.

Soon Helen heard below the step of Mrs. Wells, the good woman to whose care Kate was entrusted. She descended the stairs to speak to her.

"Ah! are you here Miss? It's been so hot today that I have let the fire out, so I had just run into the next cottage to get a few lighted embers; for I thought may be, poor Kate will be better for something warm. She has been longing to see you all the morning, but she is much too bad now to be able to say a word to you. It is a pity you should have had the trouble of coming."

"She will be better soon I hope," said Helen, "I will wait here awhile."

Miss Molesworth busied herself in making up the fire, while Mrs. Wells gave some composing medicine to her patient, who, after taking it, soon fell into a torpor. Helen seated herself by the bed side, and leaning back in the chair, was fearful almost of breathing. And as she gazed on that faded countenance, still beautiful in the hour of death, her thoughts turned in sorrow to the mournful history of the sufferer.

Kate Medley was once the beauty and the pride of Hartlebury. Her father who was a wild young man, enlisted for a soldier shortly after his marriage, and never was again heard of: and his wife, a very young girl he had brought from a distant place, pined away in the midst of strangers, and died almost immediately after the birth of Kate. Thus completely an orphan, she was brought up the child of parish bounty; but instead of belonging to no one, she was a subject of common interest to all. There was much in her friendless situation to excite the compassion of these simple people; but there was also a rare beauty and peculiar character in the child, which unconsciously affected them. Not an old person in the village passed her without an encouraging nod, or a kind word, and amongst the young it was a dire offence which all resented, to say an unkind word to poor little Kate.

Nothing could spoil Katie's good heart; but it must be acknowledged that all this consideration made her at times a little wilful. Mrs. Molesworth who took a real interest in her, was most anxious to prevent the ill consequences of this misjudging kindness, which she could not however condemn; but Dame Harrald even seemed blind on these occasions. Wherever Kate was, she ruled. Among her play-mates the boys were devoted to her, and the girls never envied her; for she was generous, and good-natured, and ever ready to share with them the gifts that were showered on her. And numerous were Kate's presents; the first bunch of primroses, the first handful of violets, the longest string of daisies, and the greatest number of birds' eggs, were always offered up to Kate.

Thus passed her days of childhood; nor did the interest she created cease when she grew up into a most beautiful woman. She had many lovers, some even the sons of farmers: but she rejected them all for the sake of Harry Drewe. Everybody except the rejected, agreed that she had chosen well. Harry Drewe was the handsomest young man in the parish, the best cricketer, and the best son. He was also well to do in the world; for he was an only child, and his father kept the shop, a most flourishing concern at Hartlebury. The old man if he were rich, was also prudent, and he thought his son too young to settle; so that our lovers were not to think of marrying for a year or two. But who could be happier than Kate, caressed by all, with a devoted lover, and the kindest friend in the world in good old Mrs. Drewe, who loved her already almost as much as she did Harry!

It was a beautiful summer evening, and the setting sun poured a golden light on our picturesque village, gay groups of animated cricketers, and eager spectators who were spread over the rural green. The beauty of the scene startled from his reverie a young man who was carelessly pursuing his evening ride. He stopped to gaze, and soon the animated game rivetted his attention; for he was himself the most scientific of bowlers, and the most skilful of batters. The villagers touched their hats to him, for he was known to many as a Mr. Mounteney, who was residing with a clergyman four or five miles from Hartlebury.

Each good hit made, catch missed, or well-pitched ball, equally excited Mr. Mounteney's enthusiasm: he thought he would offer to take a bat. "These fellows," he mentally exclaimed, as he rested on his saddle, "have really a very good notion of the game: I am sure in a month I could make them play quite respectably. A little good fielding is all they want."

But his generous intentions of instruction were speedily put to flight. However, *en passant*, I can assure him that they would have been very ill-received. A good rustic game of cricket depends entirely on pure physical force, all strong hits and long runs, and is a very different affair to the skilful handling of the bat, and the scientific playing with the ball of our brothers at Eton and Winchester.

The two systems do not work well together, I speak from knowledge, for I have seen it tried. I have said that Mr. Mounteney soon forgot all his intentions — his ruminations were disturbed by a noisy troop of villagers, gathering round a young man, who was eagerly relating the cause of his speedy discomfiture. His most interested auditor was a beautiful young girl, to whom the orator often appealed in support of his facts. Mr. Mounteney drew near, that he also might hear all the interesting particulars — of how the sun had dazzled the eyes of the defeated hero — and how, at that moment, Will Johnson had bowled a regular grounder — and how finally and fatally, the ball had struck the wicket. Mr. Mounteney showed so much proper interest, and asked such pertinent questions, that the beautiful girl herself turned to him to explain all the detail, which he was evidently so worthy of knowing. He entirely agreed with her view of the case; and how could he do otherwise, when Kate throwing back her auburn tresses, looked up in his face with her speaking blue eyes.

From this day, for some weeks Mr. Mounteney might be seen every evening on the cricket ground. But ere long he perceived that he was looked upon with suspicious eyes. The young men regarded him as an interloper who made Harry Drewe jealous, and consequently play a very bad game, and the old men shook their heads, and feared he meant no good. So he came no more openly to the village green, but late in the evenings he might still be met sauntering in the green lanes, or reclining on the banks of the meandering stream. Kate became spiritless and absent, Harry Drewe passionate and capricious. Here were elements of discord. The lovers quarrelled, they quarrelled more than once, until the maddened temper of Harry Drewe incited him to sever the contract for ever.

The next morning, Kate had disappeared: the most diligent search could find no trace of her, and Mr. Mounteney who was still in the neighbourhood, denied in the most positive manner that he had the slightest knowledge of her flight.

While these misfortunes clouded the usual serenity of Hartlebury, the affectionate and active friend who was the unfailing resource in all troubles was on his bed of death. The sudden and fatal illness of the Rector had overwhelmed almost with equal sorrow the Molesworths, and the Latimers, and their poor neighbours sympathising in their affliction, and respecting their grief, had hesitated to intrude upon them this little history, which they never guessed would end so fatally. These simple minded people could not understand poor Kate's impetuosity, which their own indulgence had nurtured.

When therefore the intelligence at last reached Mr. Molesworth and his daughter, they were painfully shocked. Kate had been a favourite of one whose memory they both adored, and Helen's tears flowed fast as she reproached herself with having betrayed her darling mother's confidence, in thus suffering her protegée to fall into such cruel snares. Mr. Molesworth shared her sorrow, and endeavoured to mitigate it by the most active search. The Clergyman with whom Mr. Mounteney had resided used every means in his power to assist them, but every effort was equally vain, and when after the lapse of some time they learnt that Mr. Mounteney had accepted an appointment in India, the only clue by which at last they had hoped to discover Kate seemed lost for ever.

This fatal event for a long time occupied the villagers of Hartlebury, it was long their morning wonder, and their evening lamentation. Unlike the inhabitants of a bustling city, whose teeming day brings forth a thousand catastrophes, where the bell tolls, and the funerals glide along the street, and no one thinks of death, these honest people felt all their sympathies enlisted in the unaccustomed misery, and there was one amongst them, the colour of whose life was for ever changed.

When the first days of Kate's flight were past, when there was no longer any clue to trace, when all pursuit was found to be hopeless, and all search vain, Harry Drewe gave himself up to all the abandonment of grief. But he had a bold spirit, and he condemned himself, and thought all others would despise him, for such womanish wailing. He endeavoured to rouse himself, but his heart was heavy, and he felt all the lassitude that bitter grief brings. He tried to forget himself, and his hollow laugh resounded from the village Alehouse, and he sought excitement amongst wild and desperate companions. Arthur Latimer beheld him with compassion, and sought by mild and tender remonstrances to turn his mind aright. Poor Harry made a thousand good resolves, but his new companions laughed them all to scorn, and this fine spirit seemed about to sink for ever into a vicious drunkard. But Providence works its ends by means unforeseen by us. Soon Harry Drewe was on the bed of sickness, his wild irregular mode of life, his state of unnatural excitement, producing a raging and virulent fever. For many days his recovery was utterly despaired of, but at last he did recover, a changed, and altered man. His beauty and his youth seemed to have flown together, he was serious, for he could not forget Kate, and he no longer sought to drown the melancholy remembrance in riot and debauchery. But he endeavoured to carry his grief with a patient endurance, and to subdue it by constant occupation. Mr. Latimer strengthened him in all his good resolves, by his patient friendship and advice, and Mr. Molesworth in confiding a small portion of land to his care, encouraged him to exertion. Thus two years had rapidly converted the high-spirited Harry Drewe, the leader of all village gaiety, into a quiet domestic thriving farmer. But his parents were happy again in their child.

At last, when everyone had ceased to wonder, to expect, or even to hope, news came of Kate. Mr. Latimer received a letter from the clergyman of a distant village, to inform him that some weeks previously a young woman travelling, he believed, to Hartlebury, had been detained in his parish, by a severe attack of illness. For some time he had expected her to die, but she was now better again, and again eager to proceed home. He thought it his duty to inform Mr. Latimer of the circumstance, as she might have some friends who would be willing to assist her on her journey. Not that she seemed in want of money, but she was so weak and exhausted, that it was perilous for her to travel alone, as she might again sink under the fatigue of the journey. Her days were numbered, and it seemed but her eager energy to see her home that stayed her spirit on its flight. The writer added that she was not aware of his sending this letter. She was so averse to speaking of herself, or her friends, that it was only during the last day or two that he had learnt sufficient to write this.

No one at Hartlebury could a moment doubt that this poor sufferer was their Kate. Her affectionate yearning after her home, her resolute eagerness to see it again before she died, proved that she was still in some things unchanged. Mr. Latimer hastened to arrange the most easy and expeditious manner of her conveyance, and Mrs. Wells a good woman who had a quiet civil husband, and whose children were all out in the world, agreed with Miss Molesworth to receive her into her cottage, and to nurse and protect her.

In a few days Kate Medley was again at Hartlebury. But how changed! There was no vestige of her former self but in the eager and impetuous love she felt towards everyone around her, even to the least forgiving of her friends. She came with the reviving spring, and the bright days, and the kind faces cheered her, and lent her strength. But it was only for a time, it was but too soon evident that all that was left for kindness and friendship was to smooth the pillow of death. Kate wished to die, and her patient and unmurmuring waiting for death was a beautiful lesson to those who had known her in her days of health and wilfulness.

Helen visited her almost daily, and as she now sat by her bedside perhaps for the last time, she felt sad and oppressed.

A slight movement of the invalid caught her listening ear, she gently undrew the curtain, and the poor girl looked on her and smiled. Helen took her hand, and knelt by the bedside.

"My dear Kate, what do you want of me?" she asked, in the softest, kindest voice.

Kate pressed her hand, as she answered, "I could not go in peace without thanking you again. The Lord will bless you, I cannot, cannot," her words failed her.

"Hush," said Helen, "you must not exert yourself."

Kate turned upon her the most seraphic look. In a few moments she closed her eyes. Helen thought she slept, and as she held her hand she feared to move, even to rise from her knees, and so hiding her face in the bed, in prayer she endeavoured to still her emotions. Kate breathed a gentle sigh, her last breath. At this moment Mrs. Wells came into the room, she saw that it was all over, and gently touching Helen she whispered, "you had better go down below, Miss."

"I fear to wake her," said Helen.

"She will never wake again," said the old woman, and she raised Helen from the ground; "pray go down stairs Miss."

Helen descended the stairs, and throwing herself into a chair, she covered her face with her handkerchief, and gave way to the feeling she had so long repressed. She wept long and unrestrainedly.

A sympathising voice roused her, she looked up. Arthur Latimer was gazing on her with the deepest emotion.

"Dearest Helen," he said, "I fear I ought not to have brought you here."

"Do not say so, I never should have forgiven myself if I had not come."

He drew her arm within his, and led her from the cottage towards her home.

"Dear Helen," he said as he parted from her in the Hall, "go you at once to the quietness of your room away from my noisy nephews, you will alarm your father if you are not more composed by the time we meet at dinner."

CHAPTER XII

In which is announced
most unexpected intelligence

Pleasure however innocent and delightful, is not eternal; the reflection is mortifying, but let us not forget that our griefs also are not interminable. And now our friends at Hartlebury were suffering the gentle sorrow of parting from their loved visitors.

Mr. Boscawen, who was a great builder and a great planter, having now exhausted all Mr. Molesworth's buildings and plantations, began to think that he must be sadly wanted amongst his own. "Charlotte, my dear, you forget what a large party we are, we shall tire out our kind friends, we must be thinking of going home" — was an observation which he made at the close of a visit of six weeks, and which each following day was repeated, and each time in a more determined tone. So at last the hour of departure was fixed, and now it was near at hand.

For the last time had the young Boscawens their scamper on the breezy common with Helen's favourite dog; for the last time had they taken their ride round the paddock on Helen's old pony, which now spent its life in gambolling about, except when its services were required by such cavaliers; for the last time had they been to thank Dame Harrald for their worsted socks; and for the last time had they made their bows to Mrs. Collins' fair daughters. Tomorrow they were to set out on their journey.

This morning had been grey and cloudy, and Mr. Boscawen who was an inveterate brother of the angle, had early sallied forth for another day's sport in the Hartlebury preserves. Towards noon Helen, accompanied by his two sons, went in search of him. Her youthful companions were in the highest and noisiest spirits, quite enchanted to be permitted each to take hold of cousin Helen's hand.

They proceeded along the velvet margin of the stream which wandering in fantastic turns, through the smiling meads of Hartlebury, glided into the glades of Bohun Park. The children stopped every minute to gather the wild flowers they were treading under their feet, and to pluck whole handfuls of the luxuriant daisies. When they were tired of stooping, they began to look out for their Papa. Henry the volatile one and the wit, who was eager to be the first to make the discovery, fancied every minute that he saw him, while Walter more slow and sage, reproved his younger brother for mistaking a broken post, or an old stump of a tree, for their Papa. At last a sudden turn of the river shewed them Mr. Boscawen in the distance.

"Who is that?" said Helen.

"Papa! papa!" exclaimed the children, shouting and clapping their hands.

There was Mr. Boscawen in his fishing costume and his tight jacket, and his wicker basket slung round his waist, apparently at that moment intently occupied in landing some weighty prey, for he was standing at a little distance from the stream, carefully drawing in his line, while his attendant stooping down even with the edge of the bank, was engaged with the landing net. Helen slackened her pace, that her noisy companions might not disturb his sport. It was with difficulty she could restrain them, and when they were permitted to advance, they rushed forward, each claiming their first peep into the basket.

At this moment the sun, which had been all the day veiled in clouds, burst forth, and so Mr. Boscawen gave up his fishing to his sons, and having sent home the fruits of his morning's diversion, he set about instructing his boisterous young pupils in this dexterous art. But soon throwing the line degenerated into throwing stones. The children were far more delighted in watching the spreading circles over the surface of the water, and scarcely less so, in seeking for the means of producing them. It was difficult to obtain ammunition enough to please them.

While they were thus busily employed, Helen who was wearied by her walk sought the inviting shade of a broad oak, which at some little distance spread its wide branches. The sun was now shining forth in full glory, and everything was still, save the ever ceaseless hum of insects, and every now and then, the drowsy tinkling of some distant sheep-bell, or the bleating of an anxious dam, who was seeking its straying offspring. She fell into the most agreeable reverie, and some time had elapsed, when she became suddenly conscious that someone on horseback seemed most anxiously beckoning to her from the other side of the hedge. It was not her father or Arthur Latimer. Who could it be? As she advanced, she discovered to her infinite astonishment, that it was Mr. Chace.

"My dear Madam," said Mr. Chace, "ten thousand apologies, pray excuse the liberty I have taken, but at such a moment I could not pass you without a word."

Helen looked at him. Serious, matter of fact Mr. Chace, appeared to be labouring under a great state of excitement, his cheek was flushed, his voice was hurried.

What is the matter, thought Helen, there cannot be another insurrection in the Bohun Colliery, he looks too joyful.

"I have great news for you, Madam," continued Mr. Chace. "I should certainly have called at Hartlebury to inform Mr. Molesworth of it, as it is befitting I should do, but when you hear it, you will not be surprised that as yet I have not had time. Would you believe it, Miss Molesworth? Mr. Bohun is coming to live amongst us."

"Is it possible?" said Helen.

"Quite possible I assure you. Here is his letter," said Mr. Chace, burying his hand deep into his pocket in search of it. "It only arrived this morning — it is great news, is it not?"

"And does he give any reason for his sudden determination?" enquired Miss Molesworth.

"None whatever."

"And I suppose then we are to be so grateful to him for his coming, that we are not to trouble our heads about his reason for doing so."

Mr. Chace laughed. "Why, Ma'am, it certainly will be a great thing for the county. It is a very short letter you see," said Mr. Chace, unfolding it. "No, he gives no reason for coming, but you see here he says that he shall soon follow his letter. And here you see," said Mr. Chace, pointing to a particular paragraph, "he begs that he may find no work-people in the Castle, when he arrives: you see, he says, 'Let me have the pleasure of finding my home, as if I had only left it last week.' So you may believe that I have a great deal to do."

"Well Mr. Chace," replied Helen, "I am sure that Mr. Bohun ought to be indeed grateful to you, that such an unreasonable desire can be gratified, but I will not detain you now, you must be so much engaged. Goodbye, and thank you for stopping to tell me the wonderful news."

Mr. Chace galloped away.

"My dear Mr. Boscawen," said Helen, as she hastened to the group who were still occupied at the river; "My dear Mr. Boscawen, you must not go away tomorrow, you must stay and see a most wonderful person. Mr. Bohun has signified his gracious intention of dwelling amongst us."

CHAPTER XIII

The unexpected intelligence proves true

The intelligence that Mr. Bohun was about to return to England, to reside in his long-deserted Castle, soon spread from one end of the County to the other. It was a subject of universal congratulation. But nowhere did it excite so much real interest as at Hartlebury. Their immediate vicinity to Bohun involved them in some of its evils, which Arthur Latimer hoped that Mr. Bohun's arrival would mitigate.

The Minister of Bohun was an old and an infirm man, who never left his house, but to shuffle through one service on the Sunday; the consequence was that ignorant fanatics usurped his neglected post. The people of England are essentially a devout people. Heavy therefore is the sin of that careless pastor, who heedless of the great charge committed to him, permits his unguarded flock to fall into the snares of the ignorant and the designing.

Poor Mr. Chace was too full of bustle to be able to think even of what he had to do. In a few weeks he had to furnish the stables, and to complete the household on the most extensive scale, for Mr. Bohun had written that he should bring no servants with him, but a valet, an Englishman, whom he had lately taken into his service.

At length Mr. Chace rested on his oars — Mrs. Brand declared all things perfect, and in order, and soon the bonfires blazed, the bells rang their gayest peal, and the poor were feasted.

Aubrey Bohun was again in the Castle of his fathers.

CHAPTER XIV

The owner of the castle

Aubrey Bohun combined a fine poetical temperament, with a great love of action. The combination is rare. He was a man of genius. But with great powers he possessed what does not always fall to the lot of their possessors — a great destiny. If a theory hitherto erroneous, had induced him to waste his youth in what some would style unprofitable and unsatisfactory pleasure — but which he would define as that unbounded pursuit of experience without which no powers are available — so fortunate was his lot in life, that at this moment with energy unsubdued though matured, a career was at his command in which he might redeem those years that had been wasted, or exercise the wisdom which had been acquired. As he now gazed upon his rich possessions, and thought upon his vast resources, did he grieve that thirty years of his life had flown away, apparently without producing a result? No: to sigh over the unchangeable past was not in the nature of Aubrey Bohun. The exciting present was the world in which he ever lived, and remorse and regret were phantoms that never disturbed his reveries.

Within the walls of his castle, surrounded by its massive grandeur and its feudal magnificence, what brilliant and stirring scenes rose before his creative imagination! If he did not with Miss Molesworth exactly project a tournament, his thoughts were equally chivalric. Devoted vassals rose up in numbers around him, his willing tools to some great, though as yet indefinite end. He knew he could work upon men's minds, he felt he had all those powers of eloquence that could excite and command.

Nor did he over-rate his abilities. His sanguine disposition was the consequence of his energetic nature. It had indeed often deceived him; but when he had failed, reflection convinced him that the failure had arisen from supposing that his instruments were as efficient as the ideas with which he endeavoured to inspire them.

Many reasons had united to induce him to return to his long-neglected country, but none had influenced him more strongly than the passing of the Reform Bill, that great and misconceived event, which already its enemies have ceased to dread, and its friends have begun to abuse. Our eager cry for Reform had created a great sensation among our Continental neighbours. Mistaking our habits, and ignorant of our customs, they had totally misconceived that state of agitation which our newspapers so forcibly depicted, and England, that envied country, in a state of anarchy and confusion, was an image too consolatory not to be worshipped. Mr. Bohun must be pardoned, if a long residence in the midst of the enslaved and repining descendants of heroes, had made him forget the peculiar characteristics of his own free-born countrymen. At the prospect of insurrection, he turned with more affection towards a country he had hitherto condemned as too uneventful for a man of genius. The immortality of a season, that fame that is the guerdon of the happy invention of a waistcoat, or the ingenious creation of a carriage was somewhat too limited for his ambition, but now he felt that all was stirring, and with his great stake and influence in the country, he should no longer be wanting.

With him to will and to act were one. He returned, and astonished everybody.

Mr. Chace met his principal, with all the consciousness of having done his duty; he was eager to explain his arrangements: he was surprised to find Mr. Bohun a complete man of business. If he shrank a little from minute detail, he far surpassed his agent in clear and rapid perception. Gifted with a rare memory, he confounded poor Mr. Chace with the velocity of his acquisition. In a few days Mr. Bohun was acquainted with the names and characters of his principal tenants, could judiciously approve, and even ventured to suggest.

The first to welcome the long lost Lord of Bohun to his home were Mr. Molesworth and Mr. Latimer. An early visit was dictated by their feeling of what was right, but it was an intercourse from which they expected no pleasure. He must be full of foreign affectations — a Virtuoso or a Carbonaro, both equally detestable to Mr. Molesworth, whose acquaintance with Mr. George Gainsborough had by no means improved his opinion of our modern Greek heroes. He must affect singularity, which Arthur Latimer thought unendurable.

They found Mr. Bohun, in every respect, the reverse of what they expected. If Mr. Chace was astonished at detecting in him a complete man of business, they were not less so at finding a man of sense. Graceful and easy in his address, mild and unaffected in his manners, he seemed as eager to please as he appeared agreeably impressed by them.

When the visit was returned to Hartlebury, and Miss Molesworth had an opportunity of forming her opinion, it was by no means less favourable than her father's. Indeed, Mr. Bohun's appearance could not fail to captivate. An air of elegance and refinement particularly distinguished him, and a most musical voice recommended his slightest observation. His delicately moulded features would have perhaps been effeminate, but for the intelligence and passion which beamed in his deep grey eye. He wore neither whisker nor moustachio, which might have been a little coquetry, in order to rivet attention on his rich brown curls.

Mr. Bohun had a great deal to say which pleased Helen. He praised the country, admired Hartlebury, he said all that was proper about Bohun. And if he did not actually declare that he was sorry that he had stayed so long away, it was sufficiently evident that now he had come back, he was charmed with the people he had fallen amongst. He asked many questions about the principal families in the county and enquired more particularly about the immediate neighbourhood. The Gainsboroughs were mentioned; he seemed struck with the name; the family was described; he said he had met George Gainsborough on the Continent.

Helen was particularly charmed by the deferential tone he assumed towards her father. He wished to lose no time in commencing that line of duty which he thought incumbent on a resident country gentleman. And a resident he should now certainly be; and he sought advice and assistance from Mr. Molesworth. He should, certainly, attend the ensuing sessions, and he asked as a particular favour, that Mr. Molesworth would introduce him. In short, he was in every way eager to be obliged, a readiness which is always most captivating in a person who is really in no want of your favours.

CHAPTER XV

Mr. George Gainsborough's bad memory

While these interesting events were occurring at home, George Gainsborough was absent on a visit to his brother-in-law Dr. Maxwell. He remained away a fortnight; but, as it was no part of his system to allow Helen to forget him, on the morning of his return he walked up to the Hall.

"You have just missed our new neighbour," said Helen, after she had received all Mr. George Gainsborough's compliments. "Mr. Bohun is only just gone. But you know him," she added.

"I have not yet that pleasure. My father, I believe left his card yesterday; but you know I have been away," said George Gainsborough a little piqued that his absence had made no impression.

"I know that; but I mean that you have seen him abroad."

"Not that I am aware of."

"Oh yes; you may depend you have," said Helen. "Mr. Bohun made no doubt about it; he spoke as if he knew you very well."

"Indeed," said George Gainsborough, musingly, "it is odd I cannot bring such a name to my mind. But," he added, a little grandly, "one really meets so many English on the Continent, in all the hurry and bustle of travelling, that without one has a wonderful memory, which I do not pretend to, it is impossible to be even with people."

"And yet," said Helen, "I should have thought Mr. Bohun's manners would have distinguished him from the herd."

"His manners are so very delightful, then?" said George Gainsborough, with as much of a sneer as he dared venture to Helen.

"Did Mr. Bohun mention where he had met me?" continued George Gainsborough, in a careless tone, after a few minutes' pause.

"No, I do not think he did — No I am sure he did not — he merely said he had seen you several times."

George Gainsborough fell into a reverie. Helen endeavoured to find conversation.

"Dr. Maxwell has a very nice parsonage, I believe."

"Very."

"Have you had any good shooting?"

"Yes."

"Is Dr. Maxwell a sportsman?"

"No."

Helen gave up her endeavour in despair. George Gainsborough made an effort to rouse himself.

"Yes, I quite agree with you; I think Maxwell's is an excellent house. I should not have stayed so long, but he persuaded me to remain over the first. There is capital sport in his neighbourhood, as you were saying."

But his loquacity did not long continue; he soon became again very silent, and said he believed his long ride had tired him; he felt so very stupid that he must bid her goodbye, or she would turn him out.

As George Gainsborough pursued his way home, he was at liberty to indulge his meditations: but they did not become more satisfactory. A train of associations had been awakened, which excited emotions which almost overpowered him. The picture he had seen at Bohun castle returned to his mind. Was it possible? — could it be? — could his evil star so predominate? — He endeavoured to rally — he endeavoured to throw off his emotion — he allowed shadows to frighten him. What indeed could be more unlikely than that two men, whom extraordinary occurrence had thrown together in a distant country, should suddenly meet in an obscure village in England! It were absurd to have supposed it even for a moment. After all Mr. Bohun would of course prove to be some uninteresting person he had once encountered at the top of a mountain, or perhaps the passing hero of some Anglo-Italian coterie. And yet something whispered that nowhere could Mr. Bohun be a very insignific-ant person; Helen had noticed his manners as remarkable — remarkable manners and his high station — surely, he must have been everywhere of sufficient importance to be remem-bered. Though George Gainsborough was very vain, he was no fool, and he could not but consider Mr. Bohun's recollection of him however flattering, a little puzzling. But whether fear or hope predominated, there was one thing very certain — his coming — and just at this moment, was most unlucky. After he had stayed away all his life-time, that he just should take it into his head to return now, was infinitely provoking. Six months later, and George Gainsborough flattered himself it would have been of no consequence: but as yet he could not feel secure of Helen. He was satisfied with his position; and after all the pains he had taken, it was very annoying that a stranger should suddenly drop down among them, and spoil everything. But was he a stranger? Tomorrow should determine: he could no longer endure this painful state of incertitude — he almost added — this agony of suspense. He would ride over early and alone, to the castle.

CHAPTER XVI

Which he endeavours to refresh

George Gainsborough passed a moody evening, and was not refreshed by a restless night. He longed for the morning to arrive, yet the first streak of dawn seemed the herald of an unlucky day. He had no appetite for his breakfast. It was too early to call at Bohun. He knocked about the balls of the billiard table, unconscious of his exploits, till involuntary hazards cleared the table of his sources of occupation, and he found himself cutting the cloth with his cue. At length it was noon, and he mounted his horse.

As he slowly ascended the hill to the castle, he was struck by the change a few weeks had produced. He met grooms exercising horses, persons of every description hurrying to and fro. Everybody seemed full of bustle and business. As he passed over the draw-bridge, a porter threw open the massive gates, which no longer creaked upon their hinges. In the quadrangle many servants were passing and repassing: as he approached the entrance, the doors flew open, a liveried servant took his horse, another ushered him up the great staircase, which he had trod so lately, with so gay a party, and such different feelings. He was in the ante-room, through which he had on that day passed to the state apartments. Now he followed his conductor by a door on the opposite side, through one or two smaller rooms, to a spacious drawing-room, where the servant begged him to be seated, while he apprised Mr. Bohun of his arrival.

A voice close to him awoke George Gainsborough from a reverie which he could not have told whether it had lasted five minutes or fifty. The servant said Mr. Bohun begged that Mr. Gainsborough would do him the honour of visiting him in his dressing-room, and the servant led him from the drawing-room through a long gallery. At the end of the gallery he threw open a door.

Mr. Bohun was reclining on a sofa, smoking a long Turkish pipe. He was wrapped in a silk dressing gown, and as he emitted a cloud of smoke, an imagination a little disturbed might have conceived a turkish robe, and a turkish divan.

"Ashurst!" exclaimed George Gainsborough, as the vision arrested him at the threshold — he hesitated, he seemed for a moment almost bent on flight, but at length he advanced.

"I venture from our old acquaintance, to hope that you will excuse my receiving you with so little ceremony," said Mr. Bohun, with some dignity.

George Gainsborough attempted to speak, but his words were inaudible, he sank into a chair, the servant left the room. For a few minutes there was a silence which George Gainsborough thought would never end. Mr. Bohun smoked on. If

he were giving his old acquaintance time to recover his composure, his kindness was of no avail; if he were enjoying his
emotion, he must have been fully gratified.

"My apparition appears to surprise you," at length observed
Mr. Bohun. "You probably thought our acquaintance had terminated, but fate seems to have determined otherwise."

George Gainsborough rose from his chair and bent against
the tall mantel-piece, and hid his face in his folded arms.

"It is remarkable," continued Mr. Bohun, in a quiet specula-
tive tone, as he stretched himself on the sofa, "it is certainly
remarkable that two men so strangely connected as we have
been, should suddenly again fall together in such different
characters, in such a quiet out of the way place as this. I dare say
you think it devilish unlucky."

George Gainsborough made no answer: he still leant against
the mantle-piece, he had somewhat subdued the violence of his
emotion, and he thought it political to leave the conversation in
Mr. Bohun's hands until he had ascertained his intentions. Mr.
Bohun had no wish to conceal them. Whatever might have
passed between them elsewhere, now at any rate he wished to
conciliate, and as George Gainsborough made no sign, he soon
added in a more familiar tone; "But our adventures, my good
fellow, however they may have suited the land of the brave and
the free, will not do for this dull clime; the less therefore that is
said of them here the better for us both. From this moment I
forget everything."

As Mr. Bohun said this, he raised himself on the sofa, and he
caught the eye of Gainsborough, whom his easy address had
brought to a more erect position, something of a sneer was
evident, as he added, "you, I suppose have no particular pleasure in cultivating the remembrance of the past."

George Gainsborough had now something to say; he was still
confused when he spoke of his sorrow for the past, but he grew
more intelligible and more eloquent, as he most sincerely
agreed in the advantage of silence at the present.

They now endeavoured to talk of indifferent things, but the
effort was principally on the part of Mr. Bohun, who seemed
desirous of reassuring his companion by appearing unconscious
of his want of ease. After some desultory conversation in which
he asked and answered most of the questions, he said:

"You have some months the advantage of me in acquaintance with this part of the world, do you think the people about here very revolutionary?"

"Not in the least, it is the most Tory county in England. You will be surprised at the people in this country," added George Gainsborough, now in his turn venturing a slight sneer, "if you have had no better data to judge by than Continental reports."

"After all, then, you think the people generally, entirely indifferent to the Reform bill?"

"Entirely."

"But it must however afford a good opening for a stirring man to excite."

"It may certainly suit you, if you retain your old tastes and capabilities."

"What sort of people have I fallen amongst? I see that Molesworth is entirely of the old school, but his daughter is very beautiful."

"Very," assented Gainsborough.

"Is she going to be married? Who is this Latimer?"

"There is no danger from him. He is a cousin you know, not likely to think of such a thing."

"You have ascertained that," said Mr. Bohun with a slight emphasis, as he turned his keen eye on Gainsborough, and rang for a fresh pipe.

"Gainsborough will you take a pipe?" he enquired: but George was in no humour for smoking, and was glad to find in all the bustle of the entrance of servants, and of the change of pipes, a good opportunity for departing.

In the open air once more he felt a little relieved from his suffocating emotions, but he could with difficulty command sufficient presence of mind to mount his horse with that air of graceful dignity, which he flattered himself usually characterised the ascent into the saddle of Mr. George Gainsborough.

CHAPTER XVII

Mr. Bohun is visited by his relations.
A fine lady and a most gentlemanlike fellow

A week had not elapsed since the arrival of Mr. Bohun, and the whole neighbourhood had not yet in the slightest degree, recovered from the thunder-stroke of his return, when some visitors arrived at the Castle.

His cousin Colonel Neville hastened to congratulate him on the flag of Bohun once more waving on the keep. Colonel Neville was Mr. Bohun's nearest relation on his father's side, and in his early career had been his constant companion. Though of late, in common with others, Colonel Neville had heard little of his cousin, he was really glad to learn his safe return, which is saying a great deal for the next in entail of the Bohun property.

Colonel Neville was a fine tall military-looking personage — one of those men who are unanimously declared by their co-mates and contemporaries, to be most gentlemanlike fellows, which means that they eat, talk, and dress according to the most approved models, and have the capability of following, where they have not wit enough to lead.

Mrs. Neville, for he had lately married, accompanied him in his visit. She was eager to see her extraordinary cousin, and his fine castle, which one day might be hers.

On the morning after their arrival, Mr. Bohun introduced his cousin at Hartlebury; and on the next day, Helen and her father promised to call on Mrs. Neville.

A pretty low phaeton was in waiting, driving round the quadrangle, several servants were lounging about with an air of indifference and sang froid, as if they had never lived anywhere else, when Mr. Molesworth's carriage drove up to the entrance.

"Does it not seem, Papa," said Helen, struck by the look of habitation, "as if some good fairy had suddenly touched this enchanted Castle, where everybody has been so long asleep?"

"There certainly is a great change," answered Mr. Moles-worth, "but I must see something better than half-a-dozen idle men before I decide, Helen, that your fairy is a good fairy."

Helen could only smile in reply, as her father handed her from the carriage, and they were ushered up the grand stair-case. Mr. Bohun advanced to receive them with the most evident pleasure, and introduced a fashionable looking woman, who languidly rose from the sofa. Two little dogs with collars covered with silver bells, ran about the room, and by their noise and the confusion they created, skilfully covered their mis-tress's languid advances.

Though Mrs. Neville had been only two or three days at Bohun, she had diffused the most modern air over the antique apartment, for all the indispensible furniture of a fine lady's travelling chariot, was spread in all directions. Scented sachets impregnated the room with the most refined odours, overpow-ering Mrs. Brand's dried rose leaves, and bunches of lavender. A massy table was sinking under a load, which for the centuries it had existed it had never before sustained — to wit, a heap of modern publications from Ebers, fashionable novels, senti-mental travels, and authentic memoirs. On another table was a work basket, containing the most seducing incentives to indus-try. All gold and mother-of-pearl, filagree and sandal wood, and on a table nearer to the lady, was an open desk, without all Russia leather, and within all satin and gold, and agate. At the feet of its mistress was a round basket, quilted with rose col-oured silk, the abode at pleasure of the favoured puppy.

Conversation proceeded, as conversation usually proceeds between well-bred persons, who mean to be civil to each other. Mrs. Neville exerted herself to say that she understood Hart-lebury was a most beautiful place. Helen hoped she would soon judge for herself, and asked if she admired the Castle. All these subjects duly discussed, there was a slight pause, when Mrs. Neville said, "I think you have but a small neighbourhood about here. I noticed, as we travelled, how few gentlemen's seats I saw — no park palings along the road."

"Now," said Helen smiling, and glancing at Mr. Bohun, "Now I can say we have a small neighbourhood; we have just arrived at the dignity of a small neighbourhood — a month ago,

I must have honestly confessed that we had no neighbourhood at all."

"You must be very dull if you live much here," said Mrs. Neville.

"I live always here, but I do not think I am very dull."

"Indeed," said Mrs. Neville, with a look of civil surprise. "I suppose you mean, you go occasionally to London— I wonder I have never met you."

"No, I really mean no such thing. I have not been in London for these four or five years, and then I am afraid I was too ignorant to profit much by my advantage."

"You look as if you had been often in London," said Mrs. Neville, in an approving tone, that was meant for a compliment, but which Helen thought rather impertinent.

"You ought really, Mr. Molesworth, to take your daughter every year to London," said Mrs. Neville addressing Mr. Molesworth.

"Has Helen told you so?" answered he, "It is more than she ever hinted to me."

"No, papa," said Helen, "because I have not yet made up my mind that I want to go."

At this moment Colonel Neville entered the room. He had been trying a horse in the Park, to ascertain if it would suit Mrs. Neville who was anxious to ride.

As he advanced to pay his compliments the two little dogs jumped upon him to greet him, the bells made a great noise, and nothing was for a few moments intelligible, but "down Flora— get away Carlo — how troublesome you both are."

"Emmeline, my dear," said her husband, as soon as the culprits permitted his address, "I wish you would keep your dogs quiet, they really will be thought a regular nuisance."

The lady smiled at such a possibility.

"How did the horse go Gustavus?" was her first query.

"Oh! my dear, it will not do for you at all, it would kill you, absolutely shake you to pieces. I told John so before I got on it, but he is so confoundedly obstinate."

Miss Molesworth now pressed Mrs. Neville to accept the loan of her horse; she had a second, which she often rode, a little rougher, it would not suit Mrs. Neville, but for her own part she liked it best. She often rode it in change with her own quiet mare, which was the gentlest thing in the world, and which she insisted that she would send tomorrow, for Mrs. Neville to try.

When Mr. Bohun heard all that was passing, he was extremely obliged to Miss Molesworth and seemed somewhat annoyed at the deficiencies of his ménage.

"I hoped," he said, "from my man's description, that the horse would just have suited Mrs. Neville. Chace told me that at the time he bought it, it carried a lady."

"A farmer's wife, you mean," said the Colonel.

"I say, Aubrey," added Colonel Neville, "who can a gentleman be that I saw riding by the Park gates today, — a military man I suppose. By the bye it is not much use asking you, I must apply to Miss Molesworth."

"It must be Mr. George Gainsborough," said Helen.

"Do you know what regiment he is of?"

"Not any, I believe."

"But this man wore moustachios," pursued the Colonel.

"He does wear moustachios. Perhaps he has been in some foreign service," said Helen hesitatingly.

"He is a foreign hero," observed Mr. Molesworth.

"I knew him abroad," said Mr. Bohun, quietly, "he is most decidedly a hero."

The ladies separated with mutual expressions of good-will. Mr. Molesworth was made acquainted with the affair of the horse, and insisted that it should be sent to Mrs. Neville on the morrow.

CHAPTER XVIII

Increased intimacy
between the castle and the hall

The horse was found perfect, and most thankfully accepted, and Mrs. Neville, full of gratitude and rather dull, sought with flattering eagerness Miss Molesworth's society. The ladies rode together every morning. The gentlemen were not always able to accompany them, but they were sufficiently well-pleased with each other, to encourage their meeting nearly every evening. In the morning Mr. Bohun was now busily engaged with Chace in making himself popular: he sought the acquaintance not only of his own tenantry, but of the principal inhabitants of Fanchester. For Colonel Neville who was a keen sportsman, there was irresistible attraction in the preserves of Bohun, which he found in so much better order than he expected that he was in no haste to close his visit. The Squire and the Rector of Hartlebury were never to be depended upon, the one was too idle, and the other too busy, to be constant attendants, and our fair ladies would sometimes have been reduced to what Mrs. Neville would have deemed, a state of unprecedented and forlorn isolation, if it had not been for the polite George Gainsborough. He was ever ready, equally willing to quit his gun, or his guitar, for their sakes. Ever smiling, ever gallant, he was invaluable to Mrs. Neville, to whom a certain number of compliments were indispensible in the course of the four-and-twenty hours. She appropriated all his civil speeches, allowed him to prescribe for her dogs, and invited him to join all their rides. She did more, she procured him many invitations to the Castle, and thus the very circumstances which he feared would destroy all his scheme, only threw him more than ever into Helen's company. It was true that fully understanding the terms on which he was admitted, he did not venture to lose his footing by an exclusive attention to Helen, but he flattered himself that she could not

be insensible to all the agreeable qualities which were daily
exhibited, and that when Mrs. Neville departed, and he was at
liberty to be more decidedly devoted, he should reap the fruit of
all the good seed he was now so plentifully sowing. With this
great object in view, Mrs. Neville found him each day more
amiable, and more captivating.

The sessions week arrived. Colonel Neville wished to
accompany Mr. Bohun, and it was therefore arranged that Mrs.
Neville, who had an equal horror of the bustle in a Country
town, and solitude in a feudal Castle, should visit Helen, while
the gentlemen were absent.

On the evening of the second day, they were to return to a late
dinner at Hartlebury, and the first was drawing to a close before
Mrs. Neville, who was always late, and her dogs, and her page,
and her lady in waiting, arrived at the Hall.

Mrs. Neville exerted herself the next morning to appear at an
unusually early hour. Helen had however already passed a most
industrious morning. It was a true autumn day, the sun was just
forcing its way through a thick mist, which had enveloped
everything, it was still too wet to venture out, the ladies therefore roamed about the house, inspecting all the antiquities, and
speculating on all the traditions. Almost every room had some
quaint story, or some curious legend attached to it, and Helen
knew them all, and could point out the hero or the heroine of
her tale amongst the family portraits which hung round the
Hall.

The old oak Hall itself was well worthy of attention. It was a
favourite object of Mr. Molesworth's care, who had removed all
the modern incongruities which from time to time had crept in.

It was of great length and height, with a ceiling of most
curiously carved oaken beams. The oaken panels reached
nearly to the ceiling, and were covered with innumerable portraits of all sizes. Above the panelling, the wall was almost
hidden by arms of all sorts, coats of mail, and shields, and
helmets, and hunting spears, and stag horns, all contributed by
some warrior, or some Nimrod of the house of Molesworth.
From this hall, curiously wrought doors led into the apartments, which although connected en suite, each severally
opened into the Hall.

The ladies at last wearied of examining, retired to luncheon.

"My dear Miss Molesworth," exclaimed Mrs. Neville, fired by gratitude as she inserted her spoon into a delicate trifle, "My dear Miss Molesworth, we must really have you in London next spring."

"My dear Mrs. Neville," said Helen smiling, "I fear we must invent some more probable mode of meeting. You must come here again."

"But you really ought to be presented," urged the grateful lady.

"It has been talked of, but I think at this moment, my father is less inclined to visit London than ever."

"It is really a shame, with all your advantages to keep you shut up here."

"But I am not shut up," said Helen laughing, "I do what I like, which I could not do in London."

"Yet you must be very dull here," persisted Mrs. Neville.

"Never, I have plenty to occupy me. I never was dull that I remember but once in my life, and that was when I was in London. That really was dullness, I never shall forget how miserable I was. My father out every day, I left with my governess, masters all the morning, and then a dull ride, and a walk in the Park. How I used to sigh for my garden, my flowers, and my pony! How I longed for the liberty of dear Hartlebury! Yes! how I longed to be, what you call shut up."

"But you were a child then, it would be very different now, with all your advantages, you would be quite recherchée."

"No," said Helen more seriously, "I am sure I should not be happy in London, I might be amused, but I should not be happy. I should hate to be liked by people who would care nothing about me if I had half a dozen brothers, or sisters, as agreeable as myself."

Mrs. Neville laughed at Helen's fastidiousness.

"Do you often," she asked, "have people staying with you?"

"Yes very often, we have many relations who live in distant counties, and indeed the families who live in this county are so far apart, that when we do meet we generally remain sometime together."

"How comes it," interrogated Mrs. Neville, "that Mr. Latimer is not married? I thought all clergymen married directly that had a living; all the clergymen I know are married."

"It must be generally a great advantage to them, living so much as they do in one place, and with so many duties to perform, in which a woman can so much aid them: but Arthur Latimer does not feel so much the necessity of a wife, for his mother is often with him."

"Mrs. Latimer seems quite a lady. I dare say she is very good."

"She is an excellent woman," replied Helen with feeling. "As kind as she is judicious. I wonder who Arthur will marry," added Helen musingly, "he is too difficult to please, to choose a wife very quickly."

"I think I ought to call on Mrs. Latimer," said Mrs. Neville rising from the table, "if you like we will take our walk now."

CHAPTER XIX

The gentlemen return from quarter sessions

It was late before the gentlemen returned. They had been detained by Lord Courtland, and by Lord Courtland's polite attentions which were very famous. The Earl of Courtland was the great man of the County, he was the Lord Lieutenant, and piqued himself on being universally popular. Indeed he possessed all the requisites to secure popularity to an Earl. He had quick sight, and a long memory, and not being burthened with much knowledge, or given to much reflection, he had always a ready head for all the minute affairs of the world. He never forgot a person he had once seen, he never forgot the name, not only of the person he addressed, but of every member of his family. If a man married a daughter, Lord Courtland never failed to congratulate him, if he lost his wife his lordship never asked after her. These delicate attentions, Lord Courtland flattered himself, had met with their due reward: he believed that he had reached the juste milieu between dignity and affability.

The first appearance of a person of Mr. Bohun's consequence was a great event, and his lordship thought it incumbent on himself to make a great sensation on the occasion. He wished all the county to be aware of the gracious manner in which he had received Mr. Bohun, and of the very handsome way in which he at once considered him as a friend. He overwhelmed his unconscious protegé with a thousand civilities, and would not allow the party to return home without visiting his castle, which carried them at least three miles out of their road.

They returned therefore very weary, and very hungry, and Helen's observing eye quickly detected that her father looked as if he had been bored to death. Dinner was however soon ready, and brought with it that consolation which a good dinner seldom fails to bestow on the hungry and the weary. Mr. Molesworth was by no means insensible to the deliciae of the table and today, as the soup was good and the Matelotte well concocted, and the pheasants not without flavour, and the wine in excellent order, Helen had soon the pleasure of seeing his smiles and his philosophy return, and before the close of dinner, the mention of Lord Courtland's name only elicited a little gentle badinage.

Mr. Bohun and Mr. Latimer were men of the most opposite character, which we trust our readers will have in some slight degree detected, but on this occasion as they joined Miss Molesworth's tea-table, they were both meditating on the same subject, in a state of the most perfect, though unconscious agreement. They were both thinking of the charms of woman's society, and of the horror of having been condemned for two whole days to the company of men. It was to this happy change they both ascribed their more agreeable sensations at the present moment, and far be it from me, a woman, to insinuate that they were mistaken. The soft carpets and the downy couches of Mr. Molesworth's drawing-room, and his rich Burgundy, and his bright Claret, would not in themselves have been more agreeable than the dust and bustle of the Town-hall, and the greasy cookery and the hot Port of the Ordinary dinner, if it had not been for Helen's graceful attentions, and Helen's sweet smiles.

"I have not yet heard one word of your adventures," said Helen; "now that you are somewhat rested, you must tell me everybody that you have seen."

"That will be quite impossible Helen," said Mr. Latimer, "without we have as good memories as Lord Courtland, who almost fancied today that he remembered Mr. Bohun because he had been present at his christening. I never saw a sessions so full."

"How do you like Lord Courtland?" asked Helen of Mr. Bohun.

"I think that question quite as impossible to answer Miss Molesworth as the one you asked Mr. Latimer."

"Well then," said Helen, "how do you like his Castle?"

"I think it is magnificent," answered Mr. Bohun, "that is to say the interior. I do not like the exterior, it looks too new; you must permit me," he added smiling, "at least to profess to admire old dilapidated exteriors, as I have allowed my own to become so."

"Do not call Bohun Castle dilapidated," replied Helen: "I like that fine grey colouring. I hope you will never give it a new smart look like Courtland."

"No I promise you I never will, but I think I must have a Gallery like Lord Courtland's. Gustavus," said Mr. Bohun to Colonel Neville, who was seated by his wife on a sofa by the side of a fire, "do you not think that a Gallery, like the one we saw this afternoon, would look well at Bohun Castle opening into the Ball-room?"

"I should so like to see the ball-room at Bohun lit up," said Mrs. Neville.

"It never will be I fear," said Helen, "if in this part of the world it is to illuminate dancers."

"It shall be lit up without dancers then," said Mr. Bohun.

"Oh delightful," exclaimed Mrs. Neville. "I should like it of all things. Would not you, Helen?"

"It shall be illuminated tomorrow Emmeline," said Mr. Bohun.

But tomorrow the ladies settled was too early a day. Mrs. Brand would be offended if it were not arranged in due order, so accordingly the day after was fixed on, and Mr. and Miss Molesworth promised to attend.

"But surely," said Mr. Bohun, when this important arrangement was concluded, "surely we might fill the Ball-room. All the fathers and husbands and brothers that have been dealing out their decrees for the last eight-and-forty hours, they must have daughters and wives and sisters, who also require their amusement."

"So you think we country gentlemen only do our duty for our diversion?" said Mr. Molesworth.

"Happy country," replied Mr. Bohun with a smile, "where such a combination is practicable. Your friend Dr. Maxwell," he continued, "at any rate makes a business of pleasure. He is a very great orator."

"And he spoke today?" enquired Helen.

"Both days without ceasing I believe," said Mr. Bohun, "I voted against him and was as is my lot in life, in a terrible majority."

"And what the subject?"

"I have not an idea. Mr. Latimer what was Dr. Maxwell's motion?"

"Against open courts," replied Mr. Latimer.

"And a very sensible motion too," added Mr. Molesworth.

"And you only *voted* against him Mr. Bohun?" enquired Helen.

"Oh, I am no orator, as Dr. Maxwell is. I envy the man who can elevate his voice above a whisper in a drawing-room."

"Well it is rather singular, but I should have thought that you would have been a very intrepid speaker."

"I have lived in silent lands," said Mr. Bohun. "What is called a free government makes a talkative people."

"Well I must say," said Mrs. Neville, "that I am no admirer of orators. The pleasantest men in town never speak in the House. I wish they would all follow their example. Society would be much more agreeable. I never shall recover this *triste* season. I really must say that I think it was very ungentleman-like in Lord Grey bringing forward any measure which he was not sure to carry at once. I declare that I found myself one day at a dinner party without a single man but old gouty Lord ——, and he was complaining the whole time that he could not get down to the House."

"Were I a man," said Helen somewhat thoughtfully, "I should like to be in parliament. It must be very exciting."

"The dullest business in the world," observed Colonel

Neville, "when you are in. Trying to get in is some amusement. But every man I know in the House tells me he is bored to death. There's Crawford — Crawford never could sleep 'till he got into parliament; and Harry Stair, he always says it cured his dyspepsia. There is no place in the world where you sleep so soundly as in the House of Commons."

"There will be noise enough now in it," said Mr. Molesworth, "to rouse anyone, but I dare say very little dyspepsia. I cannot fancy the member for Birmingham or the Tower Hamlets with the dyspepsia. Can you Arthur? Oh no; dyspepsia is a very fashionable complaint indeed. None but a very idle person with a very good cook has dyspepsia."

"Gustavus," drawled out Mrs. Neville to her husband, who was standing before the fire, "do you know that Dr. Flirt thinks that Bijou has the dyspepsia?"

"New complaints are always appearing," said Mr. Molesworth, "but I suspect that they are old offenders who return from transportation with an alias."

"The cholera is awful, and I should think new," said Mr. Latimer.

"Ever since poor Lady Harriet's death, I am quite frightened by the name of cholera. Do you know, Gustavus, I am rather losing my opinion of Flirt, for if you remember, he assured us that cholera never attacked any but the canaille!"

"The plague is not so aristocratic," said Mr. Bohun, "and therefore would not at all suit this country."

"There was no cholera when I was a boy," observed Mr. Molesworth, "and then we were indeed an aristocratic nation. That is past. We are now a people of political economists. Ricks are burnt and machines shattered, and the people are starving, but then we have the advantage of being destroyed by the most scientific legislation. As for myself, I glory in being a bigot."

"Which means, Mr. Molesworth," said Mr. Bohun, "in your vocabulary, a very honest man."

Mr. Bohun surprises Mr. Chace
and everybody else, including the reader

At six o'clock the next morning Mr. Chace received a summons from Mr. Bohun. It was promptly obeyed.

"I am sorry to disturb you at such an unreasonable hour Chace," said Mr. Bohun, who was pacing his room in his dressing gown, "but I know your zeal for me. I start for Fanchester, and as I wish my address to be circulated today, there is no time to be lost."

Mr. Chace was confounded, not at the celerity of the movements required, for he was an active man, never at a loss for expedients, but at what he considered the folly of the attempt.

He looked his astonishment as he replied: "My dear Sir, you know I am ever ready, but are you not here a little too hasty — have you considered?"

"My dear Chace," said Mr. Bohun a little impatiently, "all I ask of you now is to assist me as a friend. You need not be afraid. You will have none of the responsibility; no one will suspect such a Tory as you of having sent me forth."

What could poor Chace do? He could only do that which he did, take the pen which Mr. Bohun put into his hand, and set about inditing the well rounded sentences which Mr. Bohun poured forth.

From the observations he had made during the last two days, Mr. Bohun had determined at the present time not to start for the county. He felt that his opinions would not be popular, and he thought that it would be unwise to enter into collision with any of his county neighbours until he made his way. His thoughts therefore reverted to Fanchester, which from the moment of his return had been a favourite project. There he would certainly have a contest, but as both his rivals were strangers to the county, no one would feel it necessary to be offended if he beat them.

For many years the borough of Fanchester had been represented by two wealthy and respectable individuals, who seldom appeared among their constituents. They came to be chaired at each election, and every now and then when they were travelling that road, they spent the morning in calling on their friends. Every year each sent a buck, and every year one of them, who considered himself an orator and was fond of spouting after dinner, banquetted with the Corporation: the other who was more silent and diffident, sent an additional present of rich fruits from his hot-houses. The flattering speeches and the rich fruits balanced the affair, both were equally popular. One was a Tory, the other a Whig, but side by side they bowed in amity to their constituents, and nothing would have disturbed their friendship but the overturning Reform Bill.

The Reform Bill deprived poor Fanchester of one of its members.

The Tory who had suddenly become a little liberal, confident in his oratory, canvassed the town with great ardour. The Whig who was a quiet man— who liked the distinction of being in parliament, so long as it cost him only his money, shrunk with horror from a contested election and a personal canvass, and offered his interest, which he considered preponderated, to the Treasury. Mr. Ellice instantly fixed on a proper man. He was a Radical, who had just turned Whig for the sake of the loaves and fishes. He had in a series of Junius-like compositions, written himself into sufficient notoriety to be an acceptable ally to the government, and quite a hero among the people. He would please the Whigs, and captivate the Radicals, who united, would easily beat the Tories, and moreover he could out-talk Sir George Vavasour, the voluble Tory candidate.

As Mr. Chace concluded the last sentence of the address, he ventured one more remonstrance; but Mr. Bohun, now warmed by his own eloquent appeal, was less disposed than ever to listen to him:

"All I ask of you Chace is to get this out by three o'clock," said Mr. Bohun, who, glancing over the paper, returned it to Mr. Chace. "If you do not like to act for me afterwards I shall not be offended; but we can arrange that by and bye: let me now hurry you off — come back to breakfast."

By three o'clock all Fanchester was in confusion. Mr. Bohun's address was placarded on every wall and left at every house. The chief persons in the borough, who were generally pledged to one or other of the candidates were in dismay, at the thought of disobliging such a powerful man, and one too who had been so civil to them. The lesser people were in equal consternation. One feeling was universal: Mr. Bohun who of course must lose the election, would in revenge ruin the town.

The next morning at an early hour, Mr. Bohun rode into Fanchester, accompanied by Colonel Neville and Mr. Chace. His return to England was yet so recent that he had not ceased to be an object of uncommon interest, and to create a sensation whenever he passed through the High Street. All idle boys ran after him, and all people who were not very busy stared at him, and touched their hats, and all the smart young ladies ran to the shop doors to look at him.

But today there was a great change. Knots of people were at the corners of streets whispering together; they turned their backs when Mr. Bohun rode by; for everybody was afraid that he would ask them for their vote, before they had made up their minds how they were to answer him.

"I think I will speak to the people Chace," said Mr. Bohun. He could not help smiling at his agent's long face. Mr. Chace looked as if his principal was in a false position.

"Cannot you manage it?" asked Mr. Bohun as he looked round him. They were just opposite a large house, the principal house in the High Street. A bow-windowed drawing-room was surrounded by a balcony, if so imposing a name may be employed to describe the strong iron rails which, supported by iron bars, held during the summer months Mrs. Escott's gay flower-pots.

"Whose house is this? — Is it not my friend Mrs. Escott's?" enquired Mr. Bohun.

Mr. Chace replied in the affirmative.

"That will do, exactly — that you know will compromise no one. This balcony is made for a speech."

As Mr. Bohun said these words, he jumped from his horse, and followed by Col. Neville, entered the house, while Chace went to collect an audience. Mrs. Escott who considered the compliment paid to her importance in the town, and not to the convenience of her balcony was enraptured, and was at once Mr. Bohun's most zealous supporter.

The report of a speech soon brought some hundred loiterers round the house. Mr. Bohun appeared in the balcony — a few voices, but not of voters, cried "Bohun for ever".

He took off his hat — he passed his hand through his curls — he paused a moment — and then he spoke. The music of his harmonious voice broke on their astonished ears. He spoke with mildness and with feeling of his return to dwell amongst them — of his desire to be their friend. His is interrupted by vociferous cries of "Bohun for ever". He describes the mutual advantages of their friendship. His perfect enunciation aids his powerful voice — his tones are audible at the farther end of the street. The crowd rapidly increases. He paints with energy the duties of a representative towards his constituents — the excited people listen in profound silence — all idle sounds die away — one by one a loiterer stealthily joins the mass. He asks what their late members have done for them? — "Nothing," a thousand voices respond. He tells them what he will do for them — what only a neighbour and a friend can do for them. When he pauses, they cry "Go on"; when at last he ceases, they exclaim "We must speak to him — we must speak to him."

Mrs. Escott trembled for her neat Hall, for her well polished oaken floor, as the people pressed to her door. Mr. Bohun again appeared at the window.

"My friends," he said, "we must not intrude here: meet me at the Rose."

To the Rose the crowd rapidly turned, and thither Mr. Bohun also proceeded as quickly as his new friends would permit; but he had to shake hands with nearly all his thousand auditors.

He at last safely reached the large room of the Rose Inn: there Mr. Chace who now looked very elated, seated at a table, recorded the names of all those who hastened to assure Mr. Bohun of their support. The greater number of the liberals in the town had hitherto stood aloof, undeclared for either candidate. It was little doubted that they would finally side with the ministerial gentleman who was personally agreeable to them: but they thought it more consistent to withhold for a short time their support, as he had been recommended by their late Whig

member, whom they detested. Now they rejoiced in their freedom, as it enabled them to be the first to offer their votes to
"Bohun the friend of the People".

CHAPTER XXI

A friendly dinner party at the castle

The history of this eventful morning was carried to Hartlebury
by old Mr. Gainsborough, who from his usual haunt the news-
room, had seen and heard all that passed and who could not
return home, without calling at the Hall, to unfold the astound-
ing intelligence to Mr. and Miss Molesworth.

Mr. Molesworth was a Tory of the old school, and profes-
sedly a believer in the approach of revolution and anarchy, the
fatal effects of the late measure; but he was in fact of an amiable
temper, which made him sanguine, and had a cultivated mind,
which enabled him to reason. He was apt to theorise, and it was
his favourite dogma that talents without property, or property
without talents may produce mischief, but that little danger is
to be apprehended from the union of broad lands and clear
brains. The few weeks of acquaintance with Mr. Bohun had
proved that he was the fortunate possessor of both. When
therefore Mr. Molesworth heard that the representative of the
most Tory family in the county had broached opinions somewhat subversive of the principles of his ancestors, he did not
grow either furious or sulky, but trusting that a little longer
residence in England would improve Mr. Bohun's knowledge
of the wants of his countrymen, he prepared with his usual
philosophy to perform his dinner engagement at the Castle. For
it was on the evening of this eventful morning, that Mrs.
Neville and Miss Molesworth were to be gratified by the illumi-
nation of the ball-room.

"We have heard of all your mighty deeds," said Helen, as she gave Mr. Bohun her hand, on entering the drawing-room at the Castle.

"I hope you are for me," he replied smiling, "I dare not ask Mr. Molesworth."

"You know that it is not of much consequence whether I am for or against you," replied Miss Molesworth. "If I had a vote, I dare say you would find courage to ask for it."

"My dear Miss Molesworth," said Mrs. Neville, "was it not too bad of Aubrey not to tell us he was going to speak — would you not like to have heard him?"

"I have heard a prodigious account of your eloquence," said Mr. George Gainsborough, who at this moment was announced.

"Yes I produced a sensation," answered Mr. Bohun. "I only hope both my adversaries will not retire."

Mr. Chace who had returned with Mr. Bohun from Fanchester, now entered the room arranged for dinner smirking and satisfied.

"We made a great sensation I assure you today Sir," said he, rubbing his hands, and addressing Mr. Molesworth, "I do not know what you will say to our principles, but at any rate you will agree with us in one point, you will like our abuse of the Whigs — we peppered them well."

"You cannot say anything against them which they do not deserve," responded Mr. Molesworth.

"Upon my word we gave it them well," added Mr. Chace, who dwelt with much complacency on that part of the morning's exploit which best supported his consistency.

Mrs. Latimer and her son soon arrived, and dinner speedily followed.

It was a gay meal. Helen was seated between Colonel Neville and Arthur Latimer, who was consequently talkative and very agreeable, so also was Mr. Bohun who talked to everybody, as he did not wish all his good things to be dropped alone into Mrs. Latimer's ear.

"And were you not very nervous?" enquired Helen.

"Extremely," said Mr. Bohun, "but I never can do anything without being nervous. But then you must recollect I was backed by your friend Mrs. Escott."

"Dear Mrs. Escott, I quite love her for her valiance," exclaimed Helen, "she has such a horror of a mob."

"Well, I must say I think it very provoking Aubrey that you did not tell us you were going to speak," repeated Mrs. Neville. "Very odd indeed! We could have rode in and listened to you. Gustavus I suppose you said nothing?"

"No you will not find me making a speech in a hurry," replied the Colonel. "By Jove it was a fine sight though. I liked the scene at the Rose the best. We shall have to go round to all the benefit societies," he continued addressing himself to Miss Molesworth, "make speeches, and drink beer. By Jove! it certainly was a very fine affair."

"Aubrey what are your colours?" enquired Mrs. Neville.

"You shall choose Emmeline. They must be announced tomorrow. Come Miss Molesworth, pray assist Mrs. Neville in a felicitous choice."

"Blue I suppose is engaged," said Colonel Neville. "There is always a blue in elections."

"Blue and yellow are the engaged colours," said Mr. Chace, "Blue the Whig."

"I would have both united," said Mr. Latimer.

"We must have something very pretty and becoming," said Mrs. Neville. "What do you think of green? Green becomes me very well. You know Gustavus you told me the other day that I looked very pretty in green."

"I should like a combination," said Miss Molesworth, "Green and gold is splendid."

"Lincoln green!" exclaimed Bohun. "It shall be Lincoln green and you shall be Maid Marian."

So it was settled to be green; and then many reasons were immediately discovered why the colour should be green. The Bohun liveries not the least efficient.

"We only give you five minutes Gustavus," said Mrs. Neville to her husband as she rose from table. "Remember the ball-room is illuminated tonight — you will find us there."

And to the ball-room the ladies proceeded.

"How very splendid! — How beautiful! — How enchanting!" they exclaimed dazzled by the overwhelming brilliancy. Three large chandeliers were suspended from the ceiling, innumerable girandoles hung round the room. The pale green walls, which were covered with the most fanciful gilt arabesques, were illuminated in every part. Numerous mirrors and tall glasses, magically repeated the scene which appeared without termination. On the broad hearth blazed immense piles of wood, which were supported by richly ornamented dogs of silver.

"You must have seen this beautiful room full of gay people dear Mrs. Latimer," said Helen.

"Once just after I married, there was a very gay ball, the Castle was full of visitors, and people came from the most distant parts of the county to be present at it. But it seems to me like a dream," added Mrs. Latimer, somewhat mournfully, "it was all so soon over, and the Castle deserted."

"Was not Lady Alice very handsome?" enquired Mrs. Neville.

"I think I never saw a woman of such dazzling beauty. Her son sometimes reminds me of her, though he is so much like his father."

"I think Aubrey is very handsome," said Mrs. Neville. "Gustavus says he looked magnificently today when he was speaking to those people at Fanchester. I wish we had been there. Gustavus says there is not a man in the House like him. I hope he will gain his election," pursued the lady. "It will be so amusing to go to the ventilator to hear him."

The conversation was arrested by the entrance of the gentlemen, who joined the ladies only to participate in their admiration. They all sauntered about the room as they sipped their coffee, and admired the large carved mantel-piece, the richly-adorned frames of the glasses, the splendid cabinets. The room was pronounced quite perfect. Mr. Bohun was forbidden to think of alteration.

At the top of the room there was a considerable elevated space which was intended for the orchestra. You ascended to it by a flight of steps. As Colonel Neville for the twentieth time ran up the steps, and admired the proportions of the room he said,

"Now here, Aubrey, would be a capital place for you to address us. By the bye Emmeline, does not this a little remind you of the platform we erected for our theatricals in the music room at your father's? This would make a capital theatre."

"So it would," said Mrs. Neville eagerly. "Let us get up a piece now."

"I am afraid," said Helen, "you will find us deficient in our parts."

"Oh, you need not know your parts," said Mrs. Neville: "we never learnt our parts at Wenclyffe, it is such a bore. We always improvised."

"It is very easy I assure you," remarked the Colonel, "just fix upon a story and then everybody fills up the dialogue as their wit suggests, and if they have no wit it is only the more amusing."

"But everybody has wit enough," added Mrs. Neville: "we need not have many characters: an old father, a young daughter, and a lover of course, and a few more characters just to work out the plot."

"Well then," said Helen, "since it is so easy let us get up a performance tonight. What will you be Papa?"

"I will act the most important part, Helen, which Mrs. Neville has quite forgotten. Mrs. Latimer and myself will perform the part of audience. I am sure you would none of you like to act without you had someone to look at you."

"Well, you must not be too critical, and we will permit you to take that part. Now Mrs. Neville you must be the heroine, you must be the young daughter," said Helen turning to that lady.

"No Miss Molesworth that ought to be your part," urged Mrs. Neville in reply.

"Remember I am quite a novice," said Helen, "I should not get on at all. You must take the principal part, and I will be your soubrette. Now for the others: Mr. George Gainsborough I think must be the hero," added Helen as she looked round at her company, "he will act the lover capitally."

Mr. George Gainsborough looked as if he did not like the tone of Helen's commendation.

"Tell me Miss Molesworth," asked Mr. Bohun, who was extremely amused at the whole scene, "what are the qualities necessary to act a lover capitally?"

"They are too delicate and minute to be described," said Helen laughing: "but it is indispensable to be gallant, and to be able to sing."

George Gainsborough looked as little like a lover as possible, that is to say, if a lover be always gallant and harmonious.

"Mr. Chace must be the father," said Mrs. Neville.

"My dear Madam you must excuse me. I shall make a sorry case of it," rapidly replied worthy Mr. Chace looking quite alarmed.

"Oh! no indeed Mr. Chace, we cannot spare you," cried both the ladies at once.

"Arthur what will you be?" said Helen, turning to Mr. Latimer, who stood somewhat apart from the group.

"You must let me be an observer Helen. I am a very interested one," the gentleman replied.

"I shall be afraid to act before Papa and you."

"Why should you be afraid of me Helen?"

She could not stay to tell him, for her attention was claimed by others.

"Miss Molesworth," said the Colonel, "I am to be Gainsborough's valet, and in love with you."

"Well now," answered Helen, "what are we to do with Mr. Bohun? Who can find a character for him."

"Give me Colonel Neville's."

"That will never do," said Helen: "the orator of Fanchester sent into the servant's hall! No, you must be something grand and imperious."

"Is that your opinion of me?" asked Mr. Bohun.

"What character do you think would suit you? You would never do for an old father, and I think you would make but a bad lover."

"Try me," said Mr. Bohun. He spoke in a low tone, and he fixed his eyes on Helen's countenance.

Helen blushed, and laughing said, "You forget that I have no vote."

"I do not think Mr. George Gainsborough likes the office you have given him," said Mrs. Neville in a tone of pique.

"Indeed Mrs. Neville you do me wrong," replied George Gainsborough, and he threw himself on his knee before her in a most theatrical attitude.

"Bravo," exclaimed the gentlemen.

"That is well done," said Helen: "but if you are gloomy tonight you shall give up your part to Mr. Bohun, and you shall be some moody villain, a tyrant, or an assassin."

What could be the matter with George Gainsborough tonight? Is it possible, could he really be jealous of Mr. Bohun, or was he positively, sensitively in love with Miss Molesworth? Pale, red, ghastly pale, burning red, and all in a few instants; the alternations of his countenance could escape no one's observation, and Mrs. Latimer who was privileged ventured to notice them. George Gainsborough muttered something about a dizziness which had already gone off, and while he was muttering, Mr. Bohun was suddenly seized with a desire to dance, and began to waltz with Mrs. Neville.

CHAPTER XXII

Amatory, political, and mysterious

Helen Molesworth had captivated Mr. Bohun. He had returned to England resolved against matrimony, but the more he saw of Helen, the more his resolution faltered. Her purity, her beauty, and her grace, enchanted him, and his impetuous passions soon resolved that the splendour of his destiny would be incomplete without her love.

The events of yesterday had thrown him into that state of excitement, which in itself to him was happiness. He resolved at the same time to win the Election, and to gain the heart of Helen Molesworth. The ardent love of a woman so affectionate and so refined would indeed be a rich reward for all the pleasing toil of gaining it. Mr. Bohun was too fastidious to desire an easy conquest, and he was too exacting to be satisfied with less than the most entire one. Helen must yield up to him all her young and pure affections, she must love him for himself alone, she must love even his faults and his imperfections in spite of her conviction that they were errors, and serious ones. She must be entirely his, he should be jealous even of her affection for her father. Such were Mr. Bohun's notions of love, a sort of European adaptation of a Turkish fashion. In the land of the turban, they are satisfied with the imprisonment of the body, but in these countries where the body is always running about, visiting, and dancing and shopping, Mr. Bohun was willing to substitute in its stead an entire bondage of the soul.

Though he possessed these erroneous notions on certain subjects, Aubrey Bohun was a man of nice discernment, and he had not failed to employ all his powers of observation, in endeavouring to understand his new friends. His increasing passion for Miss Molesworth made him interested for all who were likely to influence her, and above all he had attentively marked Mr. Latimer's character and feelings.

Their frequent reunions afforded him good opportunities for study. He noted how seldom Mr. Latimer's eye was averted from Helen's countenance, and how often while apparently deeply engaged in Mr. Molesworth's whist table, or while the victim of one of old Mr. Gainsborough's button-hole discussions, he would send a sudden answer to Helen's most trivial observation. Her lowest tone seemed ever to reach his watchful ear. Mr. Bohun keenly observed all these symptoms and many more, and he felt well persuaded that Arthur Latimer loved his cousin fervently and passionately. Mr. Bohun believed however that, at present, he himself was the only person in the secret. That Helen should be apparently so unconscious of what a woman almost instinctively discovers, he could ascribe only to her extreme youth and inexperience. As to the gentleman, no doubt he would soon be enlightened; the actors were thickening on the scene, and coming events would betray him to himself.

Mr. Bohun fully appreciated Mr. Latimer's character, he felt his moral dignity, he did full justice to his cultivated intellect. He did not therefore despise him as a rival, but a rival only increased the energy of his passion. On George Gainsborough he did not waste a thought; he was satisfied that Helen was alive to all that was ridiculous in his character, and a stronger guard against love he did not ask.

While Mr. Bohun with his table covered with electioneering papers, was thus alternately indulging in visions of successful love and ambition, Mr. George Gainsborough was announced.

He was quite himself again, and in good humour.

"I have come," he said, as he entered the room, and he spoke in an assured tone, and with an air even of kindness, "to renew my offers of service. Can I do anything?"

Mr. Bohun received his offers of assistance with all due expressions of gratitude, and they both were soon busily employed in examining the lists of voters. Chace had made some rough notes against each name, indicating either their political creed, or the parties by whom they could be influenced.

"I expect Chace every moment and he will explain this confusion," said Mr. Bohun, as they both stopped at a piece of private information, in one of Chace's notes which greatly puzzled them.

"He went very early to Fanchester. Today I shall issue another address, more explanatory of my principles. Tomorrow I shall begin my personal canvass. I intend to call on everybody.

"Here," continued Mr. Bohun, as he ran his finger down the list. "Here, Gainsborough, you can help me. 'Mackinnon seven daughters', I am sure you can captivate them all, and seven daughters must govern one father."

"You have plenty to do," said George Gainsborough.

"Yes I think I have," said Mr. Bohun. "I have two affairs on hand, each of which in itself is usually thought quite engrossing. I am going to contest an Election, and I am desperately in love." Mr. Bohun said these words in a careless tone without raising his eyes from the list before him, which he seemed to be perusing.

"Here Gainsborough," he continued. "I think you can aid me, but unfortunately I cannot woo Miss Molesworth by deputy."

Gainsborough was pale from passion, he pushed his chair back from the table, but Mr. Bohun did not look up.

"You are rapid in your plans," said George Gainsborough in a tone which was intended to be satirical.

"I always am," replied Mr. Bohun, still reading his lists.

Gainsborough rose from his seat and turned to the window, but he could no longer restrain himself: he was alternately pale and flushed as he exclaimed:

"Bohun you cannot think of it, surely she is safe."

"Safe," replied Mr. Bohun, "she is sacred, I worship her. She is the shrine on which I intend to devote all that I have of good."

Mr. Bohun spoke in a gay tone, and pushing the table away from him, he jumped up from the sofa, and paced the room.

"You cannot marry her," said George Gainsborough. Mr. Bohun stopped in his walk, he turned on Gainsborough a glance of lightning as he said in a most imperious tone:

"Who is there here who dares say I cannot?"

George Gainsborough was maddened by his passion: one moment had verified his worst fears, and his disappointment was embittered by the evident contempt with which Mr. Bohun treated his pretensions.

He writhed with rage, as he answered:

"Do you then so despise my power?"

"Despise you," answered Mr. Bohun in a very equivocal tone, "oh no I have the firmest reliance on your honour."

Gainsborough bit his lips, and turned away in baffled silence.

"Let us understand one another Gainsborough," said Mr. Bohun, as he threw himself again on the sofa: "I have no wish to revive old stories; I am the last person to talk about old scrapes, but when I promised forgetfulness, I considered the oblivion was to be mutual. It is for you to choose what you desire to be said. What can you tell of me? An adventure so romantic, so improbable, that in this matter of fact country no one would believe it; while if your recollections do not fail you, some of my claims on you would not fail of being perfectly understood here."

Mr. Bohun's observations appeared convincing; for George Gainsborough made no effort to deny them.

"I am determined to gain Miss Molesworth," continued Mr. Bohun, "if it be possible. I am by no means vain enough to think it certain. She may be dazzled, but she will never be confounded. To win her, one must seem at least to deserve her. Do you not think so?" added the gentleman, with a tormenting look of appeal. "But you probably have not thought about the matter as I have done, you of course have merely regarded her as an agreeable companion."

At this moment a gentle tap at the door relieved Mr. George Gainsborough from the necessity of replying, if he ever intended it: Mr. Chace entered.

"I beg your pardon," said the agent when he saw his principal was not alone. "I thought you would be so impatient, that I have run up without waiting to be announced."

"Indeed I am very glad to see you. You may say anything before Mr. Gainsborough he is my confidential friend. How fare our constituents?"

"In as healthy a state of agitation as you could desire Sir," chuckled Mr. Chace. "Everybody is eager to hear you again. There is your new address," pursued he producing a sheet almost wet from the press: "if you will just look it over, I will hasten back with it to Fanchester."

"Here is Mr Gainsborough eager to be employed," said Mr. Bohun as he took the paper, "cannot you tell him how he can be useful while I run over this?"

George Gainsborough mechanically took a list from the table, and seemed to be listening to Mr. Chace's long winded instructions. If however he were ever of any use to Mr. Bohun in his canvass, it certainly was not from anything suggested to him this morning. His thoughts were wandering. They were in distant countries, they were at Hartlebury Hall, they were anywhere but with Mr. Chace. At last it seemed to him that that gentleman was recommending him to call somewhere, he said he would do so directly, and forgetting to say Good morning, he took up his hat and bolted out of the room.

"This is indeed a zealous friend," thought Mr. Chace.

CHAPTER XXIII

Amatory only

Mr. Bohun's second address was issued. It was a pointed résumé of his speech. Helen was attentively reading it when Arthur Latimer entered the room.

"Have you become a politician Helen?" he enquired.

"Oh no I am admiring the eloquence of this appeal without understanding a word of it. Have you read it?"

"Yes, I have, and like you I admire its eloquence, without comprehending a word of its meaning."

"But do you not think Mr. Bohun very clever?" asked the lady.

"What do you think of him?" enquired the gentleman in reply, involuntarily drawing his chair nearer to her in his eagerness to hear her opinion.

"I think him very clever and most agreeable: surely you think him clever?"

The chair receded as Arthur Latimer coolly answered: "He is undoubtedly very clever. He shews it in his skill in making friends."

"We should be ungrateful not to be his friends," said Helen, "he is so eager to be ours."

"And have you forgiven him Helen for his long desertion of Bohun, which once used to excite all your eloquence?"

"I am ashamed to say how seldom I have thought of it since his return," said Helen slightly blushing.

"We seem all to have forgotten it. But do you not still think it was wrong?"

"Oh yes very wrong."

"Should we not then dear Helen be somewhat afraid of a person who thus captivates our reason, and makes us forget the difference between right and wrong?"

"And yet," urged Helen, "would it not be uncharitable to

withhold our friendship which he so agreeably solicits, until we have thoroughly gauged his character? It is true," she added, "that as yet we know nothing of his principles, or his temper, but while we see nothing to disapprove, is it not right, is it not your own doctrine Arthur, to give him credit for being what we approve?"

"Is it impossible to be at the same time charitable and cautious?" asked Mr. Latimer.

He took up the address from the table, and drawing his chair nearer to the fire with his feet on the fender he seemed to be intently perusing it. In truth his eyes were fixed on the paper, but his thoughts were wholly of Helen. He continued for some time silent, and Helen also, busied with her netting seemed plunged in thought. At last Arthur pushed back his chair from the fire, and saying something about being very hot, took his hat and seemed about to depart.

"Are you going Arthur?" asked Helen, "if you could wait for me, I would walk with you; I want to call on your mother, but perhaps you are in a hurry."

"Not so hurried but that I can wait for you."

"I will not keep you five minutes," said Helen as she left the room.

Arthur threw himself on the sofa, and covered his eyes with his hand, as if he would shut out that light that had so suddenly burst upon him. Alas! alas! how weakly he had deceived himself — the fatal truth was now revealed with bitter force. He remembered how indignant he had felt but a short time before at Gainsborough's insolent pretensions. What was it that he now felt? Alas! it was all the eligibilities of a connection with Mr. Bohun, all the probabilities, all the certainty of his success, that filled him with his heart-rending anguish. He felt that his indignation at Gainsborough's presumption, his despair at Mr. Bohun's advances, all arose from the same source: he was no longer blind, he knew he loved Helen with an overpowering, a burning passion. But never was there a human heart so totally devoid of selfishness as Arthur Latimer's. His was truly that christian benevolence, that enabled him to deny himself for others' good. He could soon ask himself if he ought to mourn his loss, if it were Helen's gain, if he ought to grieve, if her virtues and her winning graces were removed to a more extended

sphere of usefulness and felicity? But would she be valued and
cherished as she deserved? What did they know of Mr. Bohun?
a fatal reverse of the picture would obtrude itself, and Helen,
his adored Helen, the unhappy and contemned wife of a heartless libertine————, he pressed his hand to his burning brow.

At this moment Helen returned. She opened the door with so
gentle a step, that he was not aware of her presence, until she
took his hand, and asked if he were ill. He started, his disor-
dered countenance seemed but to verify her fears.

"I am sure you are very ill Arthur, tell me what I can do for
you?" she affectionately said.

"Indeed, I am not ill," he replied, "I have only a headache, a
very slight headache."

She looked incredulous.

"Indeed I am not ill," he continued in a more cheerful tone;
for the sight of Helen, her actual presence, still happy and
blooming, had already revived him.

"I will prove to you that I am not ill if you will take a walk
with me. Instead of going down to the Rectory, let us have a
stroll on the common, the fresh air, and your cheerful company, will charm away my ailment."

Helen willingly consented, and they were soon on the common inhaling all the sweet air of the breezy down.

It was a fine October day, the air was clear and exhilarating,
and the sun bright and warm, lit up the woods which were now
clad in a thousand gay colours. Rich orange, and bright red, and
pale yellow, mingling with the solemn garb of the evergreens in
the most harmonious confusion.

The trees half-thinned of their leaves more fully developed
their majestic or their graceful forms, than in their summer
dress, and every now and then, one prematurely leafless, shot
up its grey branches among its gaudy brethren. As our cousins
skirted the road, they caught glimpses of the young children,
who were busy among the rustling leaves gathering their winter
firing. They heard their wild laughter and their sudden noises,
and they could not but in some degree participate in the gaiety
which this bright day seemed to diffuse on all.

"This is a beautiful season," said Helen, "how charming is
this rich glow of colouring! — how inspiring this fresh breeze! I
think the poets are wrong to describe sadness as the feeling

attendant on autumnal scenes. I think it excites gay and stirring feelings."

"Ah, Helen!" said Mr. Latimer, "it is so to you because you are young and joyous. It is to the old and to the unhappy, that the approaching close of the year brings mournful feelings. It tells the one that they will soon be called upon to deliver up their great account! — it reminds the other perhaps, of another year passed in anguish and suffering. But is the Autumn your favourite season?"

"No! perhaps not! and yet I think an autumn breeze on this common the most inspiriting thing in the world. I cannot tell which season I most prefer, nor do I think anyone could, if they were called upon to choose which they would always live in. How delightful is spring with its gay sounds and sweet smells; and glowing summer with its brilliant flowers — its rich foliage — and its soft delicious moon-lights! And who does not love winter? — dear domestic winter."

"I agree with you, Helen, — I think a person would be very unhappy who was condemned to live without any prospect of change in the season which he fancied he preferred. I believe it is their variety far more than their beauty which enchants our inconstant hearts."

Allured by the beauty of the morning, thus conversing they pursued their way across the common. It was a most beautiful common — we have not such another in the north. It had been formerly a forest, and was yet in parts covered with magnificent and ancient trees. Helen's little dog ran bounding on before them, jumping over the now golden fern, and delighting in the rustling noise, which even his light form occasioned among fallen leaves; and quite astonished, when a quicker breeze investing with life his dead playthings, they flew in eddying circles around him.

"Little Fairy," said Helen, "is enjoying his walk — he seems to suspect that it may be his last for this year."

Fairy soon ran crouching to the side of his mistress — he was frightened at some hissing geese, who had drawn themselves up in battle array at the gate of a farmhouse.

"Here we are at Ford's gate," said Mr. Latimer. "You must be tired, Helen — would you not like to go in and rest?"

"I am not at all tired; but I should like very much to go in to pay Mrs. Ford a visit. I have not seen her since her illness."

Having dispersed Fairy's enemies, they passed through the gate across a pretty orchard, where some men were busy gathering the last apples into the farm-house. Ford, who was a most respectable and honest man, was the proprietor of the small homestead on which he lived, one of the few small farms which still managed to struggle on, in spite of political economy. Mr. Molesworth, who was no political economist, respected this man's rights, and was always glad to assist him in maintaining his independence, and both he and Mr. Latimer always treated him with the consideration his industry and good qualities so fully merited.

Our companions lifted the latch, and at once entered the tidy kitchen, where everything, as bright and neat as usual, showed that the mistress was about again. Mrs. Ford soon herself appeared from an inner room. Her eyes sparkled when she saw Helen.

"Oh dear, Miss — is it you? I am so glad to see you."

The good woman bustled to set chairs for her visitors, carefully wiping them down with her apron (a most unnecessary precaution), as she placed them.

"I hope Mrs. Ford," said Helen kindly, "that you are not moving about too much!"

"Oh thank you Miss I now feel quite strong again: it was only yesterday I was saying to my good man that I thought I could get as far as the great house to thank you for your kindness."

"You must not be in a hurry to do that," said Helen. "I shall be very glad to see you, but you must await awhile, before you take such a long walk."

"I am able to move about now without feeling a bit the worse for it, I assure you Miss. I sent the girl away last Saturday — I was quite glad to be busy again," and as Mrs. Ford spoke, she arranged some little matters upon the shelves over the dresser, which seemed to her precise eye to be misplaced. "Somehow or other, I don't seem quite to rights yet."

"And yet," said Mr. Latimer, "your house looks as it always did, the neatest in the parish."

The good woman much gratified, smiled in reply to her pastor's commendation.

"I am sure Miss," she said, turning to Helen, "that I am able to do anything again. I must thank you, for, under God's mercy! — I am sure it was that good jelly you sent me that brought all my strength back again."

At this moment the farmer himself entered. He was a fine specimen of a once numerous and noble race, now alas! nearly extinct — the blunt, the honest, the true old English yeoman.

"My man told me Sir," said he, addressing Mr. Latimer, "as how you and Miss was paying my mistress a visit; so I thought to myself I would just step in to tell you how we settled the matter about old Tom Roberts, and I wished to thank the young lady too, for all her kindnesses to my dame."

"I am glad to find your wife so well," said Helen.

"Thank ye, she is quite fierce again this last week, and I am sure she may thank you for it Miss."

Mrs. Ford taking advantage of her husband's entrance, had dived into her pocket for the key of her most favoured stores, and now approached her guests with a bottle of her best cowslip wine. Mr. Latimer and Helen could not refuse her pressing solicitations to taste the beverage on which she so particularly prided herself.

While Mr. Latimer was occupied in listening to the farmer's long history of a Vestry meeting, Helen was hearing the equally lengthened story of all the particulars of Mrs. Ford's illness and recovery.

At last, however, the visit terminated. Arthur Latimer's headache had yielded to the influence of his beautiful companion, and he returned home, thinking with Helen, that an autumn breeze on Hartlebury common was the most inspiriting thing in the world.

"I shall tell my mother," said he smiling as he parted from Helen, "that a work of charity prevented you calling on her today!"

CHAPTER I

Mr. Bohun commences his personal canvass

The next morning, amid the ringing of bells and the cheers of the populace, Mr. Bohun, attended by Col. Neville, Mr. Chace, and Mr. George Gainsborough, and half-a-dozen of the most influential of the un-whigged Liberals, commenced his personal canvass of Fanchester. In spite of the most adverse circumstances, it was by no means an unfavourable one. The Whigs rather alarmed, wrote up to town for their champion to come down instantly. The Tories not sorry to see a split in the hostile camp, watched the fray with renewed hopes. After a long morning's work, Mr. Bohun made a speech of two hours' duration, from Mrs. Escott's balcony, to the multitude. It was impossible to decide in which he was most happy, his advocacy of popular rights, or his tirades of the pseudo-popular party. Invective and ridicule were showered unsparingly upon the Ministers whom, a few days before, the good people of Fanchester had believed to be the saviours of the nation, because they were told so by the newspapers, and any reflection upon whom they would have resented with cabbage-stalks and brick-bats. After the speech, another express was sent off by the alarmed Whigs for their man, who a month ago was huzzaed round the town. Mr. Bohun passed the evening in haranguing the Benefit Societies, and inoculating them with his new system of politics. His arguments and his manners were alike irresistible. They were equally astonished at his fluency and his fun; and when he refreshed himself after an oration, by smoking with the greatest nonchalance a pipe of shag-tobacco, the victory seemed decided. All the benefit societies agreed that they had not only at length found the man they wanted, a true patriot, but that Bohun, "the friend of the people", smoked a pipe better than any man in the whole county of ——shire.

Never was a country town in such a state of agitation. It

seemed that nobody ever thought of going to bed. Long past midnight, groups of persons were still loitering about, and ever and anon, night was made hideous by a lusty cheer from some still illuminated public house. Even the children in arms were taught by their enraptured mothers to lisp, "Bohun for ever", that charming young man, who had a smile and a compliment for every petticoat: not an urchin passed the dwelling of a Whig leader without saluting the trembling owner with the odious watchword.

At length Mr. Bohun returned to the castle, flung himself on a sofa, slept for two hours like Napoleon or Wellington in the midst of a pitched battle, woke, took his bath, and by break of day was again on horseback with his train, apparently in every part of Fanchester and its extensive boundaries at the same moment.

"What shall we do this morning?" said Mr. Chace.

"Agitate," replied his principal, "agitate, agitate. That magic word is the essence of all political success."

"What shall I do, Bohun?" said George Gainsborough.

"Anything you like my dear fellow, only agitate, agitate, agitate."

So off they scampered agitating, over downs and commons, highways and byeways; hedges did not stop them; the astonished farmers were prepossessed in favour of a candidate who always rode on before his committee, and without any ceremony leaped the five-bar gates of their farm-yards.

George Gainsborough was a Patroclus worthy of this Achilles, and shared his popularity. Col. Neville was an admirable rider, but George Gainsborough could talk as well as ride. The town of Fanchester fairly lost their senses. By ten o'clock, Mr. Bohun and his friends, splashed to their chins, were again caracoling down the High Street. His train swelled every instant; every man who could mount a horse was with the Squire, all covered with green ribbons. Mr. Bohun only wore in his breast a sprig of myrtle presented to him by Miss Molesworth.

But with all this superficial appearance of triumph, the career of the new candidate was by no means so prosperous as it appeared. The Whig party at Fanchester was very strong. The oligarchy of the High Street were in general Whigs. Fanchester boasted of several considerable manufactories. Their masters, sleek sectarians of all denominations, who under the pretence of anti-slavery meetings, bible societies, and missions "to the heathen", were in fact always sapping the foundations of that church which was the only barrier against their barbarising creeds and customs again inundating the land, were all of course, supporters of the present administration, and full of what they called "gratitude" to Lord Grey. This click, though not numerous, was very powerful. Many a mortgage did they hold on the property of their less prosperous fellow-townsmen; many a small sum, at hard interest and short dates, were they in the habit of lending to the industrious without capital. This click hated Mr. Bohun. They hated him because he was a gentleman, they hated him because he had not a snub nose, because he was suspiciously curious in his linen, because his coat was not cut after their fashion, and because he rode thoroughbred horses: they hated him because he was always courteous to those over whom they tyrannised. No tyrants in the world like the sectarian oligarchy of a country town! A high Whig is at least grand in his haughtiness. He is a tyrant, but a tyrant on a great scale. He loves a coercion bill, he cares not how many infants may be sacrificed to the bloody Moloch of Manufacturing industry, but then he can talk of the bill of rights, and advocate the immediate emancipation of the Niggers; but a low Whig is the least human of all the combinations of human matter, for soul we cannot concede to those wretches with contracted minds and cold hearts. If ever a revolution come round in this once happy country, we may trace all our misery to the influence of the low Whigs. These are the real causes of Manchester massacres, though they are always abusing the magistracy; these are the men who, though they think they are only snuffing the candle in their own miserable hard-hearted parlours, are in fact lighting the torch of every incendiary in the kingdom. How the low Whigs did hate Mr. Bohun! They hated him with that intense predisposition of enmity, which cold-blooded, calculating, unsympathetic, selfish mortals always innately feel for a man of genius, a man whose generous and lively spirit always makes them ashamed of their dead, dunghill-like, existence.

Not knowing how to meet the electrical effect of Mr. Bohun,

they all declared that he was insincere. Narrow-minded, short-sighted people, who never act but from some gross impulse of immediate interest, unless their miserable minds can detect the quid pro-quo of every act of your conduct, always consider you a Charlatan. But the truth is, it was not merely a generous and confident spirit that made Mr. Bohun our advocate, and a strenuous advocate of popular rights, and even of their extension. That he was ambitious there is no doubt, and who but fools are not ambitious? but he had too great a stake in the existing order of society to precipitate a revolution, though he intended to ride the storm, if the hurricane did occur. And this I think was his duty. It is the fashion now "to go along with the people", but I think the people ought to be led, ought to have ideas given them by those whom nature and education have qualified to govern states and regulate the conduct of mankind.

Whatever might have been Mr. Bohun's fancies when absent from his country, his keen brain, on his return, soon detected the spirit of the Reform Bill. He saw it was a Whig measure, and not a democratic one. He perceived that its only object was to destroy the balance of parties in the state, and that it intrenched in power a party who by the course of circumstances, had become pledged to an anti-national policy. Mr. Bohun cared nothing about the wretched struggle of factions, but he wished to be the subject of a great empire, and not to sink into the miserable citizenship of a second-rate island. He knew the Tories could never have remained so long in power, unless they had maintained a national policy: he knew the Whigs, in expelling them from their places, were bound to maintain an adverse system, and therefore he foresaw the dismemberment of the Empire. This was the reason he opposed the Whigs.

Mr. Bohun, with great talents, extensive experience, and a mind imbued with all the profound and comprehensive spirit of modern philosophy, was not insensible to the change which must occur in the relations between the governors and governed. As a theoretical politician, he admitted this change, perhaps in its greatest possible extent: as a practical politician, he thought it the duty of a great statesman only to effect that quantity of change in the country whose destiny he regulated which could be achieved with deference to its existing constitution. As a general principle, he considered the existing constitution the fair gauge of the civilization of a country and its capability of amelioration. As a statesman, he would have proposed measures for England which would have received his opposition in Spain, and he would have legislated for France very differently to what he was prepared to do for his own country.

Mr. Bohun considered the Whigs as a party of political swindlers, who had obtained power by false pretences. They had been permitted to enter office on the pretence of making those changes which the spirit of the age required: instead of effecting this purpose, their only object had been to root up the power of their opponents, and to destroy that happy balance of parties in the state, which in an aristocratic country is indispensible to the freedom and felicity of the mass. Mr. Bohun was of opinion that with the present machinery of the constitution, it was almost impossible to dislodge the Whigs from office, and as they were pledged to pursue an anti-national policy, he consequently considered the country in imminent peril. He was desirous of seeing a new party formed, which while it granted those alterations in our domestic policy which the spirit of the age required, should maintain and prosecute the ancient external policy by which the empire had been founded, and of this party he wished to place himself at the head — a position which his high lineage — his splendid fortune — and his superior talents, justified him in contemplating. Deeming the dismemberment of the empire the necessary consequence of the Whigs long remaining in office, Mr. Bohun was of opinion that we should get rid of the Whigs at any price, and as he considered that result was impossible, according to the new constitution, he was the advocate of movement. Perceiving that the nomination of representatives, in the vast majority of the towns, was in the hands of the Sectarian low Whig Oligarchy, he thought that the only mode by which this barbarising power could be destroyed was to expand the Whig constituency into a national constituency. Mr. Molesworth and some of the old Tories denounced these doctrines as revolutionary, and thought Mr. Bohun mad, or only amusing his audience; but Mr. Molesworth, though a sensible man, spoke on this subject from prejudice, and not from thought.

The nucleus of the Tory party at Fanchester was the corporation. The corporation was most unpopular. Their chief was a jolly brewer— a regular John Bull— a member of the Pitt club, — and an abhorrer of the French. He was unpopular as a mayor, but as a man was, nevertheless, the favourite of the town. The populace laughed even when they gave him a gentle hoot. He was a portly man, with a rubicund visage, very shrewd, and nothing of a bigot. He loved to go to church in state, with his robes and aldermen— his beadles and silver maces. He was the chief supporter of Sir George Vavasour, the Tory candidate, and held up his head, though no one knew better that Toryism was at a terrible discount. However, the jolly brewer always put a good face upon public affairs, and talked of "re-action". He had faith in the good common sense of Englishmen, and though he daily declared that the country had been irretrievably ruined by Catholic emancipation, and that for his part, he did not know where the constitution was, he was equally regular in his asseverations of his readiness to die for it any day of his life.

CHAPTER II

Arrival of two other candidates, and the consequences

It was nearly three o'clock, and the people were gathering, in expectation of another speech from Mr. Bohun. The popular candidate and his committee were canvassing in the environs. It was three o'clock — the crowd was gathering fast.

"I hope he will give it them today; eh Tim!" said a mechanic to his comrade, wiping his toiling brow.

"Oh, he'll play old Harry with them. You leave him alone!"

"My eye, though— don't I wish Lord Grey was here, just to hark a bit."

"He'll hark soon enough. I'll bet two bob now, Bohun comes in."

"My eye though — if he had only started a little earlier, eh Tim!"

"Oh! we'll bring him in yet — we'll bring him in on the shoulders of the people. It's the like of him we want. He don't want no place — not he."

"Place," said Mr. Gregson, a hair-dresser, who shaved the chief Whigs, "what should he want place for? He ay'nt a needy aristocrat. No fear of his feeding on the witals of the people — That's what I said to my wife. She's just mad for Bohun — ay'nt she though? — 'Leave me alone,' says I, 'I knows my duty.' He sha'nt lose it for me — and that's plump and plain."

"Go it Gregson," exclaimed Tim and his companion, in the most encouraging tone. "Don't care nothing for old Jenkins, doey? If they turn you out we'll find you another house."

"Oh! they've been at me already," responded Gregson with a very mysterious air. "My answer's short. 'Am I woter, or am I not? — If a woter I be, I suppose I may do what I like with my wote.' — 'And I suppose we may do what we like with our beards,' says Jenkins. 'Oh!' says I, 'if it comes to that, Mr. Bohun ay'nt the gentleman what will see a man wronged for supporting him.'"

"You be hanged for a barber. What's Bohun to you?" said a Whig mobocrat.

"Cut him over," cried out the mob. "He's a Grey-beard — Bohun for ever — Cut him over — Smash him."

"Your boy has just as much chance as puss in a snare," replied the Whig Cleon.

"The one you poached last night, eh! Master Thorpe?" halloed out another voice. There was a general laugh at Thorpe, who however was a practised bully, and soon rallied.

"Well I am sorry for your young gentleman," said Thorpe, "for he don't want pluck."

"No! — he don't want no pluck," said another Whig — a cautious man, who feeling himself in the minority, deprecated hostilities.

"I know who does," said Tim.

"Do you mean me?" said bully Thorpe.

"What if I do?" said Tim.

"You'll see!" said Thorpe.

"So do I now," said Tim.

"So you shan't long," said Thorpe, "for I'll bung up your spectacles."

"Two can play at that," said Tim.

"A ring — a ring!" hallooed the crowd. "Bohun for ever. Three groans for Earl Grey. No Prigmore! — Three cheers for Bohun — Three groans for Prigmore — No Whigs — Vavasour for ever — There's a Tory! — The Tories are better than the Whigs — No, they ay'nt — Yes they are! — They are most honest — No Whigs — no taxes — no Prigmore — no nothing. Bohun for ever — He's a Tory — You be d—d — He ay'nt — Why does Squire Molesworth support him? — He don't — Yes he do — You lie — So do you — Say that twice — What then? — You'll see — So I do now — A ring — a ring! — No fight — No go — Hallo! who's this?"

For at this moment, proceeding at a very rapid pace, though somewhat impeded by the multitude, which every moment became denser, a post-chariot-and-four dashed up to the Rose Hotel. A most supreme valet lolled on the box, and seemed conscious that the mob had assembled to gaze upon him. The orange favours announced Sir George Vavasour, and soon the smiling face of the courteous Baronet was seen smirking and bowing from the window. At his last appearance, Sir George Vavasour had been very roughly treated by his intended constituents, for they were then full of gratitude to Lord Grey; but the enlightening eloquence of Mr. Bohun had already worked marvels. Scarcely one hoot was heard; the corporation candidate was received with calm indifference. Sir George a very sanguine man, was delighted with the "re-action", and already began to flatter himself that he might again sit as M.P. for Fanchester.

Past three o'clock: the afternoon coach arrived, and stopped at the Griffin, the inn opposite to the Rose. A tall, thin, young man, very plainly dressed, with a remarkably acid expression of visage, sharp nose, and sallow complexion, jumped out and hurried into the inn. Soon a murmur was heard, which every moment increased, and at length burst into a shout which rent the skies.

"Prigmore! — Prigmore!"

"Is he here?"

"Sure*ly*! He came by the coach," said Tim the Radical, with a smile of derision.

"Outside," added his companion, with a sneer.

"What do you think of your man now Master Thorpe?" enquired Mr. Tim.

Even Thorpe could not answer. It was some time before he could recover the blow of supporting a candidate who travelled by a public conveyance.

"Oh, he'll get a place soon, Master Thorpe, and then he can keep his carriage," said Tim.

"And you can be coachman Master Thorpe," said his companion, "and then you'll have a place too."

Thorpe moved away to head the Whig mob, which began to assemble beneath the windows of the Griffin.

"Prigmore for ever!" exclaimed their leader.

"Three cheers! again, again, again! one cheer more! Prigmore for ever. He's the man."

But the cheering was very faint indeed.

"Bohun for ever!" cried out a voice.

"Bohun for ever!" responded ten thousand.

"Nine times more. Again! again! again! Again! again! again! Nine cheers more! We will have him."

At this moment Mr. Bohun's band of music with colours flying, one glorious standard touching almost the opposite houses with its flowing drapery, passed in martial pomp down the High Street. The cheering was enthusiastic, and amid all this excitement, the High Street crowded, the windows of the houses filled with anxious spectators, and dressed out in the opposite colours, Sir George Vavasour smiling and bowing at the parlour window of the Rose, and Mr. Prigmore still invisible, Aubrey Bohun and his train cantered up to the Rose Hotel.

There was a shout that rent the skies.

"God bless him," said the men.

"God bless his curly locks," said the women. "We will have him, we must have him. Bohun for ever."

"I'll never kiss the lips that don't shout Bohun," cried out a beautiful bold girl, the leader of those unhappy victims of our virtue, who in moments of popular excitement generally distinguish themselves, and it is curious are then only treated with consideration.

"Bravo Kitty!" exclaimed a thousand voices.

"Here goes, Bohun for ever!" shouted a young man. "Mr. Bohun, I promise you my vote and they may turn me out if they like. I don't care."

"Well done Ned Hathaway," said Kitty. "I'll send you a favour for that."

"I thank you my friend," said Mr. Bohun as he shook hands with his new supporter, "but I would sooner lose my election than injure one honest man."

"Bravo," shouted the mob.

"That's noble!" exclaimed one.

"I'd get up in the night to serve him," shouted another.

"He's the man!" said a third.

"We will have him," was the universal exclamation.

Aubrey had now reached the portico of the Rose, and was about to dismount. The mob were ranged in rows to shake his hand. The women were even more unreasonable. But Aubrey Bohun had the art of never appearing in a ridiculous position. Without the least bustle he seemed to shake hands with a thousand at once, and taking up one very pretty little girl in his arms made her the representative of her sex, and pressing on her lips one graceful embrace, escaped into the Hotel, amid the enthusiastic cheers of an immense multitude, hundreds of whom at that moment would literally have sacrificed their lives in his service with delight.

"Gentlemen excuse me," said Mr. Bohun, as he entered his crowded committee-room, and threw himself upon a sofa, "Gainsborough my dear fellow, this is harder work than the Morea. For God's sake get me something to eat. The quantities of ale and brandy water that I have poured down this unhappy throat today have given me a most unnatural appetite."

Away bustled George Gainsborough, and in a few minutes Mr. Bohun was refreshing himself with a cold pasty.

"This is existence!" he exclaimed, "why don't you eat Gainsborough? After all there is nothing like physical gratification."

"You will speak of course Mr. Bohun?" said his chairman.

"Of course, but let my tongue do other duty for a short while, my dear Scroggin. Besides I should like to hear Prigmore, I long to answer him."

"Gentlemen, Mr. Prigmore is going to speak," shouted the entering waiter.

"Io triumphe!" exclaimed Aubrey Bohun. "Now comes the tug of war. Waiter bring me a potato if you have such a thing. Gainsborough my dear fellow just reconnoitre a moment."

Away again bustled George Gainsborough, and shortly returned.

"Don't hurry yourself Bohun. Prigmore has not yet made his appearance."

"Perhaps the cock will not fight," said Mr. Scroggin, "I should not wonder."

"He must," said George Gainsborough. "Besides several of his supporters are on the portico of the Griffin."

A faint cheer was heard, and then a loud mixed shouting which seemed to increase in violence every instant.

"Gentlemen!" shouted an entering waiter, "Mr. Prigmore is out."

Up jumped Mr. Bohun, and followed by Col. Neville, George Gainsborough, Mr. Scroggin, and several other of his supporters, ran up stairs, and unnoticed by the mob observed the scene.

There was Mr. Prigmore with his hat off looking like patience on a monument, though not smiling. Every time he attempted to address the multitude, the lulling uproar burst forth with renewed clamour.

"Gentlemen!" said Mr. Prigmore.

"Well, you've said that before," said one of his auditors.

"No stranger," shouted another.

"No treasury nominee."

"Resident Representatives!"

"No Whigs!"

"Bohun for ever, Hurra!"

"Bohun and Independence!"

"Gentlemen," repeated Mr. Prigmore.

"Don't look down in the mouth. Bohun won't eat you."

"Prigmore and Reform!" halloed Thorpe in a stentorian voice.

"Hurra! Prigmore and Reform," echoed Thorpe's satellites.

Now arose a hissing and hooting, which exceeded anything

that had yet occurred, mingled with shouts of Bohun for ever.

"Oh! you ugly fellow!" shouted the Amazonian Kitty. "You a member of Parliament! why you ayn't a man!"

"Go it Kitty, go it Kitty. Give it him!"

"Gentlemen," said Mr. Prigmore. "Fair play is the characteristic of (terrible hooting) Englishmen," shouted Mr. Prigmore at the height of his voice.

"That's noble," shouted Master Thorpe. "That's noble, Prigmore and fair play!"

"Hear him, hear him!" exclaimed many even of the Bohunites.

"We don't want him," responded others.

"We won't have him. We won't have him at no price. We don't want nothing of him."

"Go back to town."

"Book him an inside place!"

"Gentlemen," said Mr. Prigmore, and he put on his hat, and affected to retire.

"Don't let him retire," said Mr. Bohun. "Speak to the people Scroggin. Get him a hearing."

Mr. Scroggin jumped out on the portico of the Rose, and was received with a loud cheer. Scroggin loved to make a speech. There was comparative silence.

"Fellow townsmen," said Mr. Scroggin.

"It is the wish of Mr. Bohun that everyone should have fair play."

"That's noble!" exclaimed the Bohunites.

"That's noble!" echoed Master Thorpe.

Mr. Prigmore still continued standing with his hat on. In about five minutes there was a lull. Mr. Prigmore took his hat off. The clamour recommenced but more feeble.

"Hush! Hush!" said many of the leading Bohunites. "Hear him, hear him!"

And at length they did hear him. Mr. Prigmore was an acute, cold, fluent man. The Fanchester people thought him a great orator till they heard Mr. Bohun, because he was never at a loss for words, and spoke with authority on subjects which they did not comprehend. Mr. Prigmore was a barrister by calling; but the profession only masked the political adventurer. He commenced life as an extreme Radical, and wrote articles against

Lords and Ladies in the Westminster Review. When the Whigs juggled themselves into office, Mr. Prigmore left off abusing the Aristocracy, and only anathematised the Tories. His political economy, and his brazen assurance had quite humbugged the Whigs, who are themselves the most ignorant people in the world of all those who presume to be statesmen. Prigmore got a commissionership in one of the numerous Whig jobs, wrote a pamphlet against Corporations dedicated to Lord Durham, whom he described in the dedication as the hope of the country, and in return was sent down by Mr. Ellice as the Government candidate for Fanchester with a special letter to the eminent low Whig manufacturer, Mr. Jenkins.

Mr. Prigmore amid occasional interruptions made a speech of three quarters of an hour length full of the usual commonplaces of the click. Gratitude to Lord Grey, who had given the people "Reform", was the burthen of the song. The separate stanzas consisted of abuse of the Tories, praise of the Whigs, panegyrics of the great things they had done, promises of the great things they would do. Vague generalities about retrenchment, reform, reduction of expenditure, reduction of taxation, were mixed up with some attacks in details on the Corn Laws, corrupt corporations, and parson magistrates.

Now and then Thorpe raised a faint cheer, but the people listened with indifference and impatience. Mr. Jenkins who stood by the side of Mr. Prigmore, looked gloomy but firm. At length Mr. Prigmore put on his hat, and this was the only moment of dead silence which had occurred during the day.

At this moment Mr. Bohun, who was a perfect master of stage effect, stepped out on the portico of the Rose. An acclamation rent the skies. Individual exclamations were lost in the universal cheer. Nothing was seen but the waving of hats and handkerchiefs and flags, and Mr. Bohun's band of course immediately struck up "See the conquering hero!"

This was an opportunity Mr. Bohun had long courted. He had made so many speeches during the few days he had been a Candidate for Fanchester, that he really began to find some difficulty in discovering novel topics to vary his discourses. He longed to have an opponent to reply to, and now he had found one. Unhappy Prigmore, never was a man so scarified! It was quite evident that the speaker was himself in a state of almost ecstatic enjoyment. He seemed himself almost intoxicated with his inexhaustible sarcasm. His teeming fancy fired with the maddening shouts of the populace. There is nothing like a good thundering cheer to prompt a man's imagination. Unhappy Prigmore! His friends before Mr. Bohun's appearance had quite piqued themselves on his acid acuteness. Even after Mr. Bohun's first impassioned orations, they consoled themselves by the conviction that his "flowery verbosity" must shrink before the Prigmore powers of ridicule. But alas! what was their disappointment and mortification when they found their desolate champion with a face like an unhealthy lemon exposed to the reckless laughter of the mob. Mr. Jenkins affected to treat Mr. Bohun as rude and personal, and recommended Mr. Prigmore to withdraw into the Hotel. They did withdraw, but amid the jeers of all present.

"What you've had enough of it," said one.

"What, your cock won't fight, eh! Jenkins?" exclaimed another.

"Send him back to town," said a third.

"Book him an inside place," said a fourth.

"Oh! you snivelling wretch," said Kitty.

Amid a loud shout of "Bohun for ever", the popular candidate continued, and growing more earnest and impassioned, after the retreat of his discomfited rival, he wound up with a peroration whose elaborate gorgeousness made George Gainsborough tremble for its success. But the fact is no people relish eloquence of the highest order so much as the lowest mob. They understand or seem to understand everything. Allusion to History which they have never read, metaphorical expressions drawn from sources of which they have no experience — with all they sympathise.

"There's no one like him," said Tim to his brother mechanic. "Did'st ever hear such language?"

"I love his similies," responded his companion. "They is so purty!"

Mr. Bohun made his bow, and retired, and there arose a round of cheering which would not have disgraced a triumphant navy.

"No Prigmore, no Jenkins!" said one of the lesser agitators.

"Drive him out of the town," said another.

And accordingly the mob made a rush at the Griffin, but the door was stoutly barricadoed. The Whigs made a good resistance, and the mob only broke the windows. Perhaps the arrival at this moment of Mr. Bohun's britchka from the Castle, occasioned a diversion favourable to Mr. Prigmore's safety. The mob instantly turned to the equipage, and as Mr. Bohun, Colonel Neville, and Mr. George Gainsborough jumped in, took out the horses, and followed by the whole town dragged the candidate in triumph to the ancient seat of his fathers!

CHAPTER III

A secret interview between two very great men

About ten o'clock of the same evening that Mr. Bohun demolished the Treasury nominee, Mr. Chumfield the jolly Tory brewer, and Mayor of Fanchester, quietly opened his street-door, and perceiving that no one was observing him, he made his way down one of the most obscure back streets, and so, after much winding and dodging, he finally, like the fountain of Arethusa, which sank in Greece to rise again in Sicily, re-appeared at the top of the very High Street, at the bottom of which his own house was situate. Here, giving one or two cautious glances around, he went up to the door of a great brick house with five windows in front, and knocked very softly. The door was opened by a comely dame of a certain age.

"Is your master gone to-bed?" enquired Mr. Chumfield.

"Lawk! your worship, who can think of going to bed in these timbersome times!" responded the housekeeper of Mr. Alderman Baggs, "when we may wake in the morning and not find a single pane of glass to see through."

"Nay, good Mistress Dolly," said the jocose Chumfield, "you are not a Whig, and so you need not be afeared."

"Whigs and Tories! Mr. Mayor — I am sure I do not know what your worship means; but I think it very hard that a quiet body cannot go to bed, moreover when she is used to regular hours. It's not decorous or decent in the magistracy, I am thinking, not to have special constables to guard the aldermans' houses."

"And housekeepers too, eh Mrs. Dolly?"

"And why not Mr. Mayor?"

"Nay, I think you have the better right of the two," said Mr. Chumfield, "for you are a woman, and a very handsome one."

"Well I am sure Mr. Mayor, I wish that all the worshipful Court had as stout hearts as your worship has; but I am sorry to say that when there's anything of a mob my poor master is in a manner just nothing but an old scare-crow. He do detest mobs, that he do; and truth to speak, they are very timbersome things."

"Well, my good mistress, it is not mob-law yet; so go please you to Mr. Baggs, and tell him I would speak with him. Nay I'll wait here, for he is not used to be called on late."

Mr. Baggs was an old bachelor, and the senior alderman of the Corporation. He had retired from business with a large fortune, and lived in what was called a very handsome manner. Moreover having no relations people wondered what he would do with his money, and some thought he would build a hospital. Had it not been for the Reform Bill, he would certainly have repaired the town-hall, and as it was, he presented the church with a new clock. He was looked upon as having what is called a very long head, and some said that had he not been a Tory, he might have had a chance of being M.P. for the town himself; but others laughed at this, and said that even Chumfield and his own party would join Jenkins, and vote against him, so jealous were all these High Street oligarchs of each other. However, there was no fear of this catastrophe — for Mr. Baggs was the most timid, cautious personage in the world, without a spark of ambition out of the High Street. There all his genius was concentered — there he was really a great man — in the House of Commons he felt that he should only be a little one. Mr. Baggs's wealth entitled him to the leadership of the Corporation party — but Baggs was quite a man of the Cabinet. He detested public assemblies and active pursuits. He could not make a speech, though he was more famous in close council than any of his brethren. He worked therefore with Chumfield, he was a fearless orator, had a high opinion of his judgment, and who paid him the greatest deference.

In a few moments Mrs. Dolly came forth from the parlour, and begged his worship to enter. The mayor found his friend Mr. Baggs sitting over the fire in a meditative position, stirring with moody touch a glass of very weak brandy and water. Chumfield was going to speak, but Baggs put his finger to his mouth, and begging Mrs. Dolly to bring some fresh glasses, hot water, and sugar, and open the spirit chest, Mr. Baggs begged his friend to be seated.

"We cannot be too cautious in these times Chumfield," said his host as Dolly departed. "I have a high opinion of Dolly; but she is a woman."

"She is," said the jolly Chumfield, "and has been a remarkably handsome one. I commend your taste neighbour Baggs."

But Mr. Baggs was in no humour for a joke: he shook his head, and glancing suspiciously round the room, drew his chair still nearer to the mayor. Chumfield was mixing his tumbler of brandy and water; as the sugar melted, he looked up, and caught the countenance of Baggs, charged with mysterious meaning.

"I am glad you have come tonight, Chumfield," said he. "These are strange times. Dolly tells me there is a great dinner at Jenkins'."

"Likely enough neighbour, and I am sure however scanty the repast, today has given them plenty to digest."

"I was thinking of the same thing," responded Baggs, in a very low voice. "I don't know what to make of all this. Neighbour Chumfield, these are strange times. I don't see my way."

" 'Tis a crooked lane," replied the mayor, "but if we don't stick in the mud, we may come to the end of it."

"Only to think what times we live in," said Mr. Baggs. "Why they care no more for the corporation than they do for a set of old-clothes-men. Why what do you think? — there was a boy in the street yesterday, as I was passing along, and he halloed out 'there goes a humbug of an Alderman'. It shows the spirit of the times."

"Yes, we are certainly at a discount," replied the jolly brewer with a smile, "but things will mend Mr. Baggs — things will look up yet."

"I don't know what to say to it, my good Sir, I don't know what to say to it. Reform — open elections — When I wake in the morning I can't believe it. Aldermen laughed at by little boys in the street. I almost wished we had conceded a little now Chumfield. I wish we had made Jenkins an Alderman."

"Jenkins has it not all his own way yet," said the jolly brewer.

"You think he hasn't?" said Mr. Baggs, somewhat quickly. "Well, it does my heart good to hear it. I am sure, if we could only keep down that fellow Jenkins, I scarcely care who were in power. We have had our day Chumfield. I am content — that is, I should be content if Jenkins only could be baffled. What says Sir George?"

"Haven't you seen him?"

"Oh! dear me, no. I have not stirred out today. I know nothing that has happened, except what Dolly told me, and she generally knows all. Frightful times these — frightful! frightful! I can't bear to hear of broken windows, it always makes my blood turn cold."

"But they were not our windows," said Chumfield. "It's Jenkins that the mob are at."

"So Dolly tells me," replied Mr. Baggs with a quick tone and sparkling eye, "but I can't believe it."

"It's true enough though; and what's more, they are all obliged to dine in the back parlour."

"Well, we live in strange times! Jenkins pelted!"

"Tremendously!"

"And his windows broken!"

"Every one of them!"

"There's a good spirit in the place, if it could only be directed," said Mr. Baggs musingly.

"That's the very thing I come about," said Chumfield. "If we only look about ourselves we may gain the day yet."

"Ah! the Tories," said Mr. Baggs despondingly. "It's all over with us. A Tory wont go down now."

"Anything better than a Whig," said Chumfield.

"Mr. Bohun is a gentleman," said Mr. Baggs, "but then Sir George?"

"Has no sort of chance," said Chumfield.

"We must stick to our colours," said Baggs.

"But if we have no ship of our own, we must turn privateers," said Chumfield, who loved a nautical metaphor, "and fight under the flag of another state."

"I don't see my way," said Baggs. "I would sooner vote for Bohun than Prigmore."

"Bohun is an opposition candidate," said Chumfield, "and we are the opposition party."

"That's very true," said Baggs, "but then Sir George?"

"Is a man of sense," said Chumfield. "If we can only beat Jenkins now, we may bring in the Baronet another time."

"I wish he was of our opinion," said Baggs.

"He is," said Chumfield. "He dined with me today; and if we will support Bohun, he'll resign."

"Anything to keep down that fellow Jenkins," said Baggs. "The airs his family give themselves are quite disgusting. Dolly says they never notice her now."

"We can beat him," said Chumfield.

"He is very strong," replied Baggs. "I wish Mr. Bohun had started earlier."

"We can give him one hundred and fifty votes," said Chumfield.

"It goes against my heart to call those ten pounders votes," said Baggs.

"The Reform Act is the law of the land now," said Chumfield.

"It is indeed," agreed Baggs despondingly. "It will make the fortune of Jenkins. If he brings in Prigmore, all his sons will have places."

"I shouldn't wonder," said Chumfield.

"We shan't be able to hold up our heads," said Baggs.

"Not a man John of us," agreed Chumfield.

"I wish I could see Sir George," said Mr. Baggs. "I have voted for him these five and thirty years."

"Will you step on to the Rose?" said Chumfield.

"I dread the night air," said Baggs. "Dolly will tell you I have not been out after sunset for these thirty years."

"But think of Jenkins," said Chumfield. "If we could only coalesce with the Bohun party, it will seem as if we return our own member."

"I wish I could see my way," said Baggs.

"It is as clear as a pike staff," said Chumfield, and he took out his pocket book. "Here is the registration — nine hundred votes, and Jenkins pretends that he has five hundred promises; but promises you know are like pie-crust. Depend upon it there's a re-action. Now do come and speak a word to Sir George. I'll settle it with Dolly."

"Well I don't know," said Mr. Baggs, "well wrapped up, with a silk handkerchief over my mouth, I don't think I could come to much harm."

"It is a very mild night," said Chumfield, "quite like summer."

"No fog?" enquired Baggs.

"Not a breath," said Chumfield. "Let me speak to Dolly."

"Well my dear friend, anything for my King and country, and to keep down that fellow Jenkins. If we could but bring in Mr. Bohun, as you say, he would be in a manner the Corporation member. But they say he is a Radical?" added Mr. Baggs.

"Fiddle-de-dee, he has thirty thousand a year," said Chumfield. "I am not afeared of such Radicals as those."

"It will be a death-blow to Jenkins," said Mr. Baggs. "I wish Bohun had canvassed earlier. I am afraid they have the start of us."

"The race is never won till it is lost," said Chumfield.

"I should not like to move without we are sure," said the cautious Alderman.

"We are sure," said the sanguine Mayor — "Bohun is the winning horse, or my name is not Chumfield."

"It would be a death-blow to Jenkins," said Baggs musingly.

"He's done — he's diddled," said Chumfield. "He never would be able to hold up his head again. He was cock sure— he was indeed. It was a thousand to one in his favour. He has pledged himself to the Treasury to bring in Prigmore, — I know it, I know it as a fact. I know it from a friend in town; and then he will be Mayor next year, and go up to town and be knighted!"

"You don't say so!" said Baggs in a voice of terror. "Speak to Dolly— I'll go directly— I'll see Sir George. We can tell him we will bring him in next time— we can, can't we Chumfield? I'll ring the bell— I'll order my great coat, and I'll put a handkerchief round my mouth. I'll do anything, anything in the world to crush that fellow Jenkins."

CHAPTER IV

The perplexities of Mr. Gainsborough, senior

While all these memorable transactions were occurring, there was not perhaps, of all the characters of our history, anyone in a condition of more painful perplexity than Mr. Gainsborough senior. Long before Mr. Bohun's return to England, Mr. Gainsborough acting in pursuance of those liberal views which always regulated his public conduct, and his vanity gratified by taking what he styled "a leading part", had pledged himself to Mr. Prigmore, and not only pledged himself, but had become even one of his committee. And now, here was his son the prime counsellor and bosom friend of Mr. Prigmore's opponent; and the whole neighbourhood, whose acquaintance he had been sedulously courting for the last seven years were, whatever they might pretend, doubtless not less deeply interested in Mr. Bohun's success. Mr. Gainsborough, as he declared fifty times every day, was "most awkwardly situated". The poor man was really half out of his mind. All night Mrs. Gainsborough, and all day Miss Gainsborough, poured upon him their reproaches and their supplications.

"My dear Mary, what am I to do," in vain he endeavoured to reply. "I am pledged, I am pledged to Mr. Prigmore. I am bound not only to vote for him, but to use all my influence in his favour. I am one of his committee, one of Mr. Prigmore's committee. Was ever anything so unfortunate? No one can deny but that I am most awkwardly situated. What shall I do, what can I do?— Vote for Mr. Prigmore I must. To please you, and to gratify George, I will take as little active part as possible. I will speak to Jenkins, I will speak to Mr. Prigmore — I will speak to them as a man of the world. Jenkins is a man of the world himself— Mr. Prigmore is a man of the world— they are both men of the world: I will speak to them candidly and openly. I will tell them how I am situated— how very awkwardly

I am situated. Can I do more? My dear Mary, can I do more? Fanny is it possible for any man to do more? I am sure I admire Mr. Bohun as much as anyone. I don't quite understand his politics, but no one can admire him more than I do. I am sure George may well be proud of such a friend. George always had talents in making friends. And now he has a most distinguished friend. It is impossible to say what Mr. Bohun will not do for him. If Mr. Bohun succeed, I must say I think it is all owing to George. He seems to me never to go to bed. I hope he won't knock himself up. I am sure I wish Mr. Bohun success. No one more sincerely. I am sure I hope he will succeed, though Jenkins says it is ridiculous, and that he has no chance."

"How can he have a chance?" said Mrs. Gainsborough reproachfully, "when his friends, his particular friends vote against him."

"My dear Mary!" said Mr. Gainsborough entreatingly.

"I know nothing about politics," said Miss Gainsborough: "But all I know Papa, for our family not to support Mr. Bohun with all their influence, seems to me to say the least, quite unnatural."

"Was there ever such a girl!" exclaimed the despairing father. "Well I am sure I don't know how it will end. I wish their committees would compare notes, and that the weakest would resign. I am very ready to be arbitrator, and as I have promised Mr. Prigmore to vote for him, and really wish Mr. Bohun to succeed, I think I am just the person to be a very impartial umpire. I'll speak to Jenkins."

"What is the use of speaking to Jenkins, if he persists in saying Mr. Bohun has no chance," said Mrs. Gainsborough.

"Jenkins, indeed!" said Miss Gainsborough, "what is Jenkins to us— Jenkins! what a name. I am sure I should never think of keeping a promise to a man named Jenkins."

"My dear wife— my own Fanny— do be calm. Consider, do consider, consider how awkwardly I am situated."

At this moment the servant entered the room with a despatch from the committee-room at Fanchester. Thus it ran:

GLORIOUS NEWS!!

Rose, 10 o'clock.

Dear Father,

Vavasour has withdrawn in our favour. The Tories coalesce with us heartily. Scroggin has resigned the chairmanship to Chumfield. We shall beat them — we shall beat them. You must vote for us. Bohun for ever! Huzza!

Your affectionate son,

G.G.

"Glorious!" exclaimed Mrs. Gainsborough.

"I shall die with joy," said Miss Gainsborough.

"I wish Prigmore was at the devil," said Mr. Gainsborough. "I am certainly most awkwardly situated. I think I will ride over to Hartlebury and talk it over with Mr. Molesworth."

"Do my love," said Mrs. Gainsborough.

"Do, dearest papa," said Miss Gainsborough.

"Mr. Molesworth is a most sensible man," added Mrs. Gainsborough.

"And Miss Molesworth a most charming girl," said Miss Gainsborough. "And they are both for Mr. Bohun. You cannot refuse anything to Miss Molesworth papa. You know everybody says there is a regular flirtation between you."

Mr. Gainsborough gave a smile of complacent perplexity, and half sighing, rang the bell and ordered his horse.

When Mr. Gainsborough arrived at Hartlebury, he found a large party assembled. There was Mrs. Escott, and Mrs. Neville, and several other young ladies from Fanchester, all assisting Miss Molesworth in making green favours. Mr. Molesworth was reading the newspaper.

"Well, Mr. Gainsborough," said Mrs. Escott, "I see you have come with the good news, Mr. Bohun turned Tory, always thought he was one, but I was too brisk for you. Only think of Mr. Bohun making his first speech from my balcony. Very handsome of him wasn't it? I call it the Bohun balcony now. You can't think what a favourite I am with the people. They are so grateful for my early support of their favourite. He had not so many friends then as he has now. Early friends are valued. The

Escotts were always early in the field, quite our family motto. And the people, poor things, are so grateful for it, they gave me such a cheer as the carriage passed. Very handsome of them, wasn't it?"

"I am making this favour for you Mr. Gainsborough," said Helen. "You must wear it for my sake."

"For your sake," said the guarded Gainsborough with a courteous smile. "I am too proud to wear anything; I am sure Mr. Bohun has no sincerer well-wisher than myself, but you know my dear Miss Molesworth, how awkwardly I am situated."

"Oh! nonsense," said Mrs. Neville in a very peremptory tone: "You must vote for Aubrey, and there is an end of the affair. I never intend to speak to any person again who does not vote for Aubrey."

"But my dear Mrs. Neville," piteously poured forth Mr. Gainsborough, "consider, do consider, consider how very awkwardly I am situated."

"I make it a rule never to consider," replied Mrs. Neville, "I hate considerate people."

"What am I to do, my dear Sir?" said Mr. Gainsborough to Mr. Molesworth, taking him aside by the button, "never was a man so awkwardly situated."

"You deserve it neighbour, you deserve it for ever having anything to do with the Whigs. I always told you, you would live to repent it."

"So you did," said the unhappy Gainsborough, "but surely Mr. Bohun's politics are not such as Mr. Molesworth would approve of."

"Oh! as for me, I have no vote, so it does not signify. If I had, I should have asked Sir George Vavasour to stand as a personal favour to myself, merely for the purpose of giving him my solitary suffrage."

"Well do you know my dear Sir," replied Mr. Gainsborough, "that considering all things you may thank your stars that Hartlebury is not in the boundaries, for I cannot help thinking," and here he glanced at Helen, "I cannot help thinking, that, taking everything into consideration, you would, like myself, have been very awkwardly situated."

"Well! I do not care how it ends," said Mr. Molesworth: "For my part I wish Sir George had stood. I hate compromise, I hate coalition, I hate concession of all kinds, but still I confess it is some consolation that they pelted Prigmore."

A loud ringing at the Hall bell, the door dashed open, and Mr. Bohun entered and alone.

"My colours, delightful sight," he gaily exclaimed, as he almost seized one from Miss Molesworth's hands, and pressed it to his lips. "How do you, how are you all? Emmeline we have scarcely seen each other of late. You must come and canvass for me. A pretty woman you know," said he turning to Miss Molesworth, "especially on horseback, is worth more than a whole committee. Ah! my dear Mrs. Escott, my first, my best friend, and Mr. Gainsborough too, what should I do without your son. Allow me to express my gratitude to his father."

"Mr. Bohun," said Mr. Gainsborough, as he shook the extended hand, "I can assure you that even George cannot be a sincerer well-wisher to you than his father. I wish I could say more. Unhappily I cannot, but I am sure you will pardon me. You know, my dear Sir, how very awkwardly I am situated."

"My good Sir, not a word. Whatever you do I shall ever consider myself your debtor."

"Well! that's very handsome," said Mrs. Escott, "ayn't it? More than I should say. And for my part I agree with Mrs. Gainsborough and your daughter, and your whole family, and all your circle of friends, that if you do not vote for Mr. Bohun it will be the most ridiculous thing I ever heard of."

Unhappy Mr. Gainsborough! This was riding over to Hartlebury for advice!

"Well how do you get on?" said Mr. Molesworth to Mr. Bohun, "if it be possible to get a word of truth out of a candidate."

"Why, to speak sheer truth," said Mr. Bohun, "they have the best of it; but considering that three days ago I had not a chance, I hope in three days more that the odds will change."

"I have escaped here for half an hour's relaxation," he continued in an undertone, to Miss Molesworth, "and with, I confess it with fear and trembling, a lurking hope that I might induce you to do me a great favour."

"Indeed! And what may it be?"

"I am summoning up courage to ask it," said Mr. Bohun,

looking round as if he could scarcely venture to make the request before so many auditors.

"Come gentles all," said Helen: "luncheon has been long ready. Mrs. Escott you must need refreshment after all the excitement of your cheers."

Mr. Molesworth offered his arm to Mrs. Neville, and Helen found hers almost unconsciously in Bohun's. As they walked along to the dining-room he said: "There is only one thing can gain the day."

"What?" said Helen somewhat eagerly.

"You and Emmeline must canvass for me."

"Papa!" said Helen shaking her head.

"I know the difficulty," said Bohun, "but the Tories now openly and avowedly support me. This will render it less annoying to him. But all that I can urge, your quick mind has already perceived. Dearest Miss Molesworth, do not deny me this great, this essential service, this paramount gratification."

"Nay! ask it as a service."

"I do, I do indeed."

"We must see."

"I know you can do anything. Do you think that I have no perceptions? I had not been four-and-twenty hours in your society, before I discovered that you were one of those persons whose influence no individual could resist."

"Nay! you are in your heroics! This is not the Portico of the Rose."

Mr. Bohun had too much tact not to join in the laugh, and thus they entered the dining-room.

CHAPTER V

The ladies canvass — Parliament is dissolved — nomination day

The next day Mrs. Neville and Miss Molesworth in green riding habits cantered into Fanchester, and canvassed for Mr. Bohun. They were accompanied only by their grooms, for any male companions would have marred the effect of their mission, and they had secret instructions as to the individuals whom they should endeavour to influence.

"I am sure you cannot refuse me Mr. Spring," said Miss Molesworth to an obdurate butcher.

"We do not ask you to vote for us," said Mrs. Neville, "only not to vote against us."

"The long and the short is ladies, I won't say nothing," was Mr. Spring's surly reply.

"Well I am sure," said Mrs. Neville, "this is the rudest reception we have met with in all Fanchester."

Mr. Spring whistled.

"And everybody told us Mr. Spring," said Miss Molesworth, "that you were such a particularly polite person to the ladies."

Encore whistling.

Mrs. Neville nodded to Miss Molesworth, as much as to say, there was no use in remaining. Miss Molesworth made a last desperate effort.

"You positively refuse me Mr. Spring?"

"Positive*ly* Miss," was the Spartan answer, and the ladies retired.

"I hope we shall have better fortune at this house," said Helen: "Walter, Thomas Walter, that's our man; owes money to Jenkins — now for an ingratiating smile."

"Well Mr. Walter, we have come to pay you a visit."

"I dare say you have Miss."

"What a very pretty child!" exclaimed Mrs. Neville.

"*Two* very pretty children!" exclaimed Miss Molesworth, "Is Mrs. Walter at home?"

"Yes, but can't see her."

"Are you sure we can't see her?"

"Quite sure," said Mr. Walter composedly.

"Will you give her a message from me?" said Miss Molesworth.

"Certainly Miss."

"Tell her then to use her influence with you to vote for Mr. Bohun."

"I can't say nothing about voting, Ma'am."

"Mr. Bohun is a neighbour," said Mrs. Neville.

"We ayn't seen much of him," responded Walter.

"But now he has come to live amongst you," replied Mrs. Neville.

"I hope he is Ma'am."

"Residence is surely a strong claim," said Miss Molesworth.

"Very true," said Walter.

"Mr. Prigmore does not reside here," said Mrs. Neville.

"No, nor anywhere else as ever I could learn," says Walter. "I am sure for my part I wish we had never had anything to do with this here Reform."

"Well that's exactly what we think ourselves, Miss Molesworth and I," said Mrs. Neville eagerly. "We are both of us against Reform, and therefore I hope you will support Mr. Bohun."

"I thought Mr. Bohun was for doing still more?" said Walter.

"Only to make everything quite right," said Mrs. Neville, "and to make you quite comfortable again Mr. Walter."

"I ayn't no objections to the gentleman myself," observed Walter more promisingly, "none whatsomever. I think he is as fit to be Member of Parliament as anyone. I said so to Mrs. Walter last night. I knows nothing against him, not I. But Mr. Jenkins is for Mr. Prigmore."

"And what is Mr. Jenkins to you?" said Mrs. Neville.

"Oh! nothing!" said Mr. Walter who, being a secret debtor, was very proud of his open independence. "Mr. Jenkins is nothing to me, my vote's my own, but still —"

He hesitated and turned away.

"Well I am sure I would not vote against my conscience to

please Mr. Jenkins," said Mrs. Neville.

"Nor I either," shrieked out a shrill voice, and Mrs. Walter came forward from the back shop. "I said the very same thing last night. He is for Bohun in his heart as much as anyone. Come speak out now," continued the better half, "and pass your word to the ladies like a man."

Mrs. Neville attacked Mr. Walter. Miss Molesworth took Mrs. Walter aside.

"Let him speak to Mr. Chace," said Miss Molesworth. "He will set all right. Tell him that I am quite sure that all will be set right, now do, that's a dear good woman, because although we are sure to win, every vote tells you know."

"To be sure, that's what I was saying last night, come pass your word like a man Tom. His word's a bond. Be sure of that. Thomas Walter's word is his bond."

Thomas Walter between the supplicating Mrs. Neville, and the smiling Miss Molesworth was very much like Garrick between Tragedy and Comedy. He could not resist. He gave his word, very like a man indeed; for he was persuaded to act against his interest by a woman.

So you see our fair missionaries got on very well indeed. Ay! they did wonderful execution amid the waverers who were really independent. And Timothy Clode the gigantic and humorous mealman who had never promised no one, never did, but who had been heard to declare that he thought Mr. Bohun too much of a dandy for his money, pledged his faith to Mr. Bohun's fair partizans.

The approaching contest for Fanchester made more sensation than all the other anticipated struggles in the County together, but it was the general opinion that Prigmore's early start backed by Jenkins and the Sectarians must gain the day, though rumours were also daily about that the Bohun party gathered strength every hour. As for Mr. Bohun himself he seemed never out of his saddle, unless it was when he dismounted to lunch at Hartlebury.

"Well all I can say is your man deserves to win it," was the sarcastic observation of the Prigmorites, secretly piqued by the absence of their champion. Mr. Gainsborough still indulged the forlorn hope that one of the Candidates would resign.

At length Parliament was dissolved, the writ issued, treating stopped, the deck cleared for action, the hustings built and the trumpet sounded for the final struggle.

The first day was passed only in formalities, processions and speechifications. It was a fine early December morning. Mrs. Neville called early for the Molesworths, in order that they might enter the town before the crowd was too dense, and take up their position with comfort at the windows of Mr. Scroggin, and view the procession. The Latimers declined her invitation.

Jenkins and the Sectarians being alarmed for their heads and windows had sworn in a swarm of special constables who broke the heads of all the boys in the town under ten years of age. This they called keeping the peace. The High Street was crowded, but the road-way kept tolerably clear. The bells of all the churches rang. Everybody was covered with party ribbons.

A grand burst of music announced that Mr. Bohun's principal band followed by a large body of electors were going out to meet him. They passed by with all the bravery of their standards, and their followers took off their hats and gave a lusty cheer as they passed the Hartlebury party. The cheer was re-echoed by the crowd, and the people in the distant parts thinking from the clamour that their hero had arrived made a simultaneous rush to the High Street. In a few minutes there was general confusion, and a regular row, and the special constables set to belabouring the heads of every unoffending individual who was either motionless or seemed unresisting.

"Don't you be so cocky Master Sparkes with that ere staff of yours," said one victim.

"I say Sparkes, bees you only a constable? Lord I thought as how you was the new Alderman."

"Come move on there, move on," said Sparkes authoritatively.

"My eye! move on!"

"Move on!" said a stern Radical. "Move on! A cat may look at a king mayn't he?"

"Silence," said Mr. Sparkes.

"Silence!" echoed the indignant Radical, "why you snivelling Jack in office you! If I don't call out Bohun for ever in your old corrupt ears, you old humbug! Bohun for ever! Huzza!"

And indeed he might well exclaim, for at this moment arose the sound of distant music, and soon the loud cheers of the people who lined the road for more than a mile out of the town came rushing on the wind.

A nice observer might have detected that Helen Molesworth's face turned pale. She had never yet heard Mr. Bohun speak; they had been placed accordingly just opposite the hustings.

"He is coming," said Mrs. Neville. "I am sure he is coming. Helen, dear Helen, Aubrey is coming."

The music became louder and louder, the advanced flags approached, and passed them. The cheering seemed to rend the skies. Bounding with matchless grace on an Arab steed and at the head of nearly a thousand of his tenantry and neighbours covered with boughs of laurel, Aubrey Bohun appeared. Had he been standing for all ——shire he could scarcely have been followed by a more numerous cortège.

"He doesn't look like a radical," said Mr. Molesworth with a smile.

Mr. Bohun passed their window, he reined in his ambling steed, uncovered and waving his hat cried "Bohun for ever". How many lusty voices responded to that cry! The long procession passed, the state carriage drawn by four steeds and the household followed. Down the High Street they proceeded, perambulated the great square, and then returning, and forming at the back of the Hustings, Mr. Bohun dismounted and appeared in their front amid a sea of waving arms and a storm of cheering. During the procession Mr. Prigmore attended by Mr. Jenkins and the click had contrived to take up his position on the Hustings unnoticed.

The town clerk read the writ, his worship the jolly Chumfield came forward, and made a speech, and prayed a hearing for all parties.

"That's fair Chumfield!" said a man in the mob.

"Bravo! Chumfield!"

"Bohun for ever!"

Then advanced Mr. Jenkins, a sharp, square-built, acute looking man, with a peculiarly unamiable expression of countenance, and somewhat bald. As he came forward there rose a yell which seemed interminable. Jenkins stood quite unmoved, and an expression of contempt and consciousness of power were evident in his countenance.

"Oh! you wretch!" said Kitty.

"You'll give potatoes to the poor, will you?" said one.

"Jenkins, — how d'ye do?" shouted another.

"Jenkins, don't give up!"

"Jenkins, you're a nice man!"

"I don't think!" added a fourth.

At length, the mob being conscious that the day could not last for ever, particularly in December, and that the only way to hear Mr. Bohun was to let matters go on as quietly as possible, Jenkins obtained an audience. He was not a bad mob speaker. He made some points which gave bully Thorpe an opportunity of cheering him, and he revenged some of the snubs and sneers which he had received without a requital during the last six weeks. He ended by proposing Mr. Prigmore amid renewed yells, and the proposition was seconded by a gentleman who took off his hat, and made a bow.

Then came forward Mr. Prittle Prattle amid enthusiastic cheering, to propose Mr. Bohun. The worthy alderman, who had been hissed at all his life, seemed equally astonished and delighted with his new honours, and glanced at his old opponent Jenkins with triumph. When this proposition was seconded, Mr. Prigmore advanced; but the mob would not hear him, — and, after half an hour of fruitless endeavours, and broken sentences, Prigmore made way for Mr. Bohun. When the applause had died away you might hear a pin drop.

Today Mr. Bohun was very anxious to make a very great impression. He was now an experienced orator. He brought into practice all the results of his observation. He took care never to make a hit, unless there was a dead silence, and always to end with a point. He spoke for two hours. Helen thought that she had never listened to anything more interesting, or ever witnessed a more captivating spectacle.

The orator concluded — the business of the day was over. At nine o'clock next morning the polling was to commence. But no one in Fanchester thought of going to bed that night. Mr. Bohun immediately came over to Mr. Scroggin's, to speak to the Molesworths and Mrs. Neville; but he could not return to dine with them — he could not leave Fanchester — he must attend his committee. Their carriage was ordered. They agreed that they were not to return to Fanchester until all was over.

The business grew much too nervous. Mrs. Neville was to remain at Hartlebury till the election was terminated. Mr. Bohun promised them an hourly bulletin of the state of the poll.

He handed them to their carriage.

"Goodbye, dear Emmeline," he said to Mrs. Neville, "whether I win or lose, you have my thanks. And you dear Miss Molesworth, how can I ever repay you for all your kindness?"

"By winning! — by winning! — Mr. Bohun: I will dream of nothing but your triumph."

"Dream of me, and I care not for the triumph."

"Well, good morning to you," said Mr. Molesworth. "That Prigmore is a shocking-looking vagabond. Don't let him be a member of Parliament, for God's sake!"

The carriage drew off amid loud cheers, and Mr. Bohun repaired to the Rose.

CHAPTER VI

A midnight colloquy

It was midnight. Two of the Prigmorites met in the street.

"Well, anything new?"

"I have been the rounds. The blunt's going like the town-pump. I saw a man come out of Spring's house, muffled up with a mask on. I thought I'd dodge him. Who should it be but young Chumfield! The devil's work there, I fear."

"D—e, I'll answer for Spring. You don't mean that, do you?"

"Yes but I do. I never thought he was a true man."

"Told Jenkins?"

"I could not see him, but I met young Frisby and told him."

"Young Frisby! — I ayn't no opinion of him!"

"I thought he was as right as the town-clock."

"So I thought too. His dad owes Jenkins a thirty pound note, and Jenkins told him that there would be no odds about that if as how— who comes here?— The enemy— Rufus Parsons and Swift. Keep close."

"I'll speak to them. Good night Parsons. Up rather late tonight?"

"All fair election time. *You* ayn't snoring, are you?"

"Well, I hope the best man will win."

"I am sure he will."

"Don't be too sure."

"I'll bet you five pound we win."

"No! I never bet."

"Well, I'll bet you Parsons."

"What?"

"Five pound that Bohun don't win."

"No! — you should have taken me before. Come, I'll bet you he don't lose by twenty."

"Oh! that's a very different affair. You talked of equal betting."

"Well, I'll bet you he is at the head of the poll tomorrow, at twelve."

"No! — that's humbug — I'll bet five pounds that this day-week Prigmore is our member."

"We shall see," said Parsons.

"What, you won't bet, eh?"

"D——e, I've a good mind, now. D——e, if I ayn't sure we shall beat you!"

"Come bet!"

"Well, d——e, I will. I'll bet you five pounds that Prigmore is not our member."

"Done!"

"Done!"

CHAPTER VII

The first day

Dame Harrald stood at the gate of the almshouse surrounded by the petticoats of the village. All the men were at the 'Lection.

"I wish I had a vote," said Dame Harrald.

"The women have no votes," said Mrs. Collins mournfully.

"The more's the shame," said Gossip Faddle.

"In this world the men have it all their own way," remarked Dame Harrald pensively.

"If the men have the votes, the women have the influence, Squire Bohun says," remarked the gossip.

"And I am sure there's not a woman that's not on his side," said Mrs. Collins.

"Is it a match between the Squire and Miss Helen?" enquired Gossip Faddle.

"I am sure I hope it may be," said Mrs. Collins, "for they are just suiting I think."

"I have nursed her when she was in long petticoats," said Dame Harrald.

"Only think how she has grown!" said Mrs. Collins.

"Mr. Sideboard thinks it's a match," said Gossip Faddle.

"If Mr. Sideboard says so," said the Dame, "there's something in it. He's a sensible man, John Sideboard. I remember him when he was just a foot-boy. His father was butler before him."

"He didn't not exactly say so," remarked the gossip, "but he didn't deny it when I axed him."

"He couldn't well say Yes," observed Dame Harrald. "It wouldn't be decorous."

"Silence gives assent," shrewdly observed Mrs. Collins.

"It will be a merry day on the green," said Dame Harrald.

"An ox roasted alive, I am just thinking!" said the gossip.

"It was so when the Squire married himself," said the Dame.

"Its clearly a natural match," said the gossip, "for do not the estates join?"

"It seems a matter of providence, as our Squire has no son," remarked Mrs. Collins.

"Well! I once thought of the Rector," said Gossip Faddle. "God bless him!"

"If Squire Bohun had not returned, there's no saying," said Mrs. Collins.

"However it may be, I hope Miss Helen will be as happy as she deserves," said the Dame.

"And that's as happy as the day is long," said the Gossip.

"There's Jin Flag," said Mrs. Collins, as she looked up the lane. A horseman was galloping across the green.

"He's come from the 'Lection," said the Dame.

"Good news I trow," said the Gossip: "Maybe if we call him, he'll just stop for a chat. Jin Flag! Jin Flag, I say. He takes no notice of us. It's not very civil I am thinking. Many a time has he had his baccy box filled on trust, and never paid me for it."

"Was always a wild boy," said Dame Harrald, shaking her head.

"He'll turn out well at last, I hope," said Mrs. Collins.

"Is it a match between him and Lydia?" enquired the Gossip.

"Nay Mrs. Faddle, I wish you'd not put such things in young people's heads," said Mrs. Collins gravely.

"Well, I only axed." said the Gossip.

"There's no end to axing," said Mrs. Collins.

The horseman covered with green ribbons dashed up to the gates, which flew open as he approached. In a minute the hall bell rang loud and long.

And within the hall during the whole morning, Mrs. Neville and our heroine had been engaged in conversation not less earnest than Dame Harrald and her friends.

"The hall bell!" exclaimed Miss Molesworth.

"The state of the Poll!" exclaimed Mrs. Neville.

"It really is too nervous an affair," said Miss Molesworth.

"I can bear it no longer," said Mrs. Neville, "I am sure Aubrey will lose."

"There can be nothing very decisive yet," remarked Miss Molesworth. "It is only half past twelve."

"I wonder if he will have one vote!" said Mrs. Neville.

"Sometimes I think he won't."

The drawing-room door opened and Mr. Sideboard entered, followed by Jin Flag.

"I am to see your honoured Ladyships myself," said Jin Flag, with a reeling gait and a rolling eye.

"What news?" said Miss Molesworth.

"Have you the state of the poll?" enquired Mrs. Neville.

"I am to see your honoured Ladyships myself," said Jin Flag. "The Squire told me so," looking round to Mr. Sideboard. "I have done the three miles in ten minutes," and he unbuttoned his waistcoat, and brought out a dirty silk handkerchief which he proceeded to unfold.

"Make haste," said Mrs. Neville.

"Yes your Ladyship," said Jin Flag, and he handed to her with a bow the

STATE OF THE POLL

12 o'clock.

BOHUN 73

PRIGMORE 75

Bohun and Independence for ever!!!

"Well it's quite a relief," said Mrs. Neville. "No one can say he has not polled seventy-three votes."

"And what do they say?" enquired Miss Molesworth eagerly.

"All's right," said Jin Flag with a knowing wink. "Don't you be unasy Miss. The Squire is at the head of the poll by this time. Old Jenkins ayn't got no heart at all. Looks for all the world just as if he was going to be hanged. I knows a trick or two you see. 'Tayn't the first 'lection I've had a finger in the pie. That's why young Squire Gainsborough engaged me, d'ye see. Jin says he to me, you're used to these sort of things, meaning 'lections. I think I ought to know a trick or two, says I. I brought up twenty votes for Squire Ducie last county 'lection if I brought one. I knows how to set about it, that's the fact — it's my way, d'ye see. I knows how to come over them. Well says he, you're engaged for Squire Bohun. Done, says I; you'll see what's what. My sister married Jenkins' head clerk — you twig, Miss? enemy's camp, ah? I knows how they feel. They wouldn't give a brass farthing for their chance. That's the plain truth. They're dead beat and they know it. Prigmore will resign tonight, or I'm a Dutchman!"

Nothing like an election to make an impudent fellow of importance. Mrs. Neville and Miss Molesworth listened with eager hearts and credulous ears to all Jin Flag's revelations, they thought him almost as great a man as he pretended to be, they congratulated themselves on having such an auxiliary. They made him repeat a thousand times all his boasted secrets of the enemy's camp, they caught fresh courage from each fresh rodomantade, they asked him his opinion, they exhorted him to fresh exertions. They exacted from him a promise to be their aide-de-camp during the whole contest, and constantly let them know the state of the poll, and all the secret information he obtained from his fair relative who had so fortunately united her destinies with those of Jenkins' head-clerk.

Jin Flag became each instant more confident, more communicative, more authoritative. He promised them with a mysterious shake of his head, and a significant wink of the eye, to work night and day for Squire Bohun, to leave no stone unturned to secure his success; he assured them over and over again it was the luckiest thing in the world that young Squire Gainsborough had sense enough to engage him, that he was equal to all the sub-agents of the other side together; that all the elections in which he had been employed had been gained. "Catch Jin Flag not riding the winning horse," hiccuped the hero, "as for Jenkins and every man John of them, they ayn't worth that," said Jin Flag snapping his fingers, "they ayn't no pluck at all. I'll teach them a trick or two. You leave it to me Miss. Don't you be unasy. I'll look after you as if you were my own — children. You shall know the poll every half hour, and I'll bring it myself if I can be spared," he concluded, "but if the Squire wants me for anything wery perticular," and here he stopped short, and shook his head.

"Oh! if you be wanted for anything very particular," said Miss Molesworth, "don't think of us."

"No, no," echoed Mrs. Neville, "don't think of us, if you be wanted for anything very particular."

"Why you see," said Jin Flag oracularly, "I mustn't let the cat out of the bag Miss, but you see things will turn up — there are bits of business that the Squire can't exactly attend to himself, or even the Colonel," as he said this he nodded his head to Mrs. Neville, "or even young Squire Gainsborough, they mustn't be seen in everything, you see, and then you see they come to me and that's the truth on't," continued Mr. Jin in a chuckling strain, "for as for old Scroggin, or even Mr. Chumfield, when there's anything that requires more than two and two make four they ayn't worth *that*! Very good people your Ladyships— very good gentleman Mr. Chumfield. I wish he had declared himself sooner and Mr. Baggs too, a very good sort of person indeed, but Lord bless you they're mere children in 'lections; they don't know how to set about it, they ayn't used to this sort of thing, they don't know how to come over them, that's the fact. You twig, Miss?"

"Yes! we quite twig," said Helen, "and now Jin, I think you had better go back because you'll be wanted."

"I am always wanted," said Jin.

"Take a glass of ale before you go Jin," said Miss Molesworth. "Sideboard take care of Jin."

"Thank you Miss, I can't stop, I can't think of drinking ale or enjoying myself at all till I see the Squire in. I wish you good morning Ladies. Don't be afeared. It's all right. Take my word on't," and then in a sotto voice to Sideboard as he made his final scrape, "I'll just take one glass of brandy before I go, to drink courage to the Ladies."

What an anxious morning was this at Hartlebury. The state of the poll was forwarded by the committee every hour. Even Mr. Molesworth could not conceal his anxiety though he struggled hard. Even Arthur Latimer called twice in the course of the morning to hear the last intelligence.

"Well!" Mr. Molesworth repeated twenty times in the course of the day. "Well! I wish Sir George had stood, however as it is, I must say I hope they will send that vagabond Prigmore to the right about."

That vagabond Prigmore however, in spite of Mr. Molesworth's good wishes, and Jin Flag's secret intelligence, kept the head of the poll the whole day, although by a not very formidable majority. This was the close of the first day.

FANCHESTER ELECTION

STATE OF THE POLL

5 o'clock

BOHUN 264
PRIGMORE..280

Bohun and Independence for ever!!!

The excitement of the town cannot be described. At five
o'clock Mr. Bohun made a speech which made everybody mad.
"Today," he exclaimed, "your exertions have been glorious:
tomorrow they will be triumphant." He assured the town that
his success was certain, that the enemy's force was exhausted,
that Prigmore would, must resign tomorrow, if not tonight,
which for the sake of the peace of the town, and to save useless
vexation and expense he trusted he would. A hurried note from
the hero of Fanchester to the fair ladies of Hartlebury records
however his secret feelings on the subject.

Committee Room,   8 o'Clock.

Dear Ladies,
     Courage. The plain truth is that, though Prigmore has
apparently the best of it, the chances are yet I think equal.
I do not feel like a man who is going to be vanquished. I
have confidence in my destiny. Tonight we shall make
great exertions. I cannot leave the town for a second, or I
would ride over to Hartlebury to assure you that I am,
                                        Your devoted,
                                        AUBREY BOHUN

     Gustavus sends his love, Gainsborough is too busy even
to desire to be remembered. The whole affair is very
diverting. If I lose I shall not regret the contest. I like
electioneering better than hunting — second only to war.
The people are mad with enthusiasm. The scene gives me
an idea of the politics of the Greek republics. I suppose I
am as much like Alcibiades as Fanchester is like Athens.
Adieu!

In the meantime, long, during the night, resounded music in

every street and noisy wassailers in every tavern. A choice
selection of Mr. Bohun's committee perambulated the town in
disguise, each taking his district, to confirm the wavering, to
re-animate the drooping, and to gain over the adverse. No
inducement was wanting. George Gainsborough with two or
three aide-de-camps mounted their horses, and scoured the out
town voters. They knocked up the unpolled at midnight, and
succeeded in sending off to London, by the night coach a few
Prigmorites who were too far pledged absolutely to rat.

About four o'clock a dead stillness fell over the town. The
night was clouded. Aubrey Bohun opened the window of his
room, and looked out upon the silent High Street. Perceiving
no passengers he muffled himself up in a livery great coat, and
tying a shawl half round his face he stepped forth to enjoy one
moment of quiet. As he walked along his thoughts were quick,
and not uninteresting.

" 'Tis a strange thing this life," thought he, "who could have
supposed a year ago that my thoughts should have been centred
in an obscure country town. And Gainsborough too of all men
in the world my right hand friend! It is in vain to struggle
against the conviction; there is a destiny which moulds our
actions at its will— Aubrey Bohun, Esquire, M.P. for Fanchester. Ha! ha! ha! What would Ulysses, and my comrades say to
me, if I offered them a frank which they could not read! Well
this is life, this is excitement, and that is all I care about. I feel I
live. And yet there is something petty and vulgar in all this
bustle, which half disgusts me. I who have played deep for a
crown, am now forsooth a candidate for the representation of
Fanchester! To be baffled by Capo d'Istrias backed by the
resources of an Empire is scarcely shame— but Prigmore! oh!
Aubrey, Aubrey! I fear after all you are but a headstrong boy!
No matter, I will not think. Have I not abjured plans for ever? I
have now two objects to gain. Neither will keep me long in
suspense. Tomorrow I shall know whether my country affords
me a career or not: and as for Helen — by the blood of the
Bohuns, I am convinced that she has better taste than the
electors of Fanchester, and cannot hesitate about my fate.
Courage, Aubrey, courage. If I gain her, and gain her I will,
what is Fanchester to me. For the rest, if I live I *must* be a great
man. 'Tis a consoling conviction!"

CHAPTER VIII

The fate of Fanchester
in the hands of Mr. Gainsborough —
the perplexities of a great man

Day broke, and Alderman Baggs turned in his uneasy bed. He had been troubled with uneasy dreams. Jenkins had appeared to him in his sleep. Alderman Baggs was not accustomed to dream. The sight of Jenkins sleeping or waking always made him nervous.

"We live in awful times," pondered the nervous Alderman, "only think of my dreaming of that fellow Jenkins. Prigmore 280 — Bohun 264 — sixteen a-head. Prigmore, that is Jenkins, sixteen a-head. Well, I wonder Chumfield can laugh in these times. Sixteen! sixteen a-head — and Chumfield laughed! Good God! what spirits that man has. To laugh, to laugh in these times, when Jenkins is carrying everything before him. I must vote today. I am so nervous, but vote I must. If I were on my death-bed, I would vote. I vote against Jenkins. Thank God we are popular. Young Chumfield has promised to keep the way to the booth clear for me. He has spoken to that fellow Jin Flag. Oh! this Reform Bill. It makes even that scapegrace of Jin Flag a man of importance. I never gave my vote in my life except in a snug room in the Town Hall. The cheering of our own mob quite frightens me. What should I do were I hooted. How we came to be popular all of a sudden I cannot make out. These are indeed strange times! I wish I could see my way! I cannot go to sleep again! I should like my chocolate, but I dare not ring for Dolly!"

There were many persons in Fanchester not less nervous than Mr. Alderman Baggs, though they put a better face upon the affair. Whatever might be the hopes of the populace, the better informed of both sides were generally of opinion that Prigmore would carry the day.

"They have run us harder than we expected," said Mr. Jenkins, with a thoughtful but confident look, as Prigmore's secret committee broke up some hours past midnight, "but beat them we must. We shall beat them Dawson, we shall beat them by forty-seven."

"No fear," said Dawson: "anyone but Bohun, and we should have galloped over the course. It is his confounded gift of the gab that has done all this mischief."

"Well, well we will not quarrel with his figures of speech," said Mr. Jenkins with a sour smile, "as we have the more important figures on our side. Forty-seven! I think it is clear we shall beat him at least by forty-seven! They are moving heaven and hell against us, but our lads are out. Dawson we have everything at stake. 'Tis the old war against the Corporation again. Who would have supposed that the contest would have taken this turn! Chumfield and Baggs, I would mortgage my factory sooner than Bohun should get in. Alderman indeed! To think of their making that Prittle-Prattle an Alderman, why he compounded with his creditors, he paid my father ten shillings in the pound! And we, Dawson, warm men like us, who could buy the whole town out and out, we are slaves to Chumfield and Baggs! never!" said Mr. Jenkins, and he gnashed his teeth, "their reign is over. Their man shan't win."

The Bohunites made a great push at the opening of the second and last day's poll. At twelve o'clock thus stood the

STATE OF THE POLL

BOHUN 309
PRIGMORE...301

Bohun and Independence for ever!!!

The mob shouted, but the Prigmorites were not alarmed, because it was well known that part of Mr. Bohun's committee had polled. Mr. Jenkins and his friends were, however, mistaken in ascribing this circumstance to weakness. Mr. Bohun's strength was by no means exhausted, but his committee after long consultation, had deemed it of importance to place him early on the morrow at the head of the poll, and half of them had voted, because they were electors nearer at hand than others.

This circumstance however diffused great confidence amid the Bohunites and occasioned not a little triumph at Hartlebury.

"It's all right your Ladyships," said Jin Flag, who brought the intelligence. "I told you I knew a trick or two. The Squire spoke to me last night quite under the rose, you see quite under the rose. Says he to me, 'Jin, what's to be done, you are up to the thing my man, what's to be done!' 'I know a trick or two,' says I, 'as for Chumfield and Scroggin,' says he, 'they are very good sort of people in their way.' 'I twig,' says I, 'but they know just as much about 'lections as your grandmother.' 'You're right Jin,' says he. 'Catch a weasel asleep,' says I. 'I can see with half an eye.' And so Miss this morning we're at the head of the poll, and that's how it is. I'll just take a glass of something to bring my voice round, for I have been talking all day, and then I'll go back and see what I can do for them."

From twelve to one the polling was very brisk on both sides. All Prigmore's committee polled and the rest of Bohun's. Thus affairs stood.

FANCHESTER ELECTION

STATE OF THE POLL

1 o'clock

BOHUN 421
PRIGMORE...419

Bohun and Independence for ever!!!

During the next hour everything was very languid. It was quite clear that the strength of both parties was nearly exhausted. Sick men were brought up on their beds. A blind man led by his son, a tenant of Jenkins, wanted to poll for Prigmore. The mob would not let them come to the booth, the special constables interfered, the mob, who only wanted an opportunity, showed fight, in a few minutes there was a regular row. Mr. Prigmore, who wished to gain time, applied to the Mayor to adjourn the poll, on the grounds of general riot and that his voters were prevented from tendering their votes. The Tory Chumfield being a Bohunite, talked of the liberty of the people, saw no riot, only a fair ebullition of spirit, &c, &c., made a speech to the mob, which they cheered and refused to adjourn the poll. In the midst of this confusion, about half past two o'clock Miss Molesworth received the following note.

> Rose, ¼ past 2 o'clock.

My dearest Miss Molesworth,

My strength is utterly exhausted. I am two a-head. Prigmore has certainly two more votes, for Jenkins and Dawson have not polled, though nothing can prevent them, for they are standing at this moment in the booth. They count on old Gainsborough, and have sent a thousand messages and messengers, and letters, and heaven knows what to him. George and the womankind manage that nothing shall reach him. But, dearest Miss Molesworth, it has just occurred to me that they would not prevent you. In a word, gain him for me. You can do anything I am sure; I would change my politics, my nature, my anything for you. And old Gainsborough cannot resist you. Pardon me for this. The Mayor has no casting vote in this Borough. At the best it will then be a double return, but with Gainsborough we shall beat, yes! beat!!! Again I apologize. What incoherent stuff I have written. I can only say,

> I am
> Your obliged, your devoted,
> Aubrey

She threw the letter to Mrs. Neville, and at the same time rang the bell.

"We can but try," she exclaimed, "we can but try. Dearest Mrs. Neville, let us go instantly. The carriage, Sideboard, the carriage instantly — instantly. 'Tis an affair of life and death. Not a minute must be lost."

"Only think of that old fool Gainsborough," said Mrs. Neville. "Well! I declare if he persists in refusing us, I shall think him very rude indeed."

In five minutes the britchka was at the door. Helen and Mrs. Neville were of course ready.

"Oakfield— Johnson," said Miss Molesworth, "and drive as fast as you can."

When the carriage, after winding through the most sinuous road that ever led to a residence, finally stopped at the glass door of Oakfield Lodge, the servant, who immediately came forward, looked very perplexed when Miss Molesworth enquired whether Mr. Gainsborough was at home, and said he would go and enquire. In a few minutes he returned, and said that his master was at home to them, apologizing to the visitors for having kept them waiting, and adding that he had received strict orders from Mrs. Gainsborough to deny him to everyone.

Mrs. Neville and Miss Molesworth were ushered into the library, Mr. Gainsborough's private room. The blinds were drawn, and coming immediately from the strong sun-light, a moment elapsed before the visitors could well discover the visited. In process of time however, they detected Mr. Gainsborough sitting in his library chair, with a very rueful countenance, twirling his thumbs. A long library table was placed between him and the door, a sort of barricado that he should not escape, and two wardens, in the shape of his faithful spouse and fond daughter, were placed on each side of it, to complete the precautionary measures.

Mrs. Gainsborough gave her guests a significant and complacent look as she saluted them.

"I am sorry that you were kept Miss Molesworth, very sorry indeed Mrs. Neville. But *we* are not at home today— that is the truth. So many people have called today, so many very disagreeable people, that I thought it best for Mr. Gainsborough, and for all of us, that we should not be at home. There have been fifty of Prigmore's people here if there has been one." She added in an under tone, "but you see I have gained my point— I have gained my point. I hope all is going on well. We have the poll up to twelve — Bohun quite a-head, and winning fast."

"Affairs are not quite so bright," said Helen, passing by and saluting Mr. Gainsborough.

"How do you do, my dear Sir; I hope you are very well indeed."

"Thank you, Miss Molesworth," said the old gentleman forcing a smile. "Thank you, I am pretty well— that is to say, I am not very well. I shall be better tomorrow. I shall be better when this election is over. We shall all be quieter then. I see nothing of George. I hope he is not doing too much. He is very active for your friend Mr. Bohun, and I believe Mr. Bohun is very sensible of his kindness. They tell me here that he is quite Mr. Bohun's bosom friend. I am quite sure he cannot have a better friend. I approve of Mr. Bohun very much indeed. It would be quite impossible for George to have found a more desirable connection in every point of view. It is only in youth that these strong friendships are formed. They are generally formed at public schools and colleges. George had the advantage of the very best education. I sent him to Rugby and Oxford, but he did not become acquainted with Mr. Bohun at either of those places. They met first abroad. Travelling is a very great advantage — George has had every advantage, and I must say has availed himself of them to the utmost. Everybody talks to me of my accomplished son. He is, I assure you Miss Molesworth, a staunch friend of Mr. Bohun. Mr. Bohun has many friends under this roof. I may say that all are his friends under this roof. For my part I can truly say that I wish him well. I had no idea that he could have made such a stand. I thought Jenkins would have been too much for him. I hope he will win, with all my heart. No person wishes him success more earnestly. I wish I could do more than merely wish him success, but — but, Miss Molesworth, you know how very awkwardly I am situated."

"My dearest Sir," said Helen in her sweetest tone, and with her most winning smile, "Mrs. Neville and myself have come to ask you a very great favour."

"I am sure I am very much flattered," said Mr. Gainsborough, rather alarmed.

"But will you promise to grant it us?" enquired Helen.

"I will do for Miss Molesworth and her friends, anything that is possible," replied Mr. Gainsborough.

"It is very possible my dear Sir, very possible indeed. It is something that will make us all happy. That will delight your own family, and delight all Hartlebury, and delight papa, whom I am sure you are always glad to please."

Mr. Gainsborough bowed.

"It is," continued Miss Molesworth in a desperate tone — "it is —"

"Not to vote against Mr. Bohun," interrupted Mr. Gainsborough. "In spite of my awkward situation, I grant your
request."

"You are very good — you are very good indeed Sir," said
Miss Molesworth, "you are always very good to me. I am sure
there is no person in the world, next to papa, on whose kindness, on whose unvarying kindness, I more rely than yours."

Mr. Gainsborough seemed a little affected.

"But Sir, dear, dear Sir, the favour that we have come to ask
is not that which you have granted us, but for which we feel
grateful, very grateful indeed. It is not about not voting against
Mr. Bohun."

"What can it be?" enquired Mr. Gainsborough, very puzzled, but more at his ease.

"We want you, dear Sir," said Miss Molesworth, and she put
her arm in his, and looked into his perplexed face, "we want you
to vote *for* Mr. Bohun."

"God bless me!" said Mr. Gainsborough, and he opened his
mouth.

"Yes, dearest Sir, this is the simple truth. It is the best to
speak the simple truth; it is best to be frank. There is not
another vote left, not a single vote, and they are exactly equal.
Only think, dear Sir, dear, dearest Mr. Gainsborough, only
think, the issue of the contest is in your own hands. It is in your
power to return Mr. Bohun to Parliament. The country will be
indebted for his splendid career, for a splendid career such a
man must have, will be indebted entirely to you. Everyone will
say, when he makes one of his fine speeches, had it not been for
Mr. Gainsborough we should not have heard this."

"But my situation," said Mr. Gainsborough very agitated,
"my awkward, my unfortunate situation."

"Shall it be said," continued Miss Molesworth, "that Mr.
Bohun lost his election because Mr. Gainsborough would not
vote for him? What will the world say? How everyone will
wonder. Mr. Gainsborough — his friend, his neighbour, his
fellow-magistrate, the father of his bosom friend, the intimate
friend of all his intimate friends, one of his very set, his own
fire-side, one with whom he is in terms of daily, of hourly, of the
most cordial and complete intercourse. On whom might Mr.
Bohun count if not on Mr. Gainsborough? If Oakfield, and

Bohun, and Hartlebury, do not draw together, where is there a foundation for union!"

"But my promise— Mr. Prigmore— Mr. Jenkins," said Mr. Gainsborough, touched to the very quick by being classed with his aristocratic neighbours, and looking upon his wife and daughter who stood crying, and then at Mrs. Neville, who was not used to scenes, and was quite confused.

"What is Prigmore! What is Jenkins to you!" responded Helen. "Your promise! What promise? You promised Mr. Prigmore as against Sir George Vavasour. Sir George has resigned, and a new candidate starts. The circumstances on which you made your promise are changed. We are all governed by circumstances, Mr. Gainsborough! Circumstances are too strong for the strongest of us."

"It is most true," said Mr. Gainsborough.

"Mr. Bohun's principles are yours. He is a liberal only— he is not a Whig. Mr. Bohun agrees with you on every point. He has the highest opinion of your opinions on political subjects. I know it. I have often heard him say so. Only think how delightful, dear Sir, to have a person in the House, a leading person, one who speaks and must carry weight from his great talents and property, only think of having a friend, a most intimate friend in the House under such circumstances consulting you on all points! You will in fact be a Member of Parliament yourself without the trouble of the office, and when Mr. Bohun is Prime Minister only think of your influence, you who in fact introduced him to public life and guided his early career by your counsels!"

"Only think," exclaimed Mrs. Gainsborough sobbing.

"Only think," echoed Miss Gainsborough with her handkerchief to her eyes.

"I wonder if Aubrey will be Prime Minister," said the wondering Mrs. Neville. "It never occurred to me."

"He is certain," said Mrs. Gainsborough.

"He is sure," echoed Miss Gainsborough.

"I wish I had never acted with Jenkins," said Mr. Gainsborough: "what was Jenkins to me? I wish I had never promised Prigmore."

"But you say, my dear Sir, that you do not intend to keep a promise which was entirely provisional. The promise was provisional, and the circumstances having changed, the promise is not kept. If you are free not to keep your promise as you have decided, so also you must be free to act as you please. It may be annoying to vote against a man whom you once provisionally promised to support, but will it not be more annoying to injure and to annoy all your friends, to destroy Mr. Bohun's career, to disoblige Papa, to occasion me the greatest grief, to make your own family miserable, to cause a coolness, perhaps an enmity between your son and his friend, and wantonly to destroy a connection which may realize all your plans and hopes and prospects!"

"Yes! indeed," said Mrs. Gainsborough. "I have told him this a thousand times. If Mr. Bohun were prime minister, he would make him a Baronet."

"Psha! my dear," said Mr. Gainsborough.

"And put George in Parliament," said Miss Gainsborough.

"For God's sake leave off crying, women," said the unhappy father, "never, no never was man in such an awkward situation as I am."

"You will break my heart," said Mrs. Gainsborough.

"You have broken mine," said the daughter.

"My dear wife, my own Fanny, for God's sake be calm. I intreat you to be calm. I am thinking of what Miss Molesworth has said. I am thinking for the best. I am indeed. I wish to act for the best. I wish I could split my vote between Prigmore and Mr. Bohun, but that will not do. I wish I could oblige everybody. I am very awkwardly situated, that is the truth, no man perhaps was ever more awkwardly situated. What am I to do? How can I act? Mr. Bohun is my friend, my neighbour, a brother magistrate. And his friends are my friends. They have set their hearts on his return, that they have— and very proper too. I cannot conceive a more proper person to be a member of Parliament, great fortune, great talents, immense fortune indeed, talents not less considerable. What is Prigmore to me? Oakfield should support Bohun, that is quite clear. When I promised Prigmore I meant to say that I would vote against a Tory. I beg your pardon Miss Molesworth for abusing the Tories. I shouldn't wonder if they came in yet. If they would only give up the Church and the Corn Laws I would be a Tory myself. I have no objection to war, as much as you please. I made my fortune by war. Commerce never flourished half as well as in war time. I always supported Pitt and would again. I wish to act for the best. I always have done. The promise was provisional, that is quite clear. I wish I had never seen Jenkins. He is a long-headed fellow. I had no idea that Mr. Bohun would have made such a stand. It is not a point of honour; there is no honour in the case, it is a point of delicacy. It is rather awkward certainly to vote against Mr. Prigmore when I promised to vote for him. As against the Tory though mind — at least that was my intention, and men can only be guided by their intentions, I don't care what Jenkins says. I am the best judge of my own meaning. And as for Prigmore he will go up to town again by the coach. I shall never see him again, whereas I shall meet Mr. Bohun every day. How can I look him in the face after making him lose his election? I certainly am very awkwardly situated, but for a point of delicacy, for there is no honour in the case at all, am I called upon, as Miss Molesworth says, to injure and annoy all my friends, to destroy Mr. Bohun's career, to disoblige Mr. Molesworth, to occasion Miss Molesworth the greatest grief, to make my own family miserable, to cause a coolness, perhaps an enmity, between my own son and his friend, and wantonly to destroy a connection which may realize all my plans and hopes and prospects? That is the question, that is the short and simple question. Shall I, ought I, in short to vote for Mr. Bohun? I am surrounded by my best friends, they know all the circumstances of the case, and I shall be decided by their determination."

"It is your duty," said Mrs. Gainsborough eagerly.

"Your bounden duty," said her daughter.

"You will oblige and delight everybody," said Miss Molesworth, "and be the most popular man in the neighbourhood."

"I am sure I shall be charmed," said Mrs. Neville.

"I wish George were here to take me to the poll," said Mr. Gainsborough. "I should be sorry to meet Jenkins, or Dawson, or Prigmore. They might prevent me. What is best to be done?"

"No time is to be lost," said Miss Molesworth. "Our carriage is at the door, come with us. Mrs. Neville and I will take you up to the poll. You do not object, Emmeline?"

"Not in the least," said Mrs. Neville gaily. "I suppose it will not be a greater mob than a drawing-room, and as we are on the right side they will not be very rude." So saying, each lady took hold of one of Mr. Gainsborough's arms. Mrs. Gainsborough ran and fetched his hat, and Miss Gainsborough his cane, and in less than five minutes he was going as fast as Miss Molesworth's spirited horses could take him, to vote for Mr. Bohun.

CHAPTER IX

A member returned

It was a quarter to four o'clock, at which hour the poll finally closed. During the last hour not a single elector had tendered his vote. The mob were tolerably quiet, as they believed that Bohun was all right: among the better informed a dark rumour began to run of the real state of affairs, and there were mysterious whisperings of a double return. With the exception of the leaders each party was however sanguine that some error in the summing up would be discovered, of course in favour of their man. The candidates had just made their appearance on the hustings attended by their friends. Mr. Bohun looked gay and nodded and smiled to the populace. Prigmore was very bilious. Jenkins had lost his firm, arrogant, purse-proud scowl. He looked downcast and jaded.

"He don't like it at all," said Tim the mechanic to his comrade.

"My eye! no, doey? He's dead beat or I'm a Dutchman."

"Twig Prigmore Tim: he looks for all the world like a mouldy lemon."

"Or a rotten egg."

"I say Thorpe how's your man?"

"He pretends he don't hear nothing."

"I say Thorpe what's the matter with Muster Prigmore? He ayn't got the mulli-grubs, have he?"

"Prigmore!" halloed one of the mob, who caught this delicate enquiry, "how are you off for cholera?"

"Bohun for ever! No Treasury Nominee!" shouted a hoarse voice.

Ten minutes to four. A loud cheer is heard in the distance. A britchka appears, the spirited horses champing their bits and caracoling amid the mob. Mrs. Neville and Mr. Gainsborough sit at the back of the carriage, Miss Molesworth opposite to them. Jin Flag runs before them clearing the way.

"Make way there, make way there. Make way for an Elector. A wote for Squire Bohun, Bohun the friend of the people. Make way here, make way. Go it my hearties, go it! One cheer more! — Hurra! — Bohun for ever! Now stand aside now, do, do stand aside. We shall be too late now, by G—d we shall be too late, and I shall lose all my pains. Stand aside, I say — What, you won't? — Here's a Prigmorite — knock him down, boys — toss him in a blanket — pump over him! — Bohun for ever! — Go it! go it! — One cheer more — Go it, my hearties! — Aside, aside there! — now do stand aside, my good fellow make room for a woter — room — room! — Room for Squire Gainsborough!"

"Gainsborough for ever!" — shouted the mob.

"Matchless girl!" said Aubrey Bohun, seizing George Gainsborough's arm. "By heavens, we have won the day! — Now, Gustavus, now Gainsborough, come with me — we will escort your father to the poll."

"We're done," said Jenkins to Dawson, and he clenched his arm with his pallid hand.

"The incarnate traitor!" said Dawson.

"Make room there, make room," said the jolly mayor. Special constables, do your duty. Clear the way to the poll. Clear the way for an elector."

"I demand that the poll be closed," said Jenkins. "It is on the stroke of four."

"I know my duty, Mr. Jenkins," said the mayor, in a dignified tone, "and I shall close the poll when I think proper."

"Mr. Prigmore," said Jenkins, very loudly, that all might hear, "Mr. Gainsborough has come to vote. Mr. Gainsborough, who promised you. Keep him to his word Mr. Prigmore — Keep him to his word."

Up came Mr. Gainsborough, between his son and Colonel

Neville. Mr. Bohun remained at the carriage with his fair friends.

"I hope you have come to redeem your promise, sir," said Mr. Prigmore, as Mr. Gainsborough advanced.

"I have come to do my duty," said Mr. Gainsborough very firmly, inspirited by the cheering of the mob.

"You promised your vote to Mr. Prigmore," said Jenkins, very loudly and rudely. "I am a witness."

"And I too," said Dawson.

"Against Sir George Vavasour sir," said Mr. Gainsborough.

"Against everyone," said Jenkins, losing all command over himself. "Do you call yourself a gentleman, indeed! You are no gentleman."

"You are no man of your word," said Dawson.

"I despise you," said Jenkins.

"You deserve to be kicked," said Dawson.

"I should like to see you, or any other blackguard, kick my father," said George Gainsborough.

"Bravo young squire!" shouted the mob. "Go it, young cock."

"And if you, and that man by you, do not instantly cease your insolence, I will horsewhip you before the whole town."

"Sooner said than done," said bully Dawson. "Two can play at that."

"We shall beat you yet," said Jenkins.

"For whom do you tender your vote?" said the poll-clerk to Mr. Gainsborough.

"He promised Mr. Prigmore," bellowed Jenkins to the mob.

"It won't do, Jenkins," was the answer.

"It's no go."

"You're diddled, Jenkins."

"I hopes you like it, Jenkins."

"I say, Jenkins, ayn't you a nice man?"

"Gainsborough for ever."

"You wanted to be a member of Parliament, Jenkins?"

"I say, Jenkins, Muster Prigmore looks werry ill."

"Take him home, Jenkins."

"I say, Jenkins, you've killed Prigmore."

"There'll be a Crowner's inquest!"

"It's manslaughter at the least."

"Jenkins, go to bed!"

"For whom do you tender your vote?" said the poll-clerk to Mr. Gainsborough.

There was a dead silence.

"For Aubrey Bohun, Esquire," was the tremulous answer.

"Hurra!!!" was the universal shout.

The clock struck four.

The poll-books were already summed up. This additional vote alone was to be added. In five minutes the crier prayed silence, and the final state of the poll of the famous Fanchester election was declared.

FANCHESTER ELECTION

FINAL CLOSE OF THE POLL, SECOND DAY

AUBREY BOHUN, ESQ 434
PETER PRIGMORE, ESQ 433

And the jolly Chumfield came forward, and, amid loud cheers, declared that Aubrey Bohun, Esquire, was returned to Parliament, as Burgess for the borough of Fanchester.

CHAPTER X

A ball at Bohun

That calm which succeeds excitement was not the agreeable fortune of the inhabitants of Fanchester and its neighbourhood. Christmas festivities succeeded to electioneering struggles. Mr. Bohun dined with his constituents in the town-hall, and, in return, feasted the electors in a series of banquets surrounded by the portraits of his fathers. The invitations were extended alike to opponents and supporters, and a large portion of the former attended. Twenty oxen were roasted whole by his orders in the borough on Christmas-day. He gave away two hundred chaldrons of coal, and a thousand pair of blankets. Finally he ordered Mr. Chace to advance money to the industrious at three per cent. It was quite clear that the reign of the Low Whig Oligarchs had ceased for ever. All paid off their mortgages to Jenkins and Co. No more hard interest at short dates. It was evident, as Jenkins whispered in a deadly voice to Dawson, that Fanchester was a Bohun borough.

Between the days of public banquets, Mr. Bohun amused himself with private dinner parties. The Castle was a scene of continual wassail, and finally, invitations to a grand ball were circulated throughout the whole county. Everyone was invited, from the Earl of Courtland to the family of the humblest Squireen. Notwithstanding all these calls upon his time, a day seldom passed during the fortnight, which had elapsed since the Election, that did not find Mr. Bohun a visitor to Hartlebury. Every day there was an excuse for meeting. Sometimes there was a large riding party; sometimes the ladies were to see the hounds thrown off; sometimes in-door pursuits engaged their attention, and now there were perpetual conferences and consultations about the arrangements for the ball.

"Arthur, you are to go with me to the ball," said Helen to Mr. Latimer.

"Helen, you know I detest dancing," was the reply. "I cannot conceive any man more misplaced than I am in a ball-room. You must excuse me."

"I am resolved you shall go Arthur, you are my beau. I have no idea of entering a ball-room on the arm of papa. It would be quite shocking, would it not Sir?"

"Oh! — terrible," said Mr. Molesworth, "but much more shocking for me to enter a ball-room with my daughter upon my arm. You must get Mrs. Latimer to chaperone you, Helen. I shall stay at home."

"What am I to do for a beau?" said Helen. "Arthur, you are to go."

"There is Mr. George Gainsborough," said Mr. Latimer, not very amiably. "He is a favourite of yours, or at least was."

Helen stared, but did not reply. She never remembered Arthur Latimer speaking with such an evident tone of pique.

The day of the ball arrived. Mr. Molesworth in spite of his asseverations went. Mrs. Latimer was really prevented by indisposition, but nothing could induce Arthur Latimer to leave home, and what was most provoking, he would not even make his mother's illness an excuse for his obstinacy.

Bohun Castle was illuminated. Every chamber was thrown open. The crush of carriages was worthy of a great house in Piccadilly. The quadrangle was a sea of waving flambeaus: the staircase was lined with footmen and pages in splendid liveries. As you entered the ball-room the brilliant blaze of the chandeliers, and the magnificence of the orange trees and exotic plants made you for a moment insensible to the fanciful decorations of the sumptuous chamber. The room was crowded; as the Molesworths made their way up the staircase, Mrs. Escott saluted them.

"Everybody asked," she said, "no distinction of parties, very handsome of him isn't it?"

Mr. Bohun and Mrs. Neville came forward to receive them.

"Do you think the room looks as well as the first time we lit it up?" he said to Helen, "that happy evening!" he continued.

Before she could reply, Mr. Bohun was obliged to leave her to welcome a new party. The Molesworths consequently moved away.

Colonel Neville came up, and engaged Helen to dance with him. "Aubrey you know *must* open the ball with Lady Courtland," he said with a somewhat significant smile, "otherwise I dare not take this liberty, I assure you I am acting under orders."

Helen laughed, for to such observations a laugh is the only answer.

Her father yielded her to her partner. "I suppose," was his valedictory lament, "I suppose there is no rubber."

"What a revolution Mr. Bohun's return has made!" said Helen to the Colonel. "It really seems like a dream."

"You see there was some policy after all in staying away so long," replied the Colonel, "if this had always been going on, I suppose we should have thought it a bore."

As they were dancing, she could not help smiling as she overheard Dr. Maxwell, Mr. Gainsborough's son-in-law, holding forth to a county gentleman and his spouse, who evidently looked upon him as an oracle.

"A great thing indeed for the county, a very great thing indeed; a still greater thing for the neighbourhood. The greatest thing that could possibly happen to Fanchester, Mr. Bohun's return! Quite the making of the neighbourhood. Splendid property. It's a satisfaction to see a splendid property like Bohun fall to the lot of a man who takes pleasure in assembling his friends around him. I am sure all Fanchester must be grateful to my father-in-law! Entirely owing to him, entirely, entirely! The greatest sacrifice, the very greatest possible sacrifice of feeling, I do assure you, sir, but when duty is in the case, Mr. Gainsborough never hesitates. I differ with Mr. Gainsborough, I differ with my father-in-law on some public points, I have no hesitation in saying so, I certainly do differ with him, but I defy anyone to say that when duty is concerned, when duty is in the case, that Mr. Gainsborough, that my father-in-law ever hesitates. Entirely owing to him. The people of Fanchester, and indeed the whole county, sir, may thank Oakfield Lodge for all this!"

"How do you do Chumfield?" said the Earl of Courtland to our friend the jolly brewer, "how is Mrs. Chumfield, I have not seen her here? How are your daughters? How is your eldest son? A most promising young man, your eldest son, we shall make something of him. How is your younger son? How does he like College? Let me see, at Haileybury, I think? We shall see him a Director some day. Your nephew likes Sydney? Great opening there, no doubt he will do very well, immense fortunes to be made at Sydney. What does he think of the wool? How is my friend Mr. Baggs? Pray remember me to my excellent friend Mr. Baggs. A very long head indeed has Mr. Baggs. You managed your election admirably Chumfield. The eyes of all England were on you. Things will mend Chumfield, things will mend. I saw your friend Sir George, the other day. He asked after you."

And the Earl moved on to overwhelm some other gratified county man with his flattering queries, and marvellous memory.

Mr. Bohun was dancing with Miss Molesworth.

"Are you amused?" he enquired.

"Very!" she replied, "I hope you share my diversion."

"I only reflect your feelings," he answered. "If you smile, I am happy."

He spoke in so serious a tone that Helen scarcely ventured on her customary repartee, and was silent.

"I fear you will find this room very hot. I wanted to have the quadrangle covered over but Emmeline overruled me. I perceive that it is impossible ever to have an opinion of my own, and sooth to say, I am not very anxious to enjoy that privilege. I like to be ruled."

"You have always given me that idea," observed Miss Molesworth, "you seem exactly the sort of person who would bear restraint admirably!"

"You mock me! 'Tis very true though. I have never passed three months in my life as my own master. Ruled I must be, but by a woman, Miss Molesworth, by a woman, mind you! Emmeline manages me in little things, and you in great."

"I!" said the astonished Helen.

"You," calmly replied Bohun.

"Where is my sceptre!" she gaily exclaimed. "I had no idea of my sway."

"It is absolute," said Mr. Bohun with a very serious countenance. "All I hope is that it will be merciful."

"Do you admire Miss Molesworth?" said Miss Gertrude Fanshawe to Mr. George Gainsborough, as they were dancing opposite Mr. Bohun and our heroine.

"I believe she is admired," was the cautious reply.

"So I understand," said Miss Fanshawe. "I cannot say she is at all my style of beauty. I think she has not countenance enough for her height."

"She certainly is not at all your style of beauty," thought George Gainsborough as he looked at his meagre, sallow companion. Miss Fanshawe passed the season regularly in London, and was considered a very fashionable young lady indeed.

"I suppose it's a mere flirtation between her and Mr. Bohun?" continued Miss Fanshawe.

"Assuredly," said George Gainsborough, "Aubrey Bohun is not a marrying man."

"He seems to have turned her head though," continued Miss Fanshawe, "by all we hear. All the county is talking of her interference in the Election. Un peu trop fort, I think," she

observed, looking up into Mr. George Gainsborough's face
with her brilliant black eyes, and grinning maliciously with her
brilliant white teeth.

George Gainsborough slightly shrugged his shoulders.

"Why one gets interested in an Election," said George
Gainsborough. "I did extraordinary things myself, though I am
not apt to exert myself, for what some witty writer calls 'the
brown sex'."

"You knew Mr. Bohun abroad?" enquired Miss Fanshawe.

"I did."

"And you have been a very odd sort of person yourself, I
believe?"

"The present moment is too charming to remember the
past," replied George Gainsborough mysteriously.

"I think you live near Bohun?" said Miss Fanshawe, who was
too aristocratic to know anything of the whereabouts of the
Gainsboroughs, but who was sufficiently acquainted with the
world to know that George Gainsborough, at a county ball, was
a man of mark, and likelihood, and that a son may be "very
knowing", while a father and mother and sisters may be things
too horrible even to think of.

"My father's place joins the Bohun's property."

"What is its name?"

"Oakfield; Oakfield Lodge."

"Oakfield! Dear me! I thought I knew every place in the
county, and I never heard of Oakfield."

"I know nothing about the county," said George Gainsborough rallying. "I scarcely ever live at home, and seldom in
England. It is too uninteresting. I detest the regular jog-trot
existence of English life. I require adventure, I think I shall
return to Greece."

The Corsair-like air with which this observation was made
quite silenced Miss Fanshawe, who was soon on her better
behaviour, and in the course of the evening glided very gracefully into a strong flirtation with the heir apparent of the
unheard of Oakfield.

The night wore away. The Earl of Courtland was conversing
with Mrs. Neville and Miss Molesworth. Mr. George Gainsborough approached them.

"As this ball is to celebrate our triumph Miss Molesworth,"

he said, addressing that lady in an undertone, "while we are enjoying the fruits, I hope you will remember a fellow-labourer in the vine-yard. Might I hope for the honour of your hand?"

"I had determined to dance no more," said Helen, "but you have made an appeal which I cannot resist," and George Gainsborough led her to the quadrille.

"Do you know, Mr. Gainsborough," said Miss Molesworth suddenly in one of the pauses, "it has always struck me as most singular that you should not have remembered Mr. Bohun — such a brilliant person could surely not have been forgotten."

George Gainsborough looked rather confused; but he answered, "You are quite right. Whoever once knows Mr. Bohun could never forget him."

"But you have not explained the mystery," said Miss Molesworth.

"Mystery!" said George Gainsborough.

"Yes! mystery," said Miss Molesworth, "for a mystery I am sure there is."

"You are quite right," again observed George Gainsborough, but with a more assured demeanour. "There is a mystery."

"And I am not to penetrate it?" said Miss Molesworth.

"Those eyes can penetrate anything," said Mr. George Gainsborough, who had drunk a sufficient quantity of Champagne.

"You silence me with a compliment. 'Tis discreet, but useless. I have made up my mind to know everything. Tell me."

"The revelation may not be agreeable," said George Gainsborough.

"I cannot see how it can be disagreeable to me," said Miss Molesworth.

"I wish that I could be assured of that," said Mr. George Gainsborough.

"Of what?" enquired Miss Molesworth.

"I wish I was convinced that anything I could say about Mr. Bohun could not be a subject of interest to you Miss Molesworth."

"Said I so?" enquired Helen, "indeed I meant no such thing."

George Gainsborough looked mortified, and began talking about the chandeliers.

"But you were in fact mystifying me then," continued Miss Molesworth, determined to return to the subject, "when you said that you did not remember Mr. Bohun?"

"I never mystify, Miss Molesworth," replied George Gainsborough. "I am a much franker person than you give me credit for. I did not remember the name, because I had never to my knowledge met any person abroad who bore it."

"Darker than ever," said Miss Molesworth, "and what was Mr. Bohun's nom de guerre?"

"De guerre indeed! You are nearer the truth than you imagine, but the truth is Miss Molesworth, it is no use asking me any questions, for I have at times a bad memory, and at the present moment all my recollection is concentred in this ball-room."

"With Miss Fanshawe?" said Helen laughing, who did not deem it advisable to pursue her enquiries.

"The charming, the fashionable Miss Fanshawe," said George Gainsborough laughing, "she admired you very much," he continued. "Do you know she talked to me a great deal about you?"

"Now tell me everything she said. Do not spare me. I am in a very curious humour tonight, and as you will tell me nothing about yourself, let me for the want of a better, be the subject of your discourse."

George Gainsborough laughed. "Miss Fanshawe," he said, "is of opinion that Mr. Bohun ought to be very grateful to you."

"Indeed! and for what?"

"For making him a Member of Parliament."

"There are so many persons concerned in that catastrophe," replied Miss Molesworth, "that I think Mr. Bohun may very safely be ungrateful. I assure you I had the mortification to hear your brother-in-law ascribe all our success this evening to Oakfield. And what else did Miss Fanshawe say?"

"Oh! she was curious."

"And so am I, very, very curious. Tell me all."

"Miss Fanshawe," replied Mr. Gainsborough, "appears to be a great connoisseur in what she calls flirtations."

"Well?"

"And she is extremely anxious to know whether there be a flirtation between you and Mr. Bohun."

"She applied to you for information, and you answered her.
You ought to be a judge. Well what was your response?"

"I forget."

"Nay! all your recollections you know are concentred in this
ball-room. You shall answer me."

"To be frank then, which I always am," said George Gainsborough, "I told her I thought there was not."

George Gainsborough scrutinized her countenance nar-
rowly. Miss Molesworth did not look mortified. Was she indeed
indifferent, or was she confident? He was determined to ascertain.

"I said," he continued, "that to use her own language, I did
not believe there was any serious feeling between yourself and
Mr. Bohun, for two reasons; first, because I could not conceive
that there ever could exist a man worthy of Miss Molesworth;
and secondly, because I knew Aubrey Bohun very well, and was
convinced that he would never marry."

"I think Papa is looking for me," said Miss Molesworth, in a
rather hurried tone, "just cross over, and tell him that I shall be
ready to go, when we have finished the quadrille."

CHAPTER XI

The heart chastened in a sick chamber

On the morning after the ball, Aubrey Bohun rose with the
most agreeable feelings. His recollections were delightful, his
anticipations were not less so. He determined to ride directly
over to Hartlebury. And why, thought he, should not this visit
be a decisive one? "In a week I must away to London, why
should I part from her without a word of hope to dwell upon
during separation?" He mused on all that had passed the evening before, he had said so much that he felt that Helen must

understand him, it was therefore incumbent on him to explain himself. In fact, Aubrey Bohun was in the mood to try his fate, and we none of us, even the most dull, fail of reasons in abundance to support us in doing what we have already determined on.

It was a clear frosty day, a brilliant sun made a glittering scene. This bright morning is ominous of good, thought Mr. Bohun as he vaulted into his saddle.

Notwithstanding the interesting mission on which he was bent, he could not be insensible to the beauty of his ride. The Park looked enchanted, everything was sparkling. The white frost hung in fantastic forms on the leafless branches, and the pendent icicles trembled under the warm sun. Every now and then a timorous hare disturbed by the horse's step bounded from its warm covert, and scampered across the path, scarcely disturbing the brilliant crystallizations that covered each blade of grass.

But on this day the triumphant Aubrey Bohun was destined to endure disappointment. When he arrived at Hartlebury he found everybody in trouble and confusion. During the preceding night Mrs. Latimer, who had been of late slightly indisposed, though without any symptom which caused alarm, had been suddenly seized with a most severe attack of paralysis, and was now lying insensible, it was feared without hope of recovery. Miss Molesworth had been at the Rectory ever since nine o'clock, and was not expected to return home.

Helen had returned from the Ball exhausted both in mind and body. Certain vague but disagreeable sensations added to her fatigue, but she was too tired to examine into the cause of them: she could only wonder how she could ever have thought George Gainsborough agreeable. But she did not wonder long even over this great mistake, for she soon sank into that dreamless slumber which follows physical exhaustion. After the refreshment of a very few hours repose her servant entered the room. She opened the shutters with a most officious bustle, she undrew the bed-curtains. She stirred the fire, she even began to prepare the toilette.

"Is it very late?" asked the disturbed sleeper plaintively.

"No not *very* late Ma'am. It is very nearly nine o'clock," answered the maid, who directly Helen spoke advanced, and took up a position by the bed-side.

"That is very early," murmured Helen, "how could you disturb me so soon Hardy?" "I dare say you are tired Ma'am, but *still* I thought you would like to get up," said Hardy with that particular air of agitating mystery with which ladies' maids are wont to communicate intelligence.

"What is the matter?" asked Helen, now thoroughly disturbed by Hardy's manner, "I am sure there is something the matter."

"Pray do not agitate yourself Ma'am, I hope it will be nothing after all, only I thought you would rather know it directly."

"Tell me quickly Hardy what is the matter? Is my father ill?" said Helen, now quite awake, and almost frightened out of her senses.

"Pray Ma'am, do not be so agitated, do not alarm yourself." Here Helen gasped for breath. "It is not my master Ma'am, my master is quite well. Don't be frightened Ma'am, Mr. Trueman has come by this time, and I dare say Mrs. Latimer is already better."

For this day and many succeeding ones, did Mrs. Hardy expatiate in the Housekeeper's room on the very *pertickler* clever way she had of conveying unpleasant intelligence.

Helen was soon dressed. As she descended the stairs she knocked at her father's door; he was already up.

"Dear Helen," he said, as he kissed her pale cheek, "you have heard the sad intelligence, I trust it is not as serious as Arthur's fears anticipate, I have this moment heard from him."

Mr. Molesworth put into her hand a few almost illegible lines from Arthur Latimer, which said that Mr. Trueman had just arrived but gave little hope.

"Poor Arthur," said Helen while the tears poured down her cheeks, "he must want help, and consolation. I am going now, dear Papa, you will soon see him."

Mr. Trueman's gig was still at the gate as Helen entered the Rectory. She turned into the breakfast parlour. Mr. Trueman and Arthur Latimer were leaning against the mantel-piece in earnest conversation. Arthur Latimer advanced to meet her.

"Is she better?" asked Helen in a low voice.

Arthur shook his head.

"May I go to her?" she asked of Mr. Trueman.

"You must not think of it," said Mr. Latimer affectionately; in the midst of his trouble he could still remember all that concerned Helen. "You have not been home very long, you can scarcely have been in bed. You must already be over fatigued."

"I had forgotten all that," said Helen, with so much truth and feeling that Arthur Latimer unconsciously pressed her hand.

"Only tell me, Mr. Trueman, what is necessary to be done," said Helen.

"Nothing my dear Madam, can be done beyond what I have already prescribed," said the solemn doctor, "now all depends on quiet, on the most perfect quiet. Entire absence of all noise. It is an attack of what we call paralysis, and all depends, my dear Madam, on quiet."

Helen lightly stepped into Mrs. Latimer's bed chamber. She advanced to the bed-side. There lay her beloved friend, with her eyes half closed, perfectly unconscious. Helen took her hand as it lay on the coverlid, it was so totally without power that she almost thought that it was all over.

"Ah! Ma'am," sobbed Nugent, the old servant of the family, "she will never recover, it is just the way my poor master went."

Helen took her station by the bed-side, which she was determined not to abandon. All through that day did she watch without hope. Towards evening Nugent persuaded her to try to sleep. Helen lay down on the sofa and closed her eyes, and endeavoured to compose herself, but during the last twenty-four hours she had experienced such varied and painful excitement that it was very long before sleep came to the aid of her overstrained nerves. At last, however, her excited senses subsided into an uneasy slumber, and she dreamt that she was at Fanchester. The streets were full of crowds of people, and they all told her that she would be too late. She was going to vote for Mr. Bohun, she looked at the great church clock, it was going to strike, in a minute she would be too late, she felt almost suffocated in the crowd. All of a sudden George Gainsborough was walking by her side; he said he could take her away from the crowd, out of the Town. He said they would soon be at the booth, for it was a private way no one knew but himself, and so on and on they went, and she grew very frightened, and a hollow malicious laugh resounded in her ear, and she turned round, and it was no longer George Gainsborough at her side, but a most malignant looking being who whispered in her ear, "While you are walking here, Mrs. Latimer is dead."

Helen awoke in great agitation, and it was some minutes before she could recall her wandering senses, before she could remember where she was, and through the flickering light of the solitary lamp perceive the servant watching by the side of Mrs. Latimer.

Trueman came again early in the morning. He still shook his head, he could give no hope. But the young are naturally full of hope, their buoyant hearts through the gloom of the deepest affliction quickly detect a glimmer of light. Hitherto Helen had been overwhelmed by the suddenness of the shock, but she now began to rally, and towards the close of the second day when she went downstairs to give her evening bulletin to Arthur Latimer, she dared to speak words of comfort.

And Helen was a comforter whom none could resist, for her manner was as judicious as it was soothing, and Arthur Latimer yielded with gratitude to her influence. Of late a somewhat colder and more distant intercourse had almost imperceptibly arisen between them. She knew that he had disapproved of much that she had been led to do in the ardour of the Election, and that he disliked Mr. Bohun for having required from her acts of friendship, which he deemed unbecoming to her delicacy and refinement. But now in this moment of sorrow all was forgotten, he thought not of the strangers, who had of late so much disturbed him, he thought only of his mother's sufferings, and of Helen's kindness.

But not so Helen, as she sat that night by Mrs. Latimer's bed-side; her thoughts insensibly reverted from her friend to others. She thought of that friend's unvarying kindness, of the sincerity of her affection. Here, mused Helen, is one who never deceived me, next to my dear father, here perhaps is my best friend. All this family love me, I can depend upon them all, for they are all truth and sincerity. Ah! there is no happiness in this life without the full consciousness of being able to trust those who profess to love you. She dwelt with earnestness on the beauty of truth; beyond her own beloved friends there seemed to be everywhere double dealing and duplicity and mystery. The truth is that Helen had lately seen more of the world. The election had shown her something of the secret springs which work poor human nature. She had seen persons apparently the most respectable and the most honest swayed only by their interest. How often had she herself been the tempter. Her conduct with regard to Mr. Gainsborough too, had for some time been rather a disagreeable subject of thought, but now in this quiet, silent room, perhaps soon to be the abode of death, all the excitement over, everything appeared in its true colours; she was disgusted with the whole affair, and with herself. This was perhaps the first time that Helen Molesworth's cogitations had been so little satisfactory. And she remembered the words of Arthur Latimer, "Ought we not to fear one who so captivates our reason that we forget the difference between right and wrong?" Alas! she felt that we ought. It was Mr. Bohun's brilliancy which had dazzled her; for that which now appeared to her so disgusting, so mean, and so dishonourable, had seemed at the time under his representations the most natural thing in the world which it would have been an over-fastidiousness to refuse. And Mr. Bohun himself, how strange and mysterious everything was about him. What did George Gainsborough mean by telling her that Mr. Bohun would never marry? Did he mean the intelligence for a warning to her? Did she need the warning? She shrank not from the question: could she yield her love, could she desert her father, her fond, her darling parent, for one whom she had known but a few months; known, could she even now say known? What did she know of him? — that he had lived under an assumed name in a mysterious manner in distant countries. She shuddered as she thought that she might perhaps have been so dazzled, her reason so captivated, that she might have been betrayed even into that. She mistrusted herself, she feared, she doubted everybody. Everybody seemed false and deceiving. She turned to the bed, she kissed the hand of her unconscious friend, and she bathed it with her tears.

In the meantime while these meditations, so little favourable to his wishes, occupied the mind of Helen Molesworth, Mr. Bohun never failed to call each day at Hartlebury, and each day a little note-lette was delivered to Helen either from him or from Mrs. Neville, to tell her again and again how much they grieved with her, how much they feared to hear that she was suffering from her exertions, and how miserable they were at the thought of leaving Bohun without again seeing her.

Earlier than usual one morning came a note from Mrs. Neville, to tell her that their journey was finally arranged for the next day, and to beg to see her if it were possible, if it were only for a minute. Helen could not refuse such a request.

At the appointed hour, Helen heard the tramp of horse's feet at the Rectory gate, she descended into the small breakfast room. She found there Mrs. Neville and Mr. Bohun.

"Dearest Helen," said Mrs. Neville as she advanced to meet her, and she kissed her pale cheek.

Helen returned her embrace, but she could not speak. For a week she had scarcely left Mrs. Latimer's bed-side, the confinement and the grief had weakened her, and coming now from the closed darkened room of the invalid into that gay room, bright in the sunshine, she felt for a moment overpowered.

Mr. Bohun looked pained at her affliction. He did not speak, but he took her offered hand with an expression of sympathy, which could not be misunderstood, and which was infinitely more grateful to her feelings than Mrs. Neville's fluent ejaculations.

"My dear Helen," said that lady, "this is indeed a grievous end to all our gaieties. I would not let Gustavus come, I thought we should be too many. I assure you he is dying to see you. I promised him I would bear to you his best love. I could not refuse to bring Aubrey. Aubrey, you know, could not go without thanking you for all you have done for him."

As Helen did not wish to hear a word of the thanks, she endeavoured to rally, and tried to speak of her grief in thus losing Mrs. Neville, and of her hope of their soon meeting again.

"Only think, we have never met since Aubrey's gay ball," said Mrs. Neville. "Was it not successful?" asked the lady with wonderful inconsideration.

Mr. Bohun felt her levity, and asked so kindly after Mr. Latimer that Helen was saved a reply.

He was the first to suggest that they ought to end their visit, but Mrs. Neville would not go until Helen had promised often to write to her.

"You must write to me Emmeline," said Helen, "for what can I tell you from here, except that I miss you. Remember how dull you thought it when first you came among us, you brought all our events, and with you they will all depart."

"I shall certainly write to you my dear Helen," answered Mrs. Neville. "I am very idle, but there is no fear of my not writing to you, for Aubrey will have so much pleasure in franking the letters that he will be sure to remind me of writing."

Helen felt that Mr. Bohun's eyes were fixed upon her as Mrs. Neville said this; she felt that she must exert herself, and she laughingly said, "But Emmeline I am vain enough to expect you to remember me yourself, so that I shall only regard an unfranked letter as a proof that you do not forget me."

"Dearest Helen who can forget you," said Mrs. Neville embracing her. "We shall never cease to talk of you, shall we Aubrey?"

"I wish I were sure of being remembered as I shall ever remember Miss Molesworth," said Mr. Bohun seriously.

In a moment they were gone.

"It may be only gallantry," said Helen to herself, "but *he* at any rate has feeling."

CHAPTER XII

Hartlebury at peace — Mr. Bohun in London

The most grateful labour of love is to watch the daily progress towards health of a loved friend, whom we have tended through an almost hopeless illness. To note each day that slight increase of strength which is imperceptible to others, to listen to tones no longer tremulous, to gaze on the smile which speaks of the thankfulness of the heart, and to share all the joy of returning health, are indeed rich rewards for all the cares and sympathies of friendship.

And this happiness was now Helen Molesworth's. Each day Mrs. Latimer grew stronger, and more able to express her gratitude and her affection for her young nurse. Mrs. Boscawen, at the time of her mother's sudden attack, had herself been too ill to come to her, and therefore during the whole of Mrs. Latimer's illness, all the duties of a daughter had devolved on Helen.

In the performance of those duties she became more satisfied with herself, and as the hope of Mrs. Latimer's recovery gradually grew into a certainty, she recovered her wonted gaiety and cheerfulness, and in time she could even see old Mr. Gainsborough, almost without a blush.

With Mr. Bohun had vanished all the unusual excitement of the neighbourhood; all the visiting and the carousing was over, everything was again quiet. Even George Gainsborough had been for some time away. Peaceful Hartlebury seemed itself again. Arthur Latimer yielded to the full enjoyment of Helen's society, she had become dearer to him than ever, and no intruders were at hand to awaken him to caution. He felt that he was happy —he staid not to ask why. He and Helen resumed their old walks and rides, and village visits; and he endeavoured to forget the last disagreeable year. But sometimes, in despite of himself, his thoughts would revert to Mr. Bohun. He could not help occasionally speculating on the terms on which he had parted with Helen: but Helen seemed happy and gay — ought he not then to be satisfied?

She, like himself, appeared to enjoy the peace which had returned to Hartlebury; for when her father urged her to go for a while away from home to seek change of air and scene, after all her exertions, she would always playfully answer, "Dear Papa, where can I find a greater change than I have here? Look at dear Hartlebury now, and think what it was two months ago." Mr. Molesworth always hated moving from home, so the matter was soon settled between them.

In the meantime they often heard of their late companions. Mrs. Neville was wonderfully punctual in her correspondence, and her letters were all of Aubrey Bohun. Mr. Bohun himself sometimes wrote to Mr. Molesworth — the avowed object of his letters was to obtain some information respecting the administration of the Poor Laws in the immediate vicinity of Bohun and

Hartlebury, but he did not attempt to conceal from his friends that he was eager to avail himself of any excuse to remind them of him. He assured them how desirous he was to escape from the crowds around him, and that he should deem himself the happiest man in the world, on the day he was again admitted at Hartlebury.

On Mr. Bohun's arrival in London, he became the object of universal attention. He was soon surrounded, and was more courted and caressed than in the days of his gay youth. the suddenness of his return had awakened curiosity respecting the secrecy of his retreat; everybody had some solution to offer of the mystery. He was the subject of general speculation. He was the fashion. Brilliant beauties, who had sought consolation in a coronet for Mr. Bohun's former indifference, and younger, and not less charming fair ones, who hoped now to find him more willing to be won, and leaders of all parties who were equally eager to secure him, all sought his notice. His election had already made a great sensation among the politicians; there was no saying what he might be. Everybody was interested about him — everybody seemed to think that he had been so long out of England, that without their advice he could not be successful; he had as many advisers as acquaintances.

"My dear Mr. Bohun," said the old fool, "Allow me to advise you — excuse the liberty I take, but age you know gives us a privilege. I have seen too many great men in my time. I have a high idea of your powers — no one can have a higher — I am sure you will equal the greatest: but take my advice, do not be in a hurry to speak — Feel your way first — All great statesmen have waited a season or two before they spoke — waited till they caught the tone of the House. Take my advice, do not be in a hurry to speak."

"I say, Bohun, my good fellow," said the young fool, "take my advice, don't be in a hurry to speak — wait till you catch the tone of the House — I have known devilish clever fellows quite done up, by not waiting until they caught the tone of the House.'

Mr. Bohun's answer to both was a bow. He knew his own powers. Parliament met. The King's speech was discussed. In a

crowded House, Aubrey Bohun arose. He spoke on our Continental policy. He addressed the House without the slightest
apparent nervousness, but with great mildness, and with an air
that the dandies decided was perfectly gentlemanly — so they
listened. The Tories listened because they were anxious to
make out whether he belonged to them or not: and the Whigs
listened because they were afraid of him. So Aubrey Bohun
soon felt that he had a perfect command of the House. Then he
warmed with his subject — he described with energy the fame
and power of England, as he had witnessed it spread over the
Continent, when he first went abroad ten years since. He drew a
degrading image of what it would be in ten years to come, if the
blighting principles indicated in the Royal Speech were
adhered to. He was fully master of his subject — he abounded in
facts, and each fact was an epigram. The Treasury Bench
writhed. It was not only the most successful debut ever made in
that House, but the most brilliant oration that had for years
been heard within its walls. And from this night he spoke in all
great debates, and ever with the same success, for he was
equally powerful in attack or defence.

There were others, as we must all remember, in the opening
of this reformed Parliament, who were induced by his success
to follow his example, and who made most extraordinary fail-
ures. Their friends say that it was all owing to their speaking
before they caught the tone of the House, but they are all wrong
— the mistake was not in speaking too soon, but in speaking at
all.

One morning the breakfast table at Hartlebury was enlivened
by an unusually long letter from Mrs. Neville. It contained an
account more dazzling than ever of Aubrey Bohun. Helen read
it to her father; and while he was occupied with the newspaper,
she re-read it to herself. Mr. Molesworth suddenly looked up,
and he saw Helen with a most serious countenance, studying
Mrs. Neville's epistle.

"What are you thinking of Helen?" he asked, "is not Mr.
Bohun eloquent enough to please you?"

Helen started from her reverie, and slightly blushing said,

"Indeed, papa, I was just thinking that we really have no reason to be ashamed of our Fanchester hero."

"I did not know that you ever thought that you had," said Mr. Molesworth, with a scrutinizing glance.

Helen made no answer, and he returned to his paper.

"Papa!" said Helen, rather suddenly, after some minutes of silence.

"Well, Helen," said her father, again looking up.

"Papa!" again commenced Helen, "Mr. Bohun is certainly a very extraordinary person."

"Fortunately he is, my dear," answered Mr. Molesworth; "it would be awkward if many resembled him: we should live always in a state of confusion."

"Should you not very much like to know what he did with himself abroad?"

"Perhaps his adventures would disappoint us."

"Why?"

"They might destroy all our romantic ideas of his extraordinary qualities, they might prove him a very ordinary sort of person."

"No papa, I am sure that you do not think so — you must feel that Mr. Bohun could not have passed ten years in a commonplace manner."

"Are you interested to know, Helen?" asked her father, with more seriousness.

"Oh! no," answered Helen, a little confused, "it is merely a woman's curiosity."

"If that be all," said Mr. Molesworth, "the discovery may safely be left to woman's wit."

"Not to mine," said Helen. After a pause she added, with more frankness, "Would it not, Papa, be satisfactory to know something of the past life of one with whom we have thus glided into intimacy?"

"You are right, my child," said Mr. Molesworth, "and I confess to you I have long desired this knowledge, but have sought it in vain."

"There is one person who could tell us much," said Helen.

"Who is that?" asked her father.

"Mr. George Gainsborough."

Mr. Molesworth remained for a few minutes plunged in

thought, he then turned away to his paper; but he seemed uneasy, and his eye often wandered from its columns to his daughter. But Helen was now at the window, speculating on the weather. This was the third morning that it had rained without ceasing, and her anxiety for a bright sun, and a clear sky, seemed somewhat to have lessened her curiosity— to unveil the dark clouds that hung around their mysterious neighbour.

CHAPTER XIII

George Gainsborough's hopes revive

About noon the clouds broke, the sun came forth— the horizon cleared. Mr. Molesworth invited his daughter to ride with him. It was one of those mornings towards the close of March that give us the first indication that Winter is leaving us, and that the beautiful Spring is about again to gladden the earth. The trees were yet leafless; but every branch was covered with bursting buds. The air was mild and soft, and as our companions pursued their way by the banks of the river, they allowed their horses to drop into a walk as they gazed on the changes which the last day or two had produced. The meadows looked green with the springing grass, and the daisies were appearing, and in the hedges, on the hazel and the nut, the long pendent blossom had opened by the side of its delicate pink companion, and the dark foliage of the yew was enlivened by its ivory flowers. And in every sheltered spot patches of snow-drops and tufts of primroses were seen.

Mr. Molesworth and his daughter rode on in silence; they were somewhat serious, and Helen was meditating on the many changes which had occurred since last she watched these same trees bursting into life. A horseman appeared in the distance: he hastened his pace when he discerned them.

"Papa!" said Helen, suddenly, and starting in her saddle. "Here is Mr. George Gainsborough."

Mr. George Gainsborough advanced smilingly to greet them, little aware how much of their thoughts he was at that moment occupying. He had just returned home, and had as usual much to say. He enquired after Mrs. Latimer, and was very complimentary to Miss Molesworth on the successful result of her exertions, and was eager to learn that she had not suffered from what he characterized as her amiable attentions. He talked a great deal, but he made no allusion to any of the important events which had of late disturbed them, though he had never seen Helen since the night of the ball. Helen's thoughts, however, were wholly of the past, and she was silent and constrained, but her father's unwonted loquacity fully covered her want of conversation. Mr. Molesworth seldom took the trouble of talking much to anybody, merely for the sake of conversing, and more especially to George Gainsborough, whose flowery style he considered intended for the woman-kind; but on this occasion he was very communicative. The truth was that it struck Mr. Molesworth that it was necessary to encourage some slight intimacy with a man from whom he desired to obtain such important information.

The following day Mr. George Gainsborough called at the hall. Miss Molesworth was with Mrs. Latimer, but he spent half an hour with Mr. Molesworth, who at the conclusion of the visit invited him to dinner on the next day.

The most honest are apt unconsciously to fall into a softer and more ingratiating manner than usual, when they address those of whom they require a service, and so it was at this time with Mr. Molesworth, when he gave his invitation to George Gainsborough. He was not the least aware of it himself, but his kindness was not lost on the object of it.

George Gainsborough's designs on Miss Molesworth had been abandoned, but they were not forgotten. He had yielded to his unfortunate destiny, he had yielded to one whom he detested, but who, alas! he had long fatally experienced he could not resist. From the moment that Mr. Bohun had so openly declared to him his intentions with regard to Helen Molesworth, George Gainsborough had withdrawn from the contest. He stood apart, a gay, and apparently an unconcerned, spectator. He felt that she could never be his, but he did not resign her without a struggle— he longed for the consolation of revenge. It was that feeling that prompted him on the night of the ball to play with Helen's excited suspicions, and to infuse into her mind doubts of Mr. Bohun's sincerity. More he dared not do, but he left that little to work its way. He quitted Hartlebury with the hope that he had converted her suspicions into certainty.

But today other feelings arose. Certainly Mr. Molesworth had greeted him with unusual warmth. He could not be deceived in his manner, and then so immediate an invitation to dine with them, and alone, seemed as if they sought a renewal of their earlier intimacy. Was it possible that what he had intended should destroy his rival should have produced a double effect, and worked good for himself? It was not improbable that Miss Molesworth should have communicated her conversation with him to her father, who perhaps had already shared her suspicions, and they might both regard him as a friend, whose timely caution had saved them from much future pain.

As he thus meditated, his passions roused. Why now should he not make a desperate effort to win her? He could trust the Molesworths: whatever he communicated to Mr. Molesworth under the seal of secrecy, he was confident that he would never divulge; he might venture to tell him much — why should he not tell him all — all that concerned Mr. Bohun — and all told, Aubrey Bohun and Helen Molesworth were eternally separated.

Thus mused George Gainsborough through that day and night, until his excited passions yearned for the morrow, which was to gratify his vengeance, and perhaps lay the foundations of his future triumph.

CHAPTER XIV

The mystery disclosed

On the morrow, in the gayest spirits, George Gainsborough entered the drawing-room of Hartlebury Hall. During dinner he amused his companions with innumerable anecdotes of his Continental adventures, gay and wonderful histories, which had greatly enlivened them on his first coming amongst them, but which somehow or other had lain dormant since Mr. Bohun's arrival.

He talked of nothing but Greece, and each moment there seemed to Helen an opportunity to lead to the explanation which she so much desired. She often looked at her father, and caught his eye; he too appeared to think as she did. She seized therefore the first opportunity to quit the room, that her presence might prove no hindrance to their conversation.

In the drawing-room, she drew her chair to the fire, and with her feet on the fender, her fancy was busy in speculating on what, after all, George Gainsborough could have to tell. An hour passed, and yet they came not; he must be telling all. Two hours had elapsed, when Mr. Molesworth entered the room and alone.

"Dear Papa, have you the least idea how late it is," said Miss Molesworth as her father entered. "Where is Mr. Gainsborough?"

"He has gone home," replied Mr. Molesworth in a very serious tone, and he began poking the fire.

"Gone home!"

"Yes, gone home, Helen," continued Mr. Molesworth after a momentary pause. "Helen I wish to speak a word to you." He seated himself by her side, he took his daughter's hand, held it for a moment and then kissed it.

"Dearest Papa!" said Helen rather alarmed. "You are very serious! What has happened?"

"Nothing, nothing I hope that should make us unhappy,

though much that should make us serious."

"Oh! tell me!"

"My own Helen, you must be aware that your felicity in life is ever the chief object of my care."

"Each instant of my existence proves that truth," replied the daughter.

"I have indeed," continued Mr. Molesworth, "no other thought but you. Providence has willed that our family name, an ancient and a time-honoured name, should apparently become extinct. I do not murmur Helen; I hope my child, that under any circumstances I should not murmur, but when I remember that the same beneficent Being that has denied me what some fathers would deem the crowning blessing of exis-tence— a son, should have compensated for this deprivation by yielding me a daughter, like yourself, Helen, I cannot talk of murmuring; I can only think of gratitude."

"Dear father!" What can have happened, thought Helen — surely, surely George Gainsborough is not about to make me a proposal.

"My child," continued Mr. Molesworth, "if you were unhappy, I should die."

"Papa! dearest Papa; am I not the happiest person in the world? Do you not love me? What, what more can I desire?"

"I love you sweetest, yes I love you," and he placed his arm round her waist, "and I am myself happy in your love. You are all in the world to me Helen, all, all. I can have no other thought but you. But with you Helen it is different. You are young, the world is yet before you, you are beautiful, you have all worldly blessings. It is impossible that your feelings can be concentred in mine, as mine are in yours. Were it possible, it is not desirable. It would be selfish, it would be wicked in me to desire it. Long, long my dear Helen, have I accustomed myself to our probable separation. Often, often have I pondered over it. I acknowledge its necessity. My mind is reconciled to the bereavement, and provided it secure your felicity, I am pre-pared to behold in this incident only a fresh blessing, and an occasion for renewed gratefulness."

"Dearest Papa," said Helen, and the tears stole down her cheek. "Talk not of such misery. Why should we ever part? What should occasion our separation."

"Your marriage Helen."

"My marriage Sir!"

"Ay!"

"I do not contemplate such a circumstance."

"Helen," said Mr. Molesworth, "do not deceive me. You, I firmly believe, have never deceived me. Yet women are artful, and on this subject even delicacy prompts deception, and as some think would authorise it."

"Oh! believe me Sir. I speak from my very heart. I do not contemplate marriage."

Mr. Molesworth looked at her very earnestly and then said, "Helen, there should be no secrets between us. I am your best friend, and you have no mother. Think, think twice of what you are saying."

"It is unnecessary. My conscience is clear."

"Mr. Bohun?" said her father with an enquiring air.

"Is to me nothing Sir. I will not deceive you, I will not attempt to conceal that I am sensible to the attentions, or even the qualities, of such a man as Mr. Bohun. But the first I have ever considered lightly of, and for the second— believe me I see much to dread in Mr. Bohun as well as to admire."

Mr. Molesworth rose and walked up and down the room. Suddenly he turned towards Helen, and taking her in his arms, "My daughter, my dear daughter, pardon the anxiety of a parent, of a father who adores you. My daughter, my dear daughter, you are not deceiving me?"

"Oh! my father, you reproach me!" said Helen sobbing. "I could not deceive you. Besides indeed Papa, you are here a little mistaken. Mr. Bohun's gallantry has not misled me; let it not mislead you. He is a practised man of the world; I do not doubt his sincerity when he affects to admire me, or any other pretty woman with whom he is thrown into contact, but I look upon him as a man who has no other object in life but to gratify his selfism, which he styles sentiment. I interested him here: some-one else, I doubt not, interests him now. Indeed, Papa, I have more respect for myself than you imagine; I am not so easily won as you imagine."

"Sweet child, speak on."

"I am too happy at home, to risk such felicity, for anything so uncertain as the affection of a man of whose character I know nothing. Besides, Mr. Bohun is exactly the sort of person of whom I cannot help fancying there is much to know. Nothing would induce me at this moment to become his wife. But, Papa, how he would laugh if he could overhear us, for I dare say he has as much an intention to offer himself to Miss Gainsborough as to myself!"

"You are wrong Helen," said her father. "You are wrong. Men trifle with women, but not with their own sex. Mr. Bohun admires you, I doubt not he is prepared to offer to unite his destiny with yours, for he has spoken to me on the subject, and I referred him to you. The illness of Mrs. Latimer could alone have prevented his coming to an explanation with you, and he must be very much changed indeed, if this crisis do not occur immediately on his return."

"You surprise me, you overwhelm me. Papa, you know my feelings. They can alone regulate my conduct. My affections are disengaged. I admire Mr. Bohun, I frankly confess that in time I might be induced to love him. But love him I do not at present, nay, although I feel ashamed at yielding to such unjustifiable suspicions, if I have any feeling for Mr. Bohun at present it is Fear. Yes, Papa, I cannot resist the extraordinary, perhaps the unfounded, the unjust conviction, but I feel assured that there is something about Mr. Bohun not right. With all his fascinating qualities, I fear him."

"Continue to fear him," said her father, in a deep, low voice. "He is a villain!"

Helen started, turned pale, nearly shrieked. "Good God! Sir."

"I repeat my word. Bohun is a villain. Let us speak no more upon this subject. As you value my honour and my happiness, let no word or look of yours at any time reveal to him your feeling. When you told me you did not love him, it was the happiest hour of my life, sweet, the happiest, happiest hour. When I first kissed that smiling face, girl, and pressed those little lips, I never felt more joy. I might be silent, but you will see him again, for circumstances, uncontrollable circumstances, will not allow me suddenly to terminate our acquaintance. You are safe now: God, who has given us so many mercies, be praised for this his chief. You are safe now; and for the future I guard you. Know then that Mr. Bohun *is married*!"

CHAPTER XV

A painful interview

This fatal secret very differently affected Mr. Molesworth and his daughter. The one could think only of the heinousness of the crime, the other dwelt alone on his gratitude for their escape. That Helen's suspicions and caution would in time have yielded to the seduction of Mr. Bohun's manners, Mr. Molesworth never doubted, and he thanked God for their deliverance from so eminent a peril, as he each day thought that he might have lived to see his darling child the victim of a heartless sensualist. But Helen was overwhelmed, she shrank with horror from the dark scenes of crime that were opened to her, she trembled to think that she had held intimate communion with one so hardened in guilt. Sometimes her pure mind, eager to discredit what was so painful to believe, would endeavour to seek relief in the hope that George Gainsborough had himself been deceived, but then her father, on whose judgment she entirely relied, had heard all the detail and had never doubted the truth of the story. True therefore she feared it must be, and then came the overwhelming thought that she must soon meet Mr. Bohun. It wanted but a week or two to Easter, when he was expected by his enthusiastic constituents. She became sorrowful and unhappy. So heavily did the anticipation of this evil press on her, that at night it was hours before she could sleep, and in the morning she woke faint and sick at heart. At times she tried to solace herself with the idea that he would not visit Bohun, which was at so great a distance from the metropolis, for so short a vacation. But she could not long indulge this delusion, for almost every day she was condemned to hear of some new engagement which the indefatigable Mr. Chace was authorised to make with the good people of Fanchester, who were eager to celebrate the visit of their hero, by many feasts and many speeches.

No, she felt that she must prepare to meet him, to receive him
as if he were still their friend, and alas! to listen to his professions as if they were not degrading and insulting to her. She
endeavoured to fortify her mind for such a meeting. And I
doubt not, for I have a great opinion of her good sense, that if
she had had due notice of the coming of such a visitor, if
Sideboard's pompous announcement had been preceded by the
barking of the dogs, and the ringing of divers bells, she would
have acquitted herself with tolerable composure. But the interview came to pass after quite a different fashion.

While her mind was for ever fixed upon this painful subject,
she could not forget George Gainsborough, and, strange to say,
her dread of seeing Mr. Bohun scarcely exceeded her dislike to
encounter him. An indescribable feeling overcame her in his
presence, he seemed mixed up with the dark villainies he had
unfolded, and she blushed that he should be the partner of the
secret that agitated her bosom.

One morning, about a week before the time Mr. Bohun was
expected to arrive at the Castle, Helen had been spending some
hours with Mrs. Latimer, when, suddenly remembering a book
she had promised to lend her, she hastened home to fetch it.
She hurried across the hall into the drawing-room, where she
had placed it the evening before. She opened the door, Mr.
Bohun was sitting at the table reading. He looked up, he flew to
meet her, and as he took her hand, he said, "You are surprised
to find me here, but I could not be turned away from Hartlebury. I have been endeavouring as patiently as I could to await
your return."

Surprised indeed Helen appeared. She turned quite pale,
and she could not speak. In fact it must, I fear, be admitted that
our heroine fairly lost her presence of mind. If Mr. Bohun had
been a coxcomb, he would have ascribed her agitation to the
unexpected pleasure of seeing him, but Aubrey Bohun's quick
observation saved him from the delusion of such flattery, and in
a moment he detected that her agitation arose rather from
consternation than joy.

The first moment of reunion is perhaps the moment most
fraught with sentiment, in the intercourse of either love or
friendship, and there is nothing which a susceptible mind so
acutely feels as to be received with coldness, where the grief of

parting had been alleviated by the interchange of kindness and affection. All the warmth of feeling with which Mr. Bohun had greeted Helen, was suddenly repressed, and he dropped her hand almost with the promptitude with which he had seized it. Miss Molesworth endeavoured to express her surprise at seeing him, and very incoherently informed him that she was not aware of his arrival at Bohun. She advanced to the fire, and observed that it was a very cold day, and then she sought the usual resource of nervous persons — she stirred it. She rang the bell to desire that Mr. Molesworth should be sought for in the grounds, and then, trusting that these few moments had restored her composure, and feeling all the necessity of exerting herself, she turned to Mr. Bohun, and made some very rapid enquiries respecting Mrs. Neville.

The manner of her visitor did not aid her, a dignified, but gentle expression of sorrow had succeeded to the gaiety and warmth with which he had first met her; his eyes were fixed upon her, and he seemed to wait until she chose the tone and subject of their discourse.

Helen felt that she must speak again, that he would not speak, and that she must exert herself. But every subject was alike, full of danger. She could not speak of the Latimers, their name was too intimately connected with the last meeting between herself and Mr. Bohun. As for the Gainsboroughs, she felt that she could not articulate their name. And then his own success which had wont to be made by Mrs. Neville, in all their conversations, the eternal subject of anticipatory triumph, why could she not speak of that now that had so far surpassed all their imaginings? To withhold her sympathy in his triumph was as ill-bred as it was unfeeling: but what words of commendation could she use, that would not re-kindle his warmth, that would not lead to the dreaded subject? She again sought relief in renewed inquiries concerning her friend.

"I hope," she said, "Emmeline has not suffered from the fatigue of her gay life. Notwithstanding all her engagements, she has been very good to me."

"I fear you may have found her troublesome," he answered, "but Emmeline is more constant" — here he hesitated.

More constant than I am, he means, thought Helen.

"More constant," he continued, "than perhaps you would

give her credit for. That she has faithfully kept one promise to you, I can vouch, she has never ceased to talk of you."

"She is very good," almost sighed Helen. "Her letters were full of animation, but you can guess," she added with a vain attempt to smile, "that she had a very interesting subject. You will find, I assure you, your friends at Fanchester in a state of renewed enthusiasm. Mrs. Escott says —" Helen suddenly stopped. Mr. Bohun's eyes were fixed upon her, and seemed to say, "How can you at such a moment so bitterly insult me, as to retail to me the praises of a silly old woman?" So at least thought Helen's conscience, and it must be confessed that hitherto, during the whole of this interview, during the whole of this interview, she had appeared the guilty party: he looked composed and dignified, and full of feeling, and she was embarrassed and agitated.

"I am glad," he mildly said, "that you are not ashamed of me. Still supported by Mrs. Escott, perhaps you do not regret all that your kindness effected for me. Shall I find all my friends here?" he suddenly asked, "is Gainsborough here?"

Helen's colour mounted to her temples, at this simple question, and she rang the bell with such violence to enquire if Sideboard had found her father, that the bell-rope fell at her feet.

Mr. Bohun continued silent, he was revolving a great matter. He had ridden over to Hartlebury that morning with no determined purpose of explaining his sentiments to Miss Molesworth, he had thought only of the felicity of being again in her presence. He had hastened to meet her, gay and animated, he found her confused and spiritless. A few moments of thought determined him, for his impatient spirit could ill brook this.

And so as Sideboard retired, with the unsatisfactory answer that might have been anticipated, Mr. Bohun rose from his seat and taking a place on the sofa by the side of Helen he said in the softest tone.

"Miss Molesworth, tell me why am I so unhappy as to have lost your friendship."

Helen started at this frank query.

"You were, I am sure, my friend when I left you, tell me what has happened to deprive me of my greatest happiness."

"You are too rapid in your conclusions," said Helen, who

endeavoured to repel a charge she could not confute. "For three months you have not seen me but for these five minutes: you cannot know anything about me."

"In friendship and in — love we count by sensations and not by minutes, Miss Molesworth. We cannot reason, we can only feel. I have sighed for this hour of meeting. Perhaps then my disappointment may have arisen only from my over excited expectation. Let me then breathe to you those hopes I have long so ardently indulged. Let me tell you that I love you, let me dare to ask for your love."

The fatal words she so dreaded to hear were uttered. She scarcely waited until he ceased to speak before she exclaimed, "Oh! Mr. Bohun, do not speak of that, indeed we are not fitted for one another. What do you know of me? think how short has been our acquaintance, how serious is what you ask."

"I cannot need to know more of you than I do," he calmly answered. "You have rather stated your objections to me. My dearest Miss Molesworth," and here he took her hand, "what is there you can desire to know of me, of my past life and feelings, that I would not willingly entrust to one whose charity so tempers her purity. Only let me hear from your lips that this day I have deceived myself — let me hope for the future."

His manner, which had hitherto been mild and dispassionate, suddenly assumed a more passionate tone, and it roused all Helen's feelings of injury. She drew her hand hastily from his, she covered her face with both her hands, and she shuddered as she said "Oh! Mr. Bohun, can you say this to me!"

Her horror was but too apparent.

"It is indeed harsh in you to believe me unworthy of all hope," said Mr. Bohun with some emotion. "But I feel that there must be here some painful misconception. But you are agitated now, I will not further distress you, at present I will only say farewell, and hope that your feelings are happier than mine are at this moment."

So saying he bowed and quitted the room, but as he quitted it a terrible expression came over his countenance. He bit his lip, a scowl settled on his face; for a moment he looked the impersonation of some evil demon. One moment, in profound thought, he remained upon the hall steps; then mounting his horse, he galloped away.

CHAPTER XVI

A friendly conversation

He galloped away in the direction of Oakfield, nor did he curb his pace until the neat gable ends and pointed windows of Mr. Gainsborough's residence were in sight. Within a hundred yards of the gate he perceived a horseman advancing in his direction. It was George Gainsborough whom he had not seen since his return. Mr. Bohun reined in his steed.

"How do you do Gainsborough?"

"How do you do Bohun?"

"I hope your family are quite well. I was just going to return your visit. I was sorry I had not arrived when you called yesterday."

"Ours was the misfortune."

"What are you going to do with yourself?"

"I was about to let my steed take its own direction."

"I have some orders to give at the castle which I omitted this morning, I should like to return there at once. Have you any objection to be my companion?"

"I am entirely at your service."

"Come on then." So saying Mr. Bohun turned his horse's head, and the gentlemen in company proceeded in the direction of the castle.

After proceeding along the high road about a quarter of a mile, they turned up a winding green lane which here divided the Bohun property from the demesne of Oakfield. On one side were open fields, on the other some recent plantations on which Mr. Gainsborough senior much prided himself. Conversation was not very fluent. Mr. Bohun asked a great many questions, but did not seem much interested in his companion's answers. He was courteous, and every now and then appeared to make an effort to be companionly, but on the whole he was distrait, and had not the invitation proceeded from himself, George

Gainsborough would have considered that he was in the way.

About half a mile up the lane, they arrived at a small piece of waste land, on which was a cottage in no very good repute among the magistrates. It was a Tom and Jerry shop, and kept by a rather lawless character and suspected poacher. When they had passed this dwelling about one hundred yards and again entered the lane, a very pretty young woman with a child in her arms met them. She was the wife of this cottager: she curtsied as she passed. Mr. Bohun smiled and seemed inclined to stop, but Mr. Gainsborough who appeared moody, gave her only a cold nod. The woman seemed very mortified.

"I detest to be ill-natured," instantly said Mr. Bohun, as it were talking to himself and he turned his horse. The woman came back. George Gainsborough stopped his horse, but did not return with his companion. Mr. Bohun was about half a dozen yards from George Gainsborough as he spoke to the woman, who was looking back as he turned and immediately met him. Mr. Bohun leant his head down and spoke to her about two minutes. She smiled and rather blushed. Mr. Bohun in a loud and gay tone wished her good morning, and then returning to George Gainsborough said "Come for a canter," and so proceeding at a rapid rate, they soon reached Bohun castle.

Dismounting, Mr. Bohun led the way to his private apartment, ushering in his guest who walked into the room before him and immediately threw himself on a sofa. Mr. Bohun turning the key of the apartment, planted himself before the fire. He was very pale and his lips quivered as he said in a very calm voice and in Greek, "Gainsborough, you have betrayed me."

George Gainsborough started from the sofa, as if instead of that still small voice he had listened to the last trump. He started from the sofa, and stared at Mr. Bohun with a countenance of indescribable consternation.

"Betrayed you," he at length exclaimed, for Mr. Bohun would not again speak, "What do you mean?"

"Exactly what I say. You have betrayed me."

"Who says so?"

"Only one person could tell me. It is unnecessary for me to mention that person's name."

George Gainsborough was silent.

"Gainsborough," said Mr. Bohun, "have not I told you a thousand times it is in vain to try to deceive me. If you have struggled with me more than once; you have ever been defeated. Madman, will you never learn to be wise? Is my magnanimity only to make you more rash? Yes! Sir, you have betrayed me, and I, Sir, I will bear this no more. I will take you like this vase, [Mr. Bohun took from the mantel-piece a precious vase of porcelain] and shiver you to pieces," and he dashed the vessel on the hearth into a thousand fragments.

George Gainsborough folded his arms, and leant against the wall silent, but determined. A dogged expression came over his countenance as he said in a subdued voice, but with deliberate utterance, "Tyrant, I defy you."

Mr. Bohun sprang forward like a tiger and seized Gainsborough by the neck. He dragged him from the wall, seemed to toss his powerful opponent in the air like a puppet, and then dashing him back to his old position, paced the chamber with awful strides.

"You are the only man who dare do this," said George Gainsborough very coolly.

"Silence, wretch," said Mr. Bohun.

"Aubrey Bohun, I will not be silent," replied George Gainsborough. "You deem me in your power, but I defy it. Death is more acceptable to me than life upon such terms as these. You accuse me of betraying you. If to save a beautiful and an innocent victim of your lust be treason, I glory in it. You boast of your triumphs over me; God knows you have triumphed. You have crossed my path once, once you have blighted all my prospects and crushed all my hopes, but I will avenge both Alexina and myself, and as there is a God in heaven, Helen Molesworth never shall be yours."

"Liar, robber, assassin, is it thou, thou gallows bird, is it thou that thus speakest to Bohun? I crush thy hopes, thou reptile! I won Alexina, as I will win Helen. Am I to suffer for your ambitious fancies? She saw me, and she loved me. What cared I for your plighted troth with the old bandit her father! Shall a thing like you stand in my way! A thing that wore my livery, my hireling, my slave!"

"Oh! that I had a sword," said George Gainsborough.

"I am not *sleeping*, Gainsborough," said Mr. Bohun with a fiend-like sneer, and suddenly stopping in his course, throwing a glance at Gainsborough, under which he quailed.

"Do you recognise this, wretch," he continued in an awful tone, and he tore open his clothes, and shewed upon his breast a scar— Gainsborough involuntarily placed his hand to his sight.

"I pardoned you: Love, disappointed passion was your excuse," continued Bohun in a more moderate and measured tone. "I am the most charitable of men, and willing to believe anything — 'Tis pity for the honour of our species, Sir, that I was your creditor as well as your rival, and that the blow which avenged your *passion* might also have discharged your *debts*."

Gainsborough shuddered.

"There is nothing like business," continued Mr. Bohun after a short pause, but never for a moment taking his eyes off his companion's. "Grant you have succeeded, grant that Helen Molesworth, through your arts, is not mine; grant that my revelations as to your real character and conduct are not credited; grant that my assassin is acquitted by the merciful laws of our enlightened country. How does he mean to act? The bond, the bond, the thing, 'I'll have my bond.' Will your father's miserable savings discharge it?"

George Gainsborough came forward and fell upon his knees. "I am in your power Bohun, I know that you are merciful, that you are generous. Dictate your terms."

"They are simple — Remove, utterly remove the evil impression that you have created, and the day that I marry Helen Molesworth the bond is yours, and I allow you a thousand a year for life. Nay! I wish to be generous — Go, go and share it, if you like, with Alexina."

"Oh," groaned George Gainsborough, "name not your wife."

"Wife, Sir," exclaimed Bohun, "but it is but fair — Yes, my wife is certainly at your service."

"But how can I remove the impression?" enquired George Gainsborough almost in despair.

"In one way only," answered Bohun very coolly. "By proclaiming yourself the villain which you are. Take Mr. Molesworth aside and inform him that you love his daughter to desperation, that in the madness of jealousy you have invented

the most infamous calumnies respecting the individual whom
you considered your fortunate rival, that all you repeated is
utterly false, that you feel it but justice to me to confess that my
character is pure as undriven snow. Remorse must be your
excuse. Believe me, when once you have screwed your mind to
the sticking point, you will not find more difficulty in telling
this lie than the thousand others in which you have indulged."
"I cannot," said George Gainsborough.
" 'Tis an awkward business, no doubt," replied Mr. Bohun:
"But in your situation a man can only balance inconveniences.
The simple question is this, do you prefer being utterly ruined
in fortune and character to an old man and his daughter knowing you to be a scoundrel? For, remember, the subject is too
delicate ever to become notorious. The Molesworths will
naturally communicate with no one but me, and I shall take care
for both our sakes that the subject is never again mooted. There
is no need, after this exposure, that you should even leave this
neighbourhood, if you care to stay. Whatsoever the Molesworths think, I shall take care to uphold you. You know I have
no antipathies, as long as I gain my ends. You will always find a
welcome here."
George Gainsborough continued silent. He seemed plunged
in thought. "Well!" continued Mr. Bohun, "take time to consider. I do not wish to hurry you. In the meantime I will smoke
a pipe. Perhaps you will follow my example. According to our
old enemies the Turks' opinion, 'tis a practice which very much
assists reflection."
"Bohun," said George Gainsborough, "I confess it is in vain
to struggle with you. You have conquered — By tomorrow I
pledge myself that Mr. Molesworth shall call upon you, and a
satisfactory explanation shall take place — may you be happy! I
make no terms, I trust to your generosity."
"It is what no one ever trusted to in vain," was the answer,
and George Gainsborough quitted the apartment.

CHAPTER XVII

A consultation

George Gainsborough returned to Oakfield for dinner, but his want of appetite very much discomposed his mother. He pleaded indisposition, and indeed confessed himself, as the evening drew on, so very unwell, that he retired to his own room about eight o'clock, and locking his door, gave orders that he should on no account be disturbed.

The bed-chamber of George Gainsborough was on the ground floor: without difficulty you stepped out into the garden. He withdrew the curtain, and, opening the window, examined the sky. It was a fair but clouded night. He stood for some moments in reverie, then taking his cloak, which was hanging up, he enveloped himself in it, put on a small Grecian skull cap, which allowed him to envelope his head in the cape of his cloak, and very quietly stepped forth, closing the curtain and the window, but leaving his lamp burning.

It was two hours before he returned — He re-entered very softly — He was extremely pale. He took off his cloak, and perceiving that the lower part was wet, he wiped it with a towel before he hung it up in its old position. Then partly undressing, and putting on his dressing-gown, he unlocked his door and rang the bell.

After answering his bell, the servant came into the drawing-room and said that Mr. George felt himself much worse indeed, that he had not succeeded in sleeping at all, as he had hoped; and that he thought it would be better to send for Mr. Trueman, who was the favourite medical attendant of all the neighbourhood. Mrs. Gainsborough and his sister immediately ran up to his room, full of anxiety and enquiries. They felt his pulse several times, and then they asked him many questions, and there they remained. Mr. Gainsborough, senior, occasionally joining them, until Mr. Trueman arrived. "I have such faith in

Trueman," said Mrs. Gainsborough, "I declare, my love, I am never happy except when Trueman is in the house. Somehow I never feel secure without Trueman. I am sure my love, if I ever be ill away from Oakfield, I do not know what I shall do without Trueman."

"And I am sure my dear, I don't know what Trueman could do without us, for really I think that Oakfield is an annuity to him."

"Well my dear, no one can say the money is ill-spent."

Happy Mrs. Gainsborough! If the Catholic dame have her confessor, Protestantism has at least not robbed its female votaries of their apothecary!

Mr. Trueman arrived; and after having examined his patient, looked very serious.

"Felt very ill when he came home, eh?" said Mr. Trueman— Mrs. Gainsborough dwelling on every accent that fell from his inspired lips. — "No appetite? Eat nothing? — Not a little chicken, not a very little? — only a potato? — bad things potatoes — part of a roasted potato — very bad things indeed, roasted potatoes, even part of a roasted potato will account for anything."

"Good gracious," exclaimed Mrs. Gainsborough, "only think."

"Not slept at all? No inclination to sleep? Has been lying quite still ever since eight o'clock, restless— very? I thought so. Nothing makes a man more restless than eating roasted potatoes. Even a very small portion of a roasted potato will make a man very restless indeed. My dear Madam, I speak to you because you have a head for these matters. My dear Madam, beware of roasted potatoes!"

"I never will look upon one again," said Mrs. Gainsborough. "But poor George, do you think it very serious indeed?"

"Very."

"Good God!"

"Fever — decided fever. He must be blooded immediately."

"What can be the matter with him?" said Miss Gainsborough.

"I dare say he has caught cold," said his mother.

"Or over exerted himself," said the father.

"Ah! that election," said the mother. "I knew he would do too

much, I always said he would do too much — but he was so
interested for his friend Mr. Bohun. Good God! he grows paler
and paler every minute — Salvolatile!"

"Vinegar!"

"Hot — hot!"

"No, cold will do," said Mr. Trueman.

"Hot — cold — anything — anything!"

But George Gainsborough did not faint, he rallied.

" 'Tis indigestion," whispered Mr. Trueman to Mrs. Gainsborough.

"I have no doubt," responded the lady.

" 'Tis over exertion, my love," whispered Gainsborough to
his wife.

"I should not wonder," she replied.

" 'Tis cold, mamma," whispered the daughter.

"Very likely, Harriet."

"He may have over exerted himself, and may have caught
cold," observed Trueman; "but no one can deny that he has
eaten a roasted potato."

CHAPTER XVIII

A catastrophe

It was a beautiful spring morning. The sun was rising in the
light blue sky, and spangled the dewy grass and glittering
hawthorns with drops of lustre. All was glad, sweet, and promising. The smoke went dancing from the cottage chimneys; the
fields and hedges were full of odour; and it seemed that during
the balmy night the fresh and vigorous buds had nearly struggled into blossom.

What a golden spring lit up our hearts last year! Lucky was
that lover whose good genius destined him to breathe his vows

under its influence. Lucky the wight who, fanned by its fragrant breath, wandered amid grey rocks and green woods, and listened to the sound of the cascade and the cuckoo.

Shall we have as bright, as glowing a season this year? Mayhap the sun will be as clear and warm, the light blue sky not less sweet, the cuckoo not less constant! Ah! but the feelings which gilt refined gold, painted the lily, and threw a perfume o'er the violet, those wonderful, those delicate, those evanescent feelings — where will they be? I am married! I am a happy man.

Perfectly true! I am a happy man. I do not repent the irreparable step. It has realized all my expectations. It was really a step that introduced me into Paradise. Nevertheless who can refrain from sighing after an existence of one long courtship.

It was a beautiful spring morning and a knacker's cart with two men in it stopped at the Tom and Jerry shop, on the small piece of waste land, which Mr. Bohun and Mr. George Gainsborough passed on their ride of the preceding day.

"Blow me tight," said the driver to his companion. "Blow me tight Thorpe, if I musn't whet my whistle."

"I'll stand a pot with all my heart Jin, but don't let's go 'till after business. We shall lose the beasty now. Nowadays there is *sich* a competition!"

Thus it appears that our respectable friends, Mr. Jin Flag, and Mr. Bully Thorpe were on an agreeable mission to purchase a dead horse of a neighbouring farmer.

"Well, we won't get out Thorpe, but I'll be blowed if I musn't have a drop."

"No sooner said than done. Here mistress, a pot of Chumfield."

There came out of the house the same very pretty woman to whom Mr. Bohun had spoken yesterday.

"Here's to your health Missus Thurston," said Bully Thorpe.

"Here's to ye," said Jin Flag, "and to your pretty eyes."

The woman looked very much offended at this familiarity, tossed her head slightly, but did not condescend to answer.

"Hope no offence missus," apologised Jin Flag.

"If I am to be offended by every low fellow who has a loose tongue, I should have enough to do," was her answer.

"My eye!" said Bully Thorpe, opening very wide the feature by which he swore.

"Wheugh!" whistled Jin Flag: "If that ayn't a good one! Well, here's the blunt, I s'pose you great folks like to be paid."

The woman took the money in silence, and withdrew.

"Hehup!" said Jin Flag, as he flanked his steed. "Them Thurstons give themselves more airs than my grandmother's tabby."

They took their way up the lane. When they had proceeded about half a mile, the horse jibbed.

"Hehup," said Jin Flag, "hehup! hehup! What can be the matter with the old girl! Hehup!"

But the mare would not budge. With eye distended and nostril stiff, it was evident there was something obnoxious very near.

"It cannot be the smell of the beasty," said Bully Thorpe.

"Fiddle-de-dee," said Jin Flag, "hehup! What you won't, won't you! Hehup! Hehup! I say Thorpe just get out and lead her a bit."

Out jumped Bully Thorpe, and ran to her head. "Why! here is somebody in the ditch, Jin, a drunken man in the ditch."

"Thurston, or I'm a Dutchman," responded Jin. "Give him a kick."

Thorpe went to the ditch, leant down, uttered a shriek, and, pale and panting, tottered back, and leant upon the horse's back.

"Why, what's the matter with the man," exclaimed his companion. "Thorpe, I say Thorpe, Bully Thorpe, why what's the matter? Why don't speak, man!"

"O—h!" groaned Thorpe.

"What's the matter?" again asked Jin.

"*Sich* a sight!" said Thorpe, trembling from head to foot.

"Speak!"

"I can't — look."

Jin Flag jumped out and ran to the ditch.

"Lord, have mercy upon us!" exclaimed Jin Flag, falling on his knees with a face like a sheet. "Oh! Oh! Oh!"

"Has't seen it?" said Thorpe.

"O—h!" groaned Flag.

"Has't seen it?"

"That I should live to see this day!"

"Come along," said Thorpe, "we must exert ourselves, we must examine the body. Come along. I won't touch it without you. Oh! how glad I am it is the morning!"

Jin Flag slowly rose and taking hold of Thorpe's arm, clambered into the ditch.

"Get in, Bully," said Jin Flag, "and lift up the legs."

Thorpe got into the ditch and raised the legs of the body — the body of Aubrey Bohun, muffled up in a cloak quite cold and stiff, the blood gushing out of the mouth.

"He has been shot in the back," said Jin Flag.

"Surely," said Thorpe, recovering his courage.

"Well, this is a deadly day!"

"What shall we do?" asked Jin.

"We must put it in the cart and drive back to town, as fast as we can," said Thorpe. "We musn't be found with a dead body. 'Tis manslaughter."

"Is that the law?" said Jin.

" 'Tis the law of the land," explained Bully Thorpe. "He who finds a dead man, and giveth no notice to the magistrates, is guilty of manslaughter, without trial."

"Pull away then," said Jin— "as I'm a sinner, if I don't feel as it were Doomeday."

"I'm all of a shake," said the bully, "t'was a sweet young gentleman."

"T'was my best friend," said Jin.

"T'was every man's friend," said Thorpe.

"I'd have given my life for him any day," said Jin.

"And so would I," said the bully. "It always go'ed a'gin my conscience at the 'lection to be t'other side."

"I knew that Bully," said Jin Flag blubbering.

" 'Tis the most grievous morning as I ever seed. My poor young Missus — 'Tis a breakheart business."

"And who's the murderer, I am thinking?" said Thorpe.

"Murder will out," said Jin Flag, "he could not have done it himself."

" 'Tis in the back. How came he here with his cloak on? T'was a night business I am thinking, for he has been long gone."

"I can't drive Thorpe, and that's the truth on't," said Flag, giving up the whip and reins, "Squire Bohun murdered!"

They drove on as fast as they could, 'till they were in sight of the Tom and Jerry shop when Thorpe ran forward and borrowed a blanket which he threw over the body, and thus they proceeded until they reached Fanchester when they stopped at the Rose, and Thorpe remaining with the cart which had driven into the yard. Jin Flag went in to break the news to the landlord.

The host and his principal waiter soon bustled out with countenances of mysterious consternation, and carried in the body and placed it on the table of the large room, which was wont to be the scene of the meeting of the deceased's committee. The Mayor and Town Clerk, who was also the Coroner for the county, were then summoned, and expresses were sent to Mr. Chace, Mr. Molesworth, Mr. Gainsborough, Senior, Mr. Latimer and other of the neighbouring magistrates. In the meantime dark rumours began to circulate, crowds collected before the Rose and in various parts of the town, and ever and anon a magistrate on horseback trotted up to the hotel. At length it was impossible any longer to conceal the terrible truth. A murder had been committed and the murdered person was their beloved member. The awful consternation that pervaded the whole town cannot be described. Of a sudden all business seemed to stop, many shut up their shops and ran to the Rose, and the bells of all the churches tolled.

The depositions of Jin Flag and Bully Thorpe were taken before the Mayor, and two Aldermen, Mr. Molesworth, Mr. Latimer, and Dr. Maxwell. The principal servants of the household were summoned. The coroner proceeded to hold his inquest. We draw up the result of the evidence from the County Chronicle.

The valet of Mr. Bohun proved, that his master dined at home alone on the preceding day at seven o'clock, having passed the morning as usual in riding and other customary amusements. His master returned about three o'clock having taken a ride with Mr. George Gainsborough. After remaining sometime with his master, and smoking, Mr. George Gainsborough had returned home. Supposed that his master went out after dinner, was in the habit of occasionally doing so. The household never knew when Mr. Bohun went out to take a stroll, as he stepped into the park from the dining-room. His master was in his usual spirits. Could offer no conjecture whatever on the catastrophe.

Several other of the domestics gave the same unsatisfactory evidence. The jury desired to see Mr. George Gainsborough. Mr. Trueman, who was in attendance to give evidence respecting the nature of the wound, said that Mr. George Gainsborough was extremely ill, but thought that he might attend without any very serious danger. An hour elapsed before his arrival. He came in a carriage attended by his father.

This witness is described by the county paper as the most intimate friend of the deceased. His appearance excited the greatest commiseration. He appeared absolutely overwhelmed with grief. He was quite pale, his limbs tottered — he leant upon his father's arm the whole time that he gave his evidence, and never ventured even to glance at the body. He was listened to with breathless attention.

George Gainsborough, Esq., deposed that he was on terms of extreme intimacy with the deceased, whom he had known abroad — that the deceased yesterday was about to call at Oakfield, he did not therefore go in, but invited witness to ride with him, who consented. After a short time, they arrived at Bohun castle. Witness remained chatting and smoking with deceased for some time — Deceased was in excellent spirits. Deceased invited witness to remain to dinner, but witness declined the invitation as he did not feel very well. On arriving at Oakfield, witness felt much worse, and was shortly taken so very unwell, that he was obliged to send for Mr. Trueman.

Being earnestly pressed upon the point whether he knew of any circumstance that could throw light upon the catastrophe, witness for some time hesitated. He said that it was very painful to speak only upon suspicion, but he intimated that there might have been some amour between the deceased and a woman of the name of Thurston, and that jealousy might perhaps account for the tragical event.

A clue seemed now obtained. Constables in a post chaise were immediately dispatched for Thurston and his wife. Thurston was from home, but his wife was without loss of time brought to the Inquest. She had heard nothing of the awful event, and was of course very much shocked when she was

introduced into a room with the dead body of Mr. Bohun
exposed— but her shock indicated no guilt. Being pressed upon
the point in question, she for a long time declined giving any
information, as she declared such queries were most unjust and
unfair: at length soothed by the kind manner in which she was
treated by Mr. Molesworth, and somewhat alarmed by Dr.
Maxwell's threats, she offered to communicate to Mr. Molesworth and Mr. Latimer in private.

Although such information was not evidence it was considered the most expedient course to comply with her offer, and
accordingly she retired with the two magistrates into another
room. She confessed to them, casting down her eyes and blushing deeply, that she had met Mr. Bohun in company with Mr.
George Gainsborough the morning of the preceding day, that
she had been acquainted with him before, that he spoke to her
aside, that he said it was probable that he might be walking that
way in the evening about nine o'clock. That accordingly about
nine o'clock she put on her cloak, and walked about a hundred
yards up the lane. She did not walk further, for she had nothing
to fear, her husband was absent from home. She said that she
remained in the vicinity of her house until eleven o'clock and
then, supposing Mr. Bohun had changed his mind, she
returned home. Being asked whether she heard the report of a
gun during the time she was out, she replied in the negative.

The magistrates returned to the great room and said that the
secret communication of the woman Thurston authorised them
in examining her husband. As the day was now advanced, and
Thurston was a man not very ready to meet with, the Inquest
was adjourned until the next morning.

But the next morning brought no satisfaction, for Thurston
appeared and proved the most satisfactory alibi that was ever
offered to the consideration of a jury. At six o'clock on the
preceding day, Thurston had attended a benefit club to which
he belonged at the Compasses, a small public house on a heath
seven miles distant. There he got very tipsy, and as his home
was a long way off, he had slept, as well as several members of
the fraternity, in an adjoining barn. He had not quitted the
Compasses until the afternoon the following day.

No other evidence was offered or could be obtained, and the
jury therefore brought in a verdict of "Wilful murder against

some person or persons unknown." Great rewards were offered
by the Crown, by the county and by the relatives of Mr. Bohun
to discover the murderer, no exertion was spared that human
energy could command. From Colonel Neville to Jin Flag all
felt alike interested — But hitherto their efforts have been
absolutely vain. The same impenetrable mystery still envelopes
the fate of the unfortunate and brilliant Bohun!

Cherry and Fair Star

When the 25-year-old Benjamin Disraeli left England in June 1830 for his tour of the Middle East, he had with him as travelling companion William Meredith, his close friend, and the fiancé of his elder sister, Sarah. The tour was to have a lasting effect on both Benjamin and his sister. To Disraeli his experiences in Spain, Greece and Turkey became a romantic re-discovery of his racial roots, for in his admiration of Semitic culture he made little distinction between Jews, Arabs and Turks. For Sarah, the outcome was a personal tragedy. William Meredith died of smallpox in Cairo, on 19 July 1831. The euphoria of the journey was smashed. In his letter to Sarah the next day, Disraeli vowed that he would do his best to fill the void in her life which this death must cause.[1]

Benjamin returned as rapidly as quarantine regulations would permit, and arrived home in October. He was as good as his word. Although the twenty-eight months between October 1831 and March 1834 were filled with frenetic activity, Disraeli kept Sarah abreast of the details of his burgeoning social, literary and political activities, making her feel by his frequent letters and visits home to Bradenham that she was participating vicariously in his own heady adventurings.

Sarah had for long cherished ambitions to write. She was always writing poems, sketches, short stories and articles, sending them to Disraeli to ask him what he thought of them, and suggesting possible outlets for publication which he might approach on her behalf. Usually he was non-committal, and it has been generally believed that Sarah never did succeed in breaking into print. Among the growing circle to Disraeli's new friends during this period there were a number of minor women-novelists: Mrs. Catherine Gore, Lady Blessington, Mrs. Caroline Sheridan, Lady Stepney and Lady Charlotte

Bury. It is possible that Sarah's ambitions were stimulated by Disraeli's reports of them.

It seems probable that the plan for the collaboration of Benjamin and Sarah to write a novel was conceived during Disraeli's extended visit home to Bradenham during September and October of 1833. It is also probable that he indulgently left the plot-line to her, and that she developed it by a method not far from the one she has her characters follow in their improvised dramatics at Bohun Castle.[2] Bradenham becomes Hartlebury, and High Wycombe becomes Fanchester. Disraeli's two unsuccessful election campaigns for High Wycombe in 1832 could provide the central event, but this time the hero would win. The evidence suggests that Disraeli had finished his part of the novel, dealing with the election, before he left Bradenham. By early November he had resumed his affair with Henrietta Sykes, and had moved in to a *menage à trois* by accepting the invitation of Sir Francis and Lady Sykes to stay with them at The Grange, Southend, Essex, in order to be able to concentrate on finishing his poem *The Revolutionary Epick*.

Sarah kept passing on messages to him from their mother, Maria D'Israeli expressing disapproval of his prolonged stay in Southend, enigmatically claiming that it was 'unhealthy' for him – which Disraeli cheerfully interpreted as referring only to the weather – and which he kept denying.[3] He returned home by the beginning of December, but before he left he wrote from Southend to the publisher, Richard Bentley: 'I forward you an MS worthy of your *particular attention*. It will make two volumes equal to the first series of "Vivian Grey". I recommend you to read it *completely*. I am very much mistaken if it do not possess the elements of very great popularity.'[4]

Disraeli had a manuscript of the jointly-written novel, without the final sections which Sarah was still writing. Presumably in urging Bentley to read all of it, he wanted to be sure that he reached Disraeli's own portion of the book, which, with one exception, did not begin until the second volume. The appeal failed, however, for the letter was endorsed: 'Declined/Jany 23–34.'

In the meantime Sarah was writing the ending, and had suggested to Disraeli that they send the book to Saunders and Otley, who had published Disraeli's fourth novel, *Alroy*, in

March 1833, and with whom Disraeli had been pleased. After his return to Southend on 5 January, Disraeli wrote to Sarah: 'Give me due notice before you send to S & O that I may write to them.' [5] He must have done so and received an answer sufficiently encouraging for Sarah to write on 12 January 1834:

... I hope to send the M.S. to S.&O. by the early coach on Tuesday [14 January]. I wrote yesterday the important chapter. [6] I therefore read to the family the conclusion, which has created a great sensation. Unanimous is the feeling of horror, and unanimous is the cry for justice on G.G. [7] I had already given the idea that the heroine had taken a great disgust to him, but still they cannot bear that he should remain quietly in the neighbourhood and are very urgent with you to make him commit suicide in a Postscript, on the discovery of the bond by Col. Neville. *Do you not think something might be done?* [8]

But Disraeli was deeply involved in trying to finish *The Revolutionary Epick*, and was becoming more than a little irascible at the complexities of novel-writing by family committee. He replied on 14 January: 'Do what you like with the end. I will have nothing to do with the suicide or anything else. Poetical justice is all stuff. I think you will spoil the book, but you are Lady Paramount.' [9]

Sarah must have come to the same conclusion, for before this letter arrived she had sent off the manuscript which had been copied by their brother Ralph, so that it would appear in one hand. She wrote on 16 January:

I sent the M.S. to S.&O. on Tuesday, and yesterday morning had an acknowledgement of its safe arrival. Do not forget to tell them to advertise with the little preface and settle about the printing as we shall I think now certainly go to Brighton the 8th or 10th.

For my own part I do not care a sous [*sic*] about poetical justice, but Mamma is in despair. Perhaps I shall see you before we go, and then that will be time enough to settle about the last dying words. If they print it discreetly, it will yield more pages than the MS, for Ralph who has copied much of it has written small – but I must confess that it is a very little book indeed. [10]

Disraeli wrote on 25 January 'If you go to town for a short time, I should like to be with you and to print my poem at the same time, if you do not go I shall have the proof [of the novel] sent to me here . . . Be not alarmed that I have not yet ratified any agreement about the Novel, I understand Bksellers.' [11]

He wrote again four days later, his *amour propre* well and truly bruised:

> Do not be nervous about the MS. as ere long I shall make a good arrangement. I am in the greatest rage with S & O. They have no opinion of the work at all, but especially the second volume. All the Election part they think most weak. I longed to tell them that I wrote it.
>
> Before you go to Brighton we shall have made an arrangement. They have only sold 150 of Cecil Hyde,[12] and this has sickened them. I only wonder they sold so much.[13]

The offer, when it came, was for £20 – £10 each. Disraeli was incensed and managed to have it increased. Sarah, however, was very pleased. She wrote on Sunday, 2 February:

> I have to thank you for two letters, that of today was a great surprise, for I intended to write to you today to assure you that one of the party concerned would have considered ten pounds an ample remuneration. I am amazed that you should have been annoyed about what had it been your own concern you would have dismissed from your mind in an instant. I begin however to think the book must be a very good book but I am afraid that they will not think it worth advertising. Do not pay the money into Curtis, but bring it here when you return.[14]

Sarah and her parents went to Brighton on schedule, but the name of the novel had still to be decided. On 12 February she wrote to Disraeli from Brighton: 'Talking of changes S & O seem to have been crucifying my poor Helen; I hope her name is to be preserved. They have *at last fixed on Aubrey Bohun* for the name! I have never written until to day that I might not interfere, in the hope that you would settle it. If it be not too late what do you think of "A year at Hartlebury or the Eln." – However it is not of much consequence.' [15]

Disraeli's intervention was obviously successful, for the title of the book was changed, literally in mid-printing. The first 72 pages of the first volume bear 'AUBREY BOHUN' at the top of each page, page 73 is headed 'HARTLEBURY', and thereafter 'A YEAR AT' heads each left-hand page, and 'HART-LEBURY' heads the right-hand page of each facing pair. On 5 March Sarah again emphasized the curious 'little preface' which she had written for the book: 'Do you not think that S & O. ought to advertize the little preface to show in what relation Cherry and Fair Star stand to one another?' [16] This is the only occasion on which the pseudonyms appear in the correspondence of either Benjamin or Sarah. *A Year at Hartlebury, or the Election* was published in two volumes by Saunders and Otley in March 1834, under the authorship of 'Cherry and Fair Star'.

Until the publication of the evidence in the Fall 1979 issue of the *Disraeli Newsletter* of the Disraeli Project (for the publication of a complete edition of Disraeli's correspondence, Queen's University, Kingston, Canada), the association of the Disraelis in this work had not been suspected. No copy of it remains among Disraeli's books at Hughenden; there is no manuscript; there is no subsequent reference to it in the later letters of Disraeli which have so far been located. The dust thrown by Sarah's 'little preface', identifying the authors as a newly-married couple, was taken up by at least one reviewer, and seems to have prevailed over the distinctively Disraelian political philosophy that otherwise, one might think, would have given the authorship away at once.

But why did they choose 'Cherry' and 'Fair Star' as pseudonyms? Research to find the answers to that question is still at an early stage, but there are clues. Brewer [17] relates the fairy story of Chery and Fairstar, royal children (first-cousins) cast adrift, rescued, restored, who eventually married. He quotes a 16th-century Italian source, and a 17th-century French one. There were no fewer than seven theatrical productions called *Cherry and Fair Star* in the 19th century, the first two (1822 and 1832) of unknown authorship. It is tempting to speculate whether this could have been the source of that money of his own which Disraeli lost during his stock speculations in 1824–6, for it is still a mystery how he had it to lose. From his father Isaac's account books it seems clear that he had not given it to him.

In a letter to Lady Blessington, on 12 January 1837, commenting on the poor reception given to Bulwer's play, *The Duchess de la Vallière*, Disraeli said: 'However, the actors of the present day are worse even than the authors; that I knew before, but E.L.B. would not believe it and I could pardon his scepticism. As for myself I have locked up my melodrame in the same strong box with my love letters; both lots being productions only interesting to the writer.' [18]

On Easter Monday, 8 April 1822, an Easter melodrame, *Cherry and Fair Star or, The Children of Cyprus* opened at the Theatre Royal, Covent Garden. Is it possible that Disraeli wrote it? The authorship of this play, which was a considerable success, would have been an extraordinary feat for a youth of seventeen. If he had written it, why would he not have boasted of it later? Yet one could ask the same of *Hartlebury*, the authorship of which is now beyond question.

Two contemporary reviews reflect the range of critical reception given to *Hartlebury* when it appeared. The first, general, short and indulgently favourable, recommended it without reservation as an excellent diversion for those wearied by three-volume novels, and praised it not only for 'its acuteness and variety' but added 'The dénouement is skilfully managed', which must have pleased Sarah and surprised Disraeli.[19]

The second, specific and analytical, treats the work seriously, and after his critical comments the reviewer gives a lengthy extract from Vol. II, chapter viii. He accepts Sarah's 'little preface' on face value, but, citing such characters as Kitty and Mrs Thurston, concludes that such 'characters and incidents . . . could neither have been imagined by a bride nor submitted to her approval . . . Indeed there is no trace of a female hand in the book, and Cherry has obviously had the whole matter to himself.' [20]

The reviewer also doubts the attribution in the preface to composition in the autumn, for, to him, *Hartlebury* is a Tory reply to the arguments in Catherine Gore's *The Hamiltons, or the New Era*, which had come out earlier in 1834. Of Aubrey Bohun he says: 'Mr. Bohun stands for the borough of Fanchester upon Radical professions, which the author, gruding them to one of such wealth, station, and genius, gives us to understand are accordant with a subtle contrivance of Ultra Toryism, that would carry reform beyond the ground upon which the Whigs have found their coigne of vantage.' This describes a position so close to the one for which Disraeli had been attacked in the campaigns of 1832 and beyond, and which he had answered in his pamphlet *What is he?* in 1833, that it is surprising that the attribution to Disraeli was not made on the spot.

To this reviewer, the ending was so full of loose ends that the only explanation he could think of was that a sequel must be in the works. Of Bohun he says 'A mystery, à la Byron, is cast around him, which is left unelucidated at the end of the book, where he is murdered. As the story cannot consistently with humanity to the curiosities conclude thus, we reckon on more years at Hartlebury.'

There is no precise description of how Sarah and her brother divided the work. However, the stylistic evidence is, for the most part, clear. All of volume I is certainly Sarah's, with the possible exception of chapter xiv – the first detailed description of the character of Aubrey Bohun. The first nine chapters of Volume II are certainly by Disraeli. The rest is by Sarah, with the possible exception of five paragraphs in chapter xii which describe Bohun's first days in Parliament, (from 'Mr. Bohun's arrival in London' to 'the mistake was not in speaking too soon, but in speaking at all.' II xii 172–3).

Sarah ('Lady Paramount') was thus responsible for the overall structural pattern of the book. She began by transforming Bradenham into Hartlebury Manor – the topography described in the first chapter is virtually identical with Bradenham's. She became the heroine, Helen Molesworth, unencumbered by mother or brothers. The Gainsboroughs were drawn from the Norrises who lived over the hill in Hughenden (the house Disraeli was later to acquire), although Hughenden was not the newly-built house that Oakfield Lodge was presented as being. Lord Carrington's Wycombe Abbey was the local 'great house', but Bohun Castle far excels it in magnificence, to make it appropriate for the dashing young hero who, as a *deus ex machina*, is dropped into the scene in the twelfth chapter. Aubrey Bohun was obviously conceived in the beginning by both authors to be the Disraeli-surrogate, as Helen was to be Sarah's. Enormously rich, handsome, clever, persuasive, he returns (as Disraeli had) from mysterious doings in the mountains of Greece where he has 'played deep for a crown' (II vii 141). He relaxes on a divan, in oriental dress, smoking a Turkish pipe (I xvi 63). The first time we meet him, Bohun is musing: 'did he grieve that thirty years of his life had flown away, apparently without producing a result? No: to sigh over the unchangeable past was not in the nature of Aubrey Bohun.' (I xiv 57). Disraeli was thirty years old in 1834, and he sometimes asked himself the same question. There can be no doubt, therefore that Disraeli saw in Aubrey Bohun a hero after his own heart. Most of the heroes in his novels contain recognizable autobiographical elements, but this one, appearing in an anonymously published work, perhaps provided a greater opportunity for uninhibited identification for his hopes and aspirations.

George Gainsborough is obviously destined by Sarah to be the 'villain' of the book. His conceit marks him for the role from his first appearance. But Aubrey Bohun, the agreed-upon hero, who has been presented as such in his portions of the book by Disraeli, turns out to be an even greater villain in the end. There is no hero, unless it is the quiet Arthur Latimer. The significance of what Sarah does to the erstwhile *alter ego* of her brother may be left to the psychologists. What is evident, is that Sarah retains a profound suspicion of disruptive elements that suddenly enter a structured and well-ordered society and bring about unforeseen changes. George Gainsborough and Aubrey Bohun have both grown up in that society, but have left it to go instead to that same wild and unordered region of Greece that had such an influence on her brother. In her parts of the book, Sarah shows both of them to have come back somehow 'tainted' by their experience. Bohun, for all his powers, can do no better in the election by his own efforts than reach a tie with his opponent. It is Helen who by *her*, quieter, powers of persuasion convinces Mr. Gainsborough to cast his vote for Bohun so that he wins. Even before she knows of Bohun's bigamous intentions, she feels guilt for her part in bringing this about, and the guilt is accompanied by a growing sense of distrust in everyone, even in herself.

Earlier in the book the curious little tale of Kate Marsden has prepared us for the larger theme. She is lured from the ordered and the known, and is destroyed in the process. Helen assures Mrs. Neville that she is never bored in the country, only in London. The title she gives to Vol. II chapter xii is surely significant: 'Hartlebury at Peace. Mr. Bohun in London.' Sarah's letters often show a shrewd perception of provincial life, mirrored in the small quirks and eccentricities of the types of people she knows best. *Hartlebury* is full of such insights when one stays alert for them. Mr Gainsborough, who 'began to have a tolerably exact idea of the Turkish Empire just when it was on the point of being dismembered' and Mrs. Gainsborough for whom two soups represented the idea of complete domestic splendour, do much to redeem the occasional lapses into melodrama and cliché.

The reader who approaches *Hartlebury* as a single unified novel will indeed be puzzled; but once the nature of the duality which is present is grasped, bemusement is succeeded by an increasing fascination, as one realizes how these two, so close to each other, looked at the world with such different eyes.

John Matthews
Queen's University

NOTES TO APPENDIX I

1 Bodleian Library, Hughenden papers A/I/B/I
2 See Vol I, ch xxi p. 86
3 Hughenden papers A/I/B/69
4 Library of Congress Ac.8033 12
5 Fitzwilliam Museum, Disraeli A4, 5 January 1834
6 Probably the last – vol II ch xviii – 'A Catastrophe.'
7 George Gainsborough
8 Hughenden papers A/I/B/505
9 Southeby's catalogue (9 May 1961) item 273, postmarked 15 January 1834

10 Hughenden papers A/I/B/506. In the Saunders and Otley edition, volume one contains vi + 292 pages, and volume two, v + 302 pp.
11 G Michelmore catalogue 3 (1922) item 43, dated 25 January 1834
12 A novel by Martin Archer-Shee. It had been published by Saunders and Otley earlier that same month, and so had hardly had time to sell in large numbers
13 Fitzwilliam Museum, Disraeli A5, 29 January 1834
14 Hughenden papers A/I/B/509
15 Hughenden papers A/I/B/511
16 Hughenden papers A/I/B/513
17 E. Cobham Brewer *The Readers Handbook* I (Philadelphia 1899, repr Detroit 1966) 353
18 Monypenny and Buckle *Life of Benjamin Disraeli* (1910) I 354–5
19 *New Monthly Magazine* XLI (May 1834) 100
20 *The Examiner* no 1369 (27 April 1834) 259–261

New light on Disraeli's early politics

The discovery that Benjamin Disraeli was the author of a hitherto unidentified novel arose from a detailed study and annotation of Disraeli's early correspondence. Though surprising, the discovery was somewhat fitting. As elusive in death as he was throughout his long political career, Disraeli seems to have succeeded in catching yet another generation of literary and political scholars unawares.

Now that the jig is up, an intriguing question arises. Is Disraeli reacting to the discovery with relief or dismay? Nor is this idle speculation, for it is clear that in *A Year at Hartlebury* Disraeli revealed more about himself and his most deeply held views of the political process that he was ever willing to deliver up to the many recipients of his early letters. More inclined to record his effect on others – witness his excited report of his first political address: 'I made them all mad. A great many absolutely cried. I never made as many friends in my life or converted as many enemies'[1] – than his own reaction to events, Disraeli was careful to avoid the kind of revelations that would provide readers of his letters with his innermost thoughts on the career he had mapped out for himself.

By March 1834, when *Hartlebury* first appeared, Disraeli was already immersed in the political process. Having participated in two unsuccessful campaigns in High Wycombe in June and December of 1832, he persisted, contesting first Bucks county in December of the same year and then the London borough of Marylebone in April 1833 – again unsuccessfully. Disraeli's letters during this period of intensive political participation make it plain that, while the substantive content of his political creed remained vague, his political dislikes were, from the start, instinctive, even visceral. The focus of his greatest hatred – the Whigs – was summed up in the claim made in a letter to Benjamin

Austen early in June of 1832, that he would never 'condescend' to be a Whig however great his desire for a seat in Parliament.[2] Yet even at this early stage, Disraeli was too well-informed not to have realized that the impending Reform Bill would radically alter the political landscape. 'Old Toryism' was dead and Disraeli knew that his political future hinged on his ability successfully to discern the changed lie of the land. On the other hand, Toryism – if not Tories – had always evoked Disraeli's sympathy. Shortly after his return from the Middle East in the fall of 1831, he adopted the tone of a somewhat crotchety 'Old Tory'. 'The times are damnable. I take the gloomiest view of affairs, but we must not lose our property without a struggle.'[3]

Such is the depth of Disraeli's comments to early correspondents about his political opinions and views. Hence the significance of *Hartlebury*. For it seems clear that at this early stage, Disraeli saw the novel as a safe forum where, protected by the mask of anonymity, he was free to think out loud – about political life, electoral campaigning and the motives and behaviour of the electors whose support he was attempting to win. Exposed enough to the political process to have come to some shrewd, if not often cynical conclusions, but not yet at a stage where his political affiliations had solidified, Disraeli used the novel as a way to sort out and analyse his reactions to these, his initial forays into the political world. It is for this reason that his hero's musings and behaviour provide valuable insights into what was going on in Disraeli's mind.

On reading *Hartlebury*, one first notices that the hero offers no explanation for his choice of politics as his life's vocation. For Disraeli no justification was necessary either for his own or his hero's decision to plunge into the political arena. The only explanation provided is indirect. When first introduced, Aubrey Bohun is described as a man who 'combined a fine poetical temperament with a great love of action'. Aware that he can 'work upon men's minds', Bohun is convinced that he has all the necessary powers of eloquence to 'excite and command' (p. 57). Moreover, Bohun's observation that 'to will and to act were one' neatly parallels Disraeli's observation in his mutilated diary: 'I am only truly great in action.'

Like Disraeli, Bohun is drawn home from foreign adventures by the political instability ensuing from the passage of the

Reform Bill, and neither ever questions the political arena as the most appropriate place to fulfil his 'love of action'. To the end of the first volume, the only hint we are given of Bohun's political beliefs is the slogan 'Bohun the Friend of the people!' (p. 82). As ambiguous as Disraeli's first campaign slogan which had so alarmed a radical like Bulwer,[4] Bohun's causes an old Tory like Mr. Molesworth little concern. From the beginning, Molesworth remains steadfastly convinced that a little longer residence in post-reform England would 'improve Mr. Bohun's knowledge of the wants of his countrymen' (p. 82). The electrical effect of Bohun's first speech in the borough apparently had nothing to do with the electors' belief that he was a man of firm principle and deep conviction.

An interesting sidelight on Bohun's decision to enter politics as the most appropriate arena in which to fulfill his 'love for action' is his explanation for contesting the borough as opposed to the county. This parallels Disraeli's decision to seek a seat in Wycombe not Bucks county. Knowing that initially, at least, his opinions were not going to be popular, Bohun reasons that it is preferable to alienate his urban neighbours rather than his county friends, 'until he has made his way' (p. 78). The borough is seen as the safest testing ground, for the relationships established with its residents are somehow perceived as being of less significance than the deeper, more lasting, rural ones.

As was the case in High Wycombe, the odds are very much against Bohun. Not only does this not deter him, it seems to provide him with a sense of mission, for he strides into the centre of borough politics and proceeds to entrance the inhabitants with 'the music of his harmonious voice' (p. 81). His persuasiveness knows no bounds for he manages to bring several Whigs over to his camp. Yet, curiously, Disraeli portrays their motives in an ambiguous light, describing the conversions as a petty and revengeful way for certain electors to act out their hostility to a past Whig member who had been impolitic enough to recommend his replacement to them! This essentially negative portrayal of politics and the nature of the political process is a theme which takes on greater significance as the novel develops.

Like Disraeli, Aubrey Bohun stations himself between the

two traditional political parties. With both, the decision to adopt this position is based on a shrewd evaluation not only of the possible long-term effects of reform, but also of certain eternal verities of human nature and self-interest. Convinced of their ability to sway people whichever way they wished, both adopt a political stance that enables them to take full advantage of the waning popularity of the Tories and an underlying hostility to the old Whig families in the borough. Nor does Bohun's own deep-seated antipathy to the Whigs lead him into unrealistic estimates of the number of converts he can accumulate. He knows that, in the end, most will return to the Ministerial candidate. Better, however, to turn their petty exercise in revenge to one's own electoral advantage than to stand aside, suspicious of their motives, thereby depriving oneself of the benefits of their support, however temporary. Sincerity here is not the issue; tactics are.

The second volume of *Hartlebury* – written largely by Disraeli – opens with a description of Bohun's effect on the political landscape of the borough. Mr. Bohun meets with more than puzzlement from his fictional Whig opponents. Frightened by Bohun's oratorical successes, they react with hatred and small-mindedness, concluding the Bohun is an overly ambitious and unprincipled charlatan. Indulging, perhaps in some rationalization, Disraeli explains their hostile reaction exclusively in terms of personal categories: no reference is made to political or ideological differences. They hate Bohun 'because he is a gentleman'; because he does not have a 'snub nose'; because he is suspiciously curious in his linen; because he rides thoroughbred horses and because he displays a paternalistic courtesy to his inferiors which the Whig families have never managed to cultivate. In short; 'they hated him with that intense predisposition of emnity, which, cold-blooded, calculating, unsympathetic, selfish mortals always innately feel for a man of genius, a man whose generous and lively spirit always makes them ashamed of their dead dunghill-like existence.' (p. 103)

The only detailed examination of Bohun's political creed, appears in the second chapter of volume two. Closer analysis of the argument presented shows that while instinctively a Tory, Disraeli found the political landscape of Bucks county better suited to the tactics of a Radical. For Bohun, as for Disraeli, it was the passage of the Reform Bill that served as the impetus for his developing interest in politics. Both recognized it as a Whig, not a democratic measure, and for both the definition of 'Whig' is anti-national. Nor is this phrase explained except for the ensuing statement that a genuine (presumably, 'national') statesman must often pursue policies in one nation which in another he would oppose. Hardly a novel idea – certainly not a radical one – and not far removed from this exposition of his political views which Disraeli had offered in the December 1832 campaign at Wycombe:

> Feeling that a real revolution had occurred in the nation, I have thought much and deeply upon what should be the duty of a statesman at such a time. If, instead of filling the humble situation of a private individual, I held a post near the person of my King, I should have said to my sovereign, 'Oppose all change, or allow that change which will be full, satisfactory and final.' I am a Conservative to preserve all that is good in our Constitution, a Radical to remove all that is bad. Have I not always said that the work of reformation must be slow to be sure, and then we shall get all we desire; for *all we ask is* for the common good.[5]

Convinced that the Whigs were a party of 'political swindlers' who had been elected to make those changes which 'the spirit of the age required' and who, instead, had devoted themselves to upsetting that crucial balance of parties 'which in an aristocratic country is indispensable to the freedom and felicity of the mass', Bohun had concluded that the country was in imminent peril (p. 105). The single over-riding item in his political creed, then, is a determination to get the Whigs out of office 'at any price'. It is this which determines his intention to form a new 'national' party of which he intends to be the leader; and it is this which informs his tactical decision to present himself as an Independent or Radical, thereby splitting the Whig camp, while at the same time never abjuring any Tory offers of aid and comfort that might come his way. For, like Disraeli, Bohun was convinced that the Whigs had ensconced themselves so firmly in office that it was safe to become an 'advocate of movement' – meaning movement of the Whigs out of power.

Throughout this discussion of Bohun's political views, no mention is made of the Tories. As late as 1834, then, Disraeli was still discounting them as a moribund party whose day was past. The two main Tories of the novel, Mr. Molesworth and Alderman Baggs, provide useful models for what 'old Toryism' meant to Disraeli. Molesworth who is described as being 'entirely of the old school' had always been a supporter of the Tory candidate Mr. Vavasour and he finds it very difficult to transfer his loyalties when Vavasour is persuaded to resign in favour of Bohun. Portrayed by Disraeli as an honest man of somewhat limited intellectual means, Molesworth is confused by the pace of recent changes and puzzled about the most appropriate position to adopt. More importantly, he is portrayed as a man who is rigid in his views and is unable to adapt to change; hence his comment 'I hate compromise, I hate coalition, I hate concession of all kinds!' (p. 125) For Disraeli this way of thinking epitomized the moribund state of the old Tory party and he leaves no doubt that it is no longer a viable position to adopt.

Two Tories who find compromise a more appetizing prospect are prominent members of the corporation – the mayor, Mr. Chumfield, and Alderman Baggs. In a secret midnight meeting they manage to convince each other that, since Vavasour is not likely to win in a contest against the Whig, Mr. Prigmore, they are better advised to throw their support behind Aubrey Bohun. Momentary concerns that Bohun might, in fact, turn out to be a Radical are dismissed with Chumfield's comment; 'Fiddle-dee-de, he has thirty thousand a year . . . I am not afeard of such Radicals as these' (p. 120). This combination of realism and pragmatism goes hand in hand with the determination of an old Tory like Baggs to 'do any thing, any thing, in the world', to crush the local Whig magnate, Jenkins.

It is, of course, the single deciding vote of another Fanchester notable – Mr. Gainsborough – that sends Bohun in triumph to London as the representative of the borough. But his conversion from Whiggery is not a matter of gradual enlightenment. It is entirely a function of family pressure combined with his admitted admiration for Bohun's character and talents. As Gainsborough observes in his characteristically bemused fashion; 'I don't quite understand his politics, but no one can admire him more than I do' (p. 122). It is a matter of personal honour, mixed with not a little fear that prevents Gainsborough from bowing to family pressure and switching his allegiance. It is the persuasive charm of Bohun's chief devotee, campaigner and advocate – Helen Molesworth – that finally convinces him to change his mind.

The arguments Helen uses to persuade Gainsborough convey important aspects of Disraeli's way of thinking. In touching on matters of personal honour they reveal a blend of pragmatism and practicality which would later give rise to numerous attacks on Disraeli's loyalty and consistency. In addition they enlarge on Disraeli's vision of the possibility of building a viable coalition of old disillusioned Tories and new enthusiastic Radicals against the hated and tyrannical Whigs.

Helen makes short shrift of the issue of personal honour, arguing that, since the circumstances in which Gainsborough had made his promise of support for Prigmore had changed, the promise was no longer binding: 'We are all governed by circumstances . . . Circumstances are too strong for the strongest of us.' (p. 149) There can be little doubt that Disraeli held to this conviction throughout his life, for it has, at base, been the source of most accusations of unprincipled conduct which echoed throughout his career.

The same sort of dispatch accompanies Helen's disposal of Gainsborough's concerns about ideological purity. Arguing, in essence, that Bohun and Gainsborough have more in common than Gainsborough realizes, for Bohun is a liberal – though not a Whig – she goes on, in the style of an experienced campaigner, to appeal to Gainsborough's ego and sense of his own importance, in telling him that 'Mr. Bohun agrees with you on every point. He has the highest opinion of your opinions on political subjects.' No further explanation is provided for how a convinced Whig would have no difficulty in voting for an Independent like Bohun. The key point of distinction, apparently, is membership in the Whig party.

This suggests, then, that Disraeli's vision of the possibility of building an alliance of Radicals and Tories was grounded in a conviction that neither of the traditional parties was based on deep-seated beliefs or principles. Just as Chumfield's and Baggs' Toryism is purely a function of their anti-Whiggism, so

Gainsborough's Whiggism is portrayed as a confusion of matters of personal honour with those of political principle. Like Bohun, Disraeli believed that such individuals were the most likely recruits for his new 'national' party that would replace the outworn traditional ones. It would take yet another defeat – in December 1834 – to convince Disraeli that forming and leading a new political party would have to await his election to Westminster as a member of a more traditional group. Yet he never abandoned the notion, and it reappeared in a variety of guises later on in his career, both in his novels and in the Young England experiment.

With the aid of Gainsborough's deciding vote, Bohun emerges victorious and leaves Fanchester to dazzle London society with his brilliance and genius. Yet his reaction to victory – to the very thing which Disraeli sought so vigorously and for so long – is curiously ambiguous. In painting a picture of a hero simultaneously attracted and repulsed by the political process, Disraeli provides us with valuable clues to his perception of the nature of his chosen career.

Consider for example, Bohun's musings on the nature of the electoral process part-way through the campaign: 'This is life, this is excitement, and that is all I care about. I feel I live.' (p. 141) Yet he cannot erase the disquieting feeling that somehow the process – the involvement – is soiling his character and ideals: 'And yet there is something petty and vulgar in all this bustle, which half disgusts me.' Attempting to dismiss these second thoughts, Bohun vows, 'I will not think' reminding himself that he has abjured plans forever. He concludes that, in his scheme of priorities, winning the hand of Helen Molesworth is of far greater importance than dedication to the public weal; that once he has won her love, winning Fanchester will be of only minimal significance.

Rationalization? Perhaps. Yet this curious inner dialogue suggests that for Disraeli political participation is in some sense a 'negative' activity requiring little in the way of rational thought or conscious self-sacrifice. For Bohun, as for Disraeli, political campaigning provided, at base, little more than a release for pent-up genius and energy. Thus Bohun's remark; 'For the rest, if I live, I must be a great man' (p. 141) provides a revealing echo of this confession in Disraeli's mutilated diary written in 1833: 'My disposition is now indolent. I wish to be idle and enjoy myself, muse over the stormy past and smile at the placid present. My career will probably be more energetic than ever, and the world will wonder at my ambition. Alas! I struggle from pride. Yes! It is Pride that now prompts me, not Ambition. They shall not say I have failed'.[6]

With Bohun, as with Disraeli later in his career, the motivation for political participation is expressed exclusively in terms of personal needs. Traditionally Disraeli's enemies have rested their case here. Friends of Disraeli, of course, would argue that an awareness of and concern for the greater common weal so fundamental to Disraeli's mature political creed had yet to develop.

In passing judgement on Bohun at the end of the book, Helen Molesworth is also Disraeli passing judgement on himself. As disillusioned with the political process as Bohun and disgusted with herself for having supported him without question, Helen provides a thumb-nail sketch of Bohun which could only be Disraeli's self-portrait so closely does it echo the Mutilated diary; 'I look upon him as a man who has not other object in life but to gratify his selfism, which he styles sentiment' (p. 180).

More than anything else, perhaps, these self-revelations explain why Disraeli never did acknowledge authorship of *Hartlebury*. More honest with himself here than anywhere else in his writings, he doubtless feared that these youthful musings would be misinterpreted and used as ammunition against him. Certainly no great significance can be attributed to the ultimate fate of the hero, for the correspondence with Sarah makes it clear that Disraeli considered it overdone and inappropriate.[7] Yet this leaves us with a tantalizing question: how would Disraeli himself have ended *Hartlebury*? This would provide valuable clues to how Disraeli saw his future – what he expected of himself and others. Certainly the ambiguity in the portrait of our hero leaves us with no firm notion as to an alternate resolution of the plot. Elusive even in anonymity, Disraeli has once again left us to watch and wonder.

Ellen Henderson
The Disraeli Project

NOTES TO APPENDIX II

1   Disraeli to Sara Austen, 10 June 1832
2   Disraeli to Benjamin Austen, 2 June 1832
3   Disraeli to Banjamin Austen, 3 November 1831
4   Distressed at Disraeli's choice of the slogan 'Grey and Reform; Disraeli and the People', Bulwer wrote: 'You don't mean it seriously or publicly to countenance the idea – that to consider the cause of the People an antithesis and opposition to the cause of Reform.' Hughenden papers, B/I/A/15
5   It would appear that the originator of this argument was Clara Bolton, who in her role as Disraeli's political confidante and some-time spy, provided him with this ingenious if somewhat confused justification for his political posture: 'I told them your object was not to preserve old things or to *recast* them into new *shapes*, but to remove them entirely away, and that it was easy for a radical without infringing on his integrity to unite with the Tories who admit or *no change* as for him to join the Whigs, who are for *all change*.' Hughenden papers A/IV/G/4.
      Early in July 1832, she summed up the meaning of Disraeli's first defeat for him: 'The ultra-Tory game is up, so my dear friend you have it all your own way.' Hughenden papers A/IV/G/5
6   The Mutilated Diary is reprinted in Monypenny and Buckle's biography of Disraeli: Volume I, pp. 234–37
7   See Appendix I.